SURVIVING MISTER NICE GUY

Loving & Leaving
the Covert Narcissist

MONICA LINSON

Surviving Mister Nice Guy:
Loving & Leaving the Covert Narcissist
Copyright © 2025 Monica Linson. All Rights Reserved.

This book is a work of nonfiction, a memoir that tells of personal narrative. It is based on the Author's experiences and opinions. In some cases, names, identifying details, and circumstances have been changed to protect the privacy of individuals. Any resemblance to actual persons, living or dead, or actual events, is purely coincidental unless expressly stated by the Author.

The views, thoughts, and opinions expressed in this book are solely those of the Author and do not necessarily reflect those of the Publisher. The Publisher has not independently verified the accuracy of the information contained herein and disclaims any liability for errors, omissions, or any outcomes related to the use of this material.

This publication is provided with the understanding that neither the Author nor the Publisher is engaged in rendering legal, medical, psychological, financial, or other professional advice. Readers should consult qualified professionals regarding their own circumstances.

No part of this publication may be reproduced, stored in a retrieval system, or transmitted in any form or by any means—electronic, mechanical, photocopying, recording, or otherwise—without prior written permission of the Publisher, except in the case of brief quotations embodied in critical articles or reviews.

To request permissions, contact the publisher at
jennifer@entouragemedia.ca.

ISBN (Paperback): 978-1-7381171-6-1
ISBN (e-Book): 978-1-7381171-7-8
First Paperback Edition: September 2025

Printed in the USA
1 2 3 4 5 6 7 8 9 10

Published by Entourage Media
www.entouragemedia.ca

To Henry and Fred,
I love you more than you'll ever know

CONTENTS

PROLOGUE xi
INTRODUCTION xvii

PART 1

WHAT'S A NARCISSIST ANYWAY? 3
    EXERCISES 10
WHAT THE DSM-5-TR SAYS AND DOESN'T SAY 13
    Overt vs Covert Narcissists 18
EXPERIENCING THE COVERT NARCISSIST 21
    The Beginning of the End 21
    My Misconceptions of Narcissism 23
    The Slip of The Mask 26
    Isolation and Exploitation 29
    Hidden Resentment 32
    EXERCISES 41
IDEALIZING. DEVALUING. DISCARDING. 43
    Idealization 44
    Devaluation 56
    Discarding 60
    EXERCISES 66
INVALIDATION 69
    EXERCISES 78
DARVO 81
    EXERCISES 88
PLAYING THE VICTIM 89
    Playing the Victim to Garner Pity 89
    Playing the Victim to Get Narcissistic Supply 90
    Playing the Victim to Protect Image 91
    Playing the Victim to Hurt and Devalue You 92
    Playing the Victim to Transfer Accountability 92

Playing the Victim to Extract Something from You 94
The Facebook Incident 96
    EXERCISES. 101

GASLIGHTING. 105
More Than a Cup of Tea 110
    EXERCISES. 115

ENTITLEMENT 117
Not in the Mood 121
The Elders' Visit 128
    EXERCISES. 136

LACK OF EMPATHY 139
Money For The Boys 157
Power. 157
Greed 158
    EXERCISES. 162

NOW THAT YOU KNOW 165
Remaining in a Narcissistic Relationship 165
Resilience. 166
Self-Preservation: 169

PART 2

FINDING MY WAY OUT 175
Questions Are the Cure 177

QUESTIONING AND SHIFTING MY BELIEFS 181
More Questions 185
The Power of Exploration & Affirmations 190
The Need for Safety 193
Self-Awareness Is a Superpower 195

GETTING UNSTUCK 199
My First Assault 200
Something to Think about 208
The File Marked "SAFETY". 208

SELF-DISCOVERY: AN ADVENTURE GUIDE 215
    Three Rules for Self-Discovery 216
    Saying YES 217
    The Greatest Man I Never Knew 226
    The Freedom of Forgiveness 227

CELEBRATING LIBERATION 229

DATING AFTER NARCISSISTIC ABUSE 235
    Online Dating with Better Instincts 235
    Dating in Real Life 238
    Setting Boundaries and Raising Standards 240
    Options 245

THE GREATEST LESSON 247

EPILOGUE 251

CREDITS 253

Warning: this book contains depictions of sexual and psychological abuse.

PROLOGUE

I had been looking forward to this appointment all day, hoping that it would give us answers. Things were bad. Really bad. I was grateful for my husband's efforts to save our marriage.

He had booked this appointment himself despite the fact that it came with a hefty out-of-network price tag.

"It's one-ninety per hour!" he said with an exasperated look on his face as he backed out of the driveway. "But it's worth it, if it can help us."

His investment in making things better had filled me with optimism throughout most of the week. My heart was open and ready for the session. I was prepared to do my part.

"I'm glad that we're doing this. I like the points made in the relationship book you bought," I told him. "Thanks for finding it."

Instead of my words making him happy, his tone changed. "Well, I wish I could say that I'm glad too, but I'm not. I'm worried you will go in there and accuse me of crimes I haven't committed."

I had let my guard down, so it took a second to register his sudden shift in mood: "Wait. What?" I thought we were both looking forward to this appointment and on the same page this time.

"You always do," he mumbled under his breath as we pulled into the parking lot. He slammed the brakes, got out of the car, and shut the door so hard that I jumped.

I wasn't surprised that he picked a fight. Just that he picked it today. Now. After all, *he* had researched the therapist, ordered the books, and scheduled the appointment.

My husband rushed ahead of me. I wasn't sure of the suite number, so I hurried to catch up. I had never falsely accused him of anything. Ever. But I wasn't about to have the argument in the lobby. We rode the elevator in silence. The burning sensation in my chest was familiar. I cursed myself for hoping that this day would be different than any other.

By the time I was seated on the sofa in Dr. Jim's office, I was desperately holding back tears. I felt dizzy. My heart raced. I could hear the pounding in my ears. *Pull yourself together!* I ordered myself. But the tears won and began streaming down my cheeks.

Dr. Jim introduced himself and started to describe the Gottman Method of Relationship Therapy. He asked if we were familiar with the book, *The Seven Principles for Making Marriage Work*, by John Gottman.

"I am," I heard my husband say. "I gave it to her, but I don't know if she read it." There was a tone in his voice. I knew it well. His I-am-the-victim, this-woman-is-so-unreasonable tone.

He knew that I'd read the book.

I couldn't seem to form words, so I simply nodded to confirm I had read the book.

This was not the first time my husband had presented himself as a loving but frustrated husband who was doing all he could to save his marriage and make his wife happy. The last therapist wasn't fooled. However, this time I was aware that I was supporting my husband's claims with my incessant crying. I appeared unstable, leaving him to look like the sane one. I wished again that I could turn off my tears.

Dr. Jim explained, "The Gottman Method proposes that the foundation of a loving, long-lasting relationship is for the couple to stand together on a solid platform based on seven principles. The couple must agree to engage with one another within the principles, each holding the marriage as highly important." He stopped and exhaled. After a noticeable pause, Dr. Jim explained that at this point he usually outlined the principles of the approach and what sessions with him would look like for us. But instead, he looked at me, acknowledging my distress for the first time.

"First, I'd like to address what's happening now," Dr. Jim said.

I willed myself to get it together. I met Dr. Jim's eyes and tried to explain how helpless I felt: "We … we … we … don't … have … a platform. He destroys them. I can't win!" A wail broke free. It came from deep down. I surprised myself—and Dr. Jim.

I knew by the look in Dr. Jim's eyes that I'd said the wrong thing. He began to preach about win-win encounters; and how we shouldn't view conflict as a fight to win, but rather, as an opportunity to hear and connect as a couple, as an opportunity to repair and strengthen our bond.

I felt my words being twisted. I inhaled deeply and said as fast as I possibly could before the next sob could silence me, "I didn't say that I can't win in the sense of winning a fight. I said that I can't win in that no matter what I do, I feel like it's not enough. No matter which way I turn, it's the wrong move! I can't win. It's always my fault. No matter—"

"She's so sensitive! That's not *my* fault," my husband interrupted.

He had Dr. Jim's attention for a moment, but the therapist just as quickly glanced my way again. He looked concerned. But I couldn't be sure. Maybe it was a look of pity.

I tried to explain. I began recounting the ways my marriage hurt—the manipulations, the lies, the betrayals, the need for control, the infidelity.

There was a burning pain in my chest. I could feel heat radiating from my body. I checked my skin for hives and redness. Nothing. The burning was localized in my heart, both arms, and the top of my thighs. These absurd sensations added to my confusion.

My husband said, "It's like she is convicting me of crimes I haven't committed yet …" He took on a conciliatory tone, as if he were pleading for an explanation and redemption simultaneously.

Dr. Jim asked, "Could you give me an example of what you mean?"

The room began to spin. My throat burned with the taste of vomit threatening to come up. I covered my mouth and swallowed, which only made me feel more nauseated.

I searched my memory for crimes of which I accused and punished this innocent, exasperated man on the couch beside me.

My husband recounted an argument we had the week before when I explained how I felt hurt and dismissed when he didn't show up for a date we had. "She insinuated I don't care about her or our marriage just because I decided to help a neighbor put together an Ikea table."

He was, of course, leaving out the part where he kept me waiting for hours without a word, not answering my texts or calls. He also left out that he failed to inform this new, young, single female neighbor that he was married (albeit separated and working on it). He was pretending that putting people before me, before us, wasn't a familiar destructive pattern of his, one he claimed he wanted to change, and supposedly one of the reasons we sat before Dr. Jim.

Worse than his denial and deflection of reality in that moment was that he was full of rage. I could feel it. He resented me at times like this, when I didn't believe his lies, when my body sensed something was amiss.

Unlike Dr. Jim, I knew my husband was hiding something about this neighbor. The two continued with Dr. Jim asking questions and my husband being irritated by them. It was my husband's irritation that gave me a small bit of comfort. It meant that this therapist wasn't falling for the performance. To my surprise, my husband admitted to a few damaging actions. Actually, it was more like he was trapped by his own words and felt compelled to choose being intelligent over playing victim.

I am not sure how much time passed before I realized that Dr. Jim was talking to me again. His words came through in bits and pieces, broken, like a poor radio connection. My ears were muffled with the echo of my pounding heartbeat. *Boom! Swoosh!* I wondered if this would be the moment I finally cracked—right there, on a shrink's couch. It seemed fitting after being treated as if I were crazy for the better part of the last thirty years.

But then I realized the starts and stops of words that I heard wasn't because I was losing my mind. It was Dr. Jim. He was hesitating, searching for an explanation, for words other than the ones he knew must be said. This was new to me. I was poised for the familiar list of changes that I needed to make to accommodate my husband.

I listened closer.

Dr. Jim met my eyes and said, "I am at a loss for helpful insight. Monica, you have extended grace." After a long, deep breath, he said, "I don't see anything else for you to do." Dr. Jim glanced at my husband, who was wearing his signature *whatever* smirk on his face. Then looking directly at me again, Dr. Jim summed up my marriage in uncanny detail: "It is apparent that you have experienced invalidation and betrayal to varying degrees, some of which have been admitted here today. Earlier you described your marriage as not having a platform. You said that it seems that you are always at fault and unable to win. I get that now. As the two of you sit here, with you in such distress, your husband has displayed more disdain than empathy. There have been no repair attempts."

My breathing slowed. *He gets it! Dr. Jim gets it!*

This was what I had needed for so long—someone to see the full story, *my* story, for what it truly was. The pounding and swooshing of my heart began to quiet for the first time since walking into the room. It was my turn to exhale! And I did. In one long exhale, I released years of held breath and self-doubt, years of questioning my sanity, and fear that I was going crazy.

Then, in a stern, clear, concise voice, Dr. Jim said five words: "You need to walk away."

With that, I got off the couch and walked out of his office.

That was the first time a therapist, someone in authority, spoke those life-changing words to me. Getting off Dr. Jim's couch and walking out of his office was the breakthrough that I needed. It was the first time I felt as if I might actually be justified (and more importantly, strong enough) to *just walk away*.

Of course, my marriage to a covert narcissist didn't end that evening. But after that appointment, I gave myself permission to step into the possibility that I was *not* responsible for my husband's unhappiness or low self-esteem. Nor was I responsible for everything that had ever gone wrong in our marriage.

I began to look at my marriage more objectively. I began searching for other explanations for what felt like endless suffering up to that point. I had been blind to such options before the session with Dr. Jim.

I realized that I had cemented myself in obligation and guilt as proof of my loyalty and love. It all made sense given the way I was raised.

My desire for clarity showed up a thousand-fold. The mask had fallen off for the last time. I began to accept that I was married to someone with narcissistic personality disorder (NPD), a diagnosis that I had heard long before meeting Dr. Jim. That evening, so many unresolved matters started to fall into place. After realizing that it made sense for me to want to walk away, my life just got better and better. I discovered that there was a reason I felt so discombobulated, lonely, and disheartened when it came to my marriage. That event in Dr. Jim's office opened my eyes to just how treacherous the covert narcissist can be. I realized that *my* experience of my husband was valid, despite how others experienced him. My field of vision widened so that I could see I hadn't been too sensitive, too demanding, or too unreasonable. I hadn't been *too* anything! Making it appear that way was all part of the covert plan.

INTRODUCTION

Hello, Dear Reader. My name is Monica Linson, and I am a relationship coach specializing in narcissistic abuse recovery. Aside from spending most of my life with a covert narcissist and now serving as a recovery coach, I am also a public school teacher, Reiki practitioner, and energy worker. As I did my work to overcome narcissistic abuse, unbeknownst to me, other women in similar situations were watching. One by one, they began asking me for support: "I don't even want to get out of bed. How did you do it? How did you get over it and learn to trust yourself again? When will it stop hurting? I feel so stupid. How do I stop dreaming about him?"

Supporting such women was my inspiration to refresh my certification as a life coach. At the time of this writing, I am working toward another certification. I've studied to become a trauma-informed teacher and coach for the sake of my students as well as my clients. My energy and somatic work have allowed me to support others to heal and to get to the root cause of limiting beliefs and subconscious behaviors. I've supported hundreds of other targets of narcissists on their recovery journey. I now offer private and group coaching. My goal is to retire from teaching and shift, full time, into supporting women in reclaiming themselves after narcissistic abuse. I don't want one more woman to spend decades with a covert narcissist, wondering if they're going crazy and feeling imprisoned by judgment and trauma.

I wrote this part-memoir, part-field guide to share with you the red flags that reveal the covert narcissist, and to give you options and strength for moving forward once you do. I want you to have the information I wish someone had shared with me long ago, so that it doesn't take you thirty years to connect the dots.

Back then, I didn't see the red flags. I didn't follow the clues and, therefore, had no real understanding of the physical and emotional damage I would undergo as a result of relationships that were infused with toxicity.

Since you are here reading these pages, perhaps you, or someone you care about, are in the same place I was all those years ago. If so, please allow my book to be your guideposts along the way.

There are so many things I want you to know, but before we get into that, let's begin with: It's *not* your fault. You were targeted. You were seen as a means to an end, as someone who would make the narcissist feel better about themselves. You were desired for your great capacity to love and forgive, for your compassion, grace, and empathy. Unfortunately, these traits were used against you. Yet, these are wonderful qualities, and you get to cherish them.

This book is a culmination of what I learned about NPD, about covert narcissists, and how they compare to the classic, or overt, narcissists. To put it simply, the classic narcissists are more overt in their grandiosity, arrogance, and attention seeking behavior. They openly display their beliefs of superiority and feelings of disdain toward others, and their rage when things don't go their way. In contrast, covert narcissists are more subtle. They appear mild and meek, and quite self-effacing on the surface, while hiding feelings of entitlement and their exploitation of others for their own gain.

Most importantly, this book is a record of what I learned about myself after digging through the aftermath of being raised by a covert narcissist, then marrying one and staying for far too long. You might say that I was steeped in the mindf*ck that is narcissistic abuse.

The point is that I made it out. *Hallelujah!* Believe me, if I can make it out, so can you. I know the way.

As I tell my story, I will give you real-life examples of the covert narcissist's tactics, motives, and likely thought process. I do this because this is exactly the information I was missing when trying desperately to connect words like grandiose, apathetic, and attention-seeking to the caring, hard-working, easy-going, shy, funny man I had fallen in love with. It was still hard to make the connection when my life, with that same man, became exhausting, unpredictable, confusing, and scary. By the time asthma, migraines, and depression had set in, I didn't have the energy, nor the mental capacity, to make the connections. I was deep in survival mode. All I could do was take it one day at a time. When my boys arrived, their safety, happiness and well-being became my priority. For years, I thought I was to blame for the problems in my marriage. As it turns out, all of the crazy-making traits of the overt narcissists are also there in the covert narcissists. It is my goal to make you aware of such behaviors. As I said before, I don't want you steeped in confusion and, what I call, toxic hope with a covert narcissist.

The stories shared within the pages you're about to read are mine. The stories are not told in a linear fashion covering the thirty years that I was trapped. While I do give some markers of where I was in my marriage, I thought it more important to provide the best real-world example of the particular covert trait. The crucial bit of knowledge for you to know is that the signs were there—all of them—from the very beginning. Through the lenses of societal norms, religious upbringing, childhood trauma, and other subconscious influences, I misinterpreted them.

The stories I share are vulnerable by choice. I've purposely revealed my wounds—wounds that I had to heal to truly thrive in the wake of being raised by a covert narcissist, and then being married to one for thirty years. These are wounds that you may also have. That's why I share them. *I want you to know.* On behalf of countless other women who have suffered the same circumstances, *I need you to know.* If you've never been there yourself, you may read about my journey and wonder how I couldn't see the obvious manipulations and red flags. You may feel sure that there's no way you would have fallen for such nonsense.

But I urge you, "Do not let your judgment of me cause you to miss out on the lesson that may be staring you right in the face." There are nuances in our personal experiences. We don't know what we don't know.

An article in Psychology Today explains it this way, "Not surprisingly, we learn certain behavior patterns and coping mechanisms during the developmental stages of life. And if those behavior patterns are unhealthy or dysfunctional, we then carry this with us into our adult relationships. Whether intended or not, the way we learn to interact with our caregivers is usually mimicked in our early relationships. If any of these interactions were dysfunctional, we could unknowingly carry on dysfunctional ways of engaging with the world."[1]

> "Until you make the unconscious conscious,
> it will direct your life, and you will call it fate."
> —Carl Jung

No truer words have been spoken when applied to the narcissist and their chosen target than those of Carl Jung, the Swiss psychologist and the founder of analytical psychology. It's the subconscious beliefs of self-loathing and inferiority that dictate the ruthless words and behavior of the covert narcissist. At the same time, it's the subconscious beliefs of the target that blinds them to the red flags, and to the narcissist's questionable behavior. Those same subconscious beliefs, along with a consistent dose of gaslighting, are what leave us questioning our sanity, which in turn leads to an inner narrative of shame and self-doubt that keeps us stuck. We start to ask ourselves, "What's wrong with me? Why do I keep doing this?!" We condemn ourselves with, "I should know better …" And you do, of course, know better, when you're not being manipulated to think otherwise.

---

[1] "Why People Can Miss Red Flags in Toxic Relationships." 2023. Psychology Today. 2023. https://www.psychologytoday.com/us/blog/invisible-bruises/202211/why-some-of-us-overlook-red-flags-in-toxic-relationships#:~:text=Due%20to%20their%20history%2C%20many,in%20a%20family%20of%20origin.

INTRODUCTION

While reading this book, at the end of each chapter you will find exercises related to the chapter topic and how it fits in your life. Consider these exercises to be invitations to take action so that you can identify and protect yourself from the covert narcissists in your life. Don't just read about my experience; do your own deep dive. Take a close, hard, objective look at your own experiences. I am sharing with you the things that I wished I'd known to pay attention to, to recognize as a pattern, to identify as emotional and mental abuse at the hands of someone who claimed to love me.

When accepting the invitations, I recommend using a journal. This will allow you to keep your evidence and *A-ha!* moments all in one place. This will prove helpful when the waters get murky. I recommend that you write out the answers to the questions I pose. Research shows that writing things down makes the information more solid and easier to recall. There will be times when I ask you to just notice. For me, just noticing means not only making a mental note of an event, but also noticing how your body responds to the situation. Our body cues are very important in our quest.

(You get to decide if your journal needs to be under lock and key. You know your specific situation better than anyone.)

You may find yourself resisting some of the questions that I ask. You may scoff as if I am being ridiculous. You may even get angry. Those are the times that I want you to pay extra close attention. Through that resistance, you will find your greatest epiphanies. I invite you to dig deeper. Revisit the question again and again, if needed. Your resistance tells a story. Something is there. Know that you are resisting for a reason. Challenge your automatic response. That's your conditioning, your subconscious programming, at work. It's what we want to uncover.

Before we dive in, there are a few other matters I want you to know.

First, for legal reasons and to protect the privacy of those who contributed to my story, names and places have been changed. When telling my own story I will refer to my then-partner as Colin. It's important to remember that this book isn't about Colin. It's about you and me. It's about you having the opportunity to learn from my mistakes, saving yourself years of pain and heartache.

Second, please understand that my words here do not constitute a mental health diagnosis for you or anyone in your life. I am not qualified to make such claims. Colin was diagnosed as having Narcissistic Personality Disorder by a licensed mental health therapist. His subtype, covert narcissist, was identified years later. Although the narcissist in your life may not be diagnosed with NPD, my research informs me that there are those who display highly narcissistic traits without the diagnosis. The issue is that narcissists are not likely to admit that they have a need to consult a mental health professional. As far as the narcissists are concerned, their interrelationship issues are someone else's fault. I invite you not to insist on an official diagnosis before you start to examine a person's behavior. The key is to recognize the toxicity in the relationship regardless of a professional diagnosis.[2] Colin's behavior was problematic long before I understood the diagnosis. If at any time you find the information and anecdotes that I share to be emotionally triggering, to the point of becoming a threat to your safety, please stop reading. Take a break. Phone a friend to help you process your reactions. Then come back to our work when you're able.

Third, although I sometimes refer to the narcissist as a male, using the pronouns he and him, I acknowledge that women can be character-disordered, have narcissistic traits, or be diagnosed with narcissistic personality disorder. In fact, there's research that suggests that many female narcissists are misdiagnosed as having borderline personality disorder, also a Cluster B personality disorder. Please know that when I refer to narcissists in the male gender it's because that has been my primary experience, and to avoid the awkward he/her, himself/herself

---

[2] "Narcissistic Personality Disorder: Causes, Symptoms, Treatment." 2023. Healthcentral.com. June 16, 2023. https://www.healthcentral.com/condition/narcissistic-personality-disorder?legacy=psycom.

phrasing. Having acknowledged that, I also want to say that I will do my best in editing to use gender neutral pronouns.

I am also aware that some readers of this book are dealing with a family member, a friend, a boss, or a workmate who may be a covert narcissist. The information within these pages still applies. The covert narcissist's tactics are still the same.

Finally, know that the purpose of the exercises in this book is not to bash anyone. This is not the "Burn Book" from *Mean Girls*. The exercises are meant to help you recognize and protect yourself from further harm. If you ever feel stuck, and can't seem to connect the dots, then you'll find free resources on my website: *ReclaimingYourselfNow.com*. Please also feel free to reach out to me. We can make sense of it all … together.

PART 1

I don't want one more woman to do thirty years with a covert narcissist!
— *Monica Linson*

CHAPTER 1

WHAT'S A NARCISSIST ANYWAY?

In the last ten years or so, the term narcissist seems to be the go-to insult for ex-boyfriends and ex-girlfriends following a bad breakup. From my observations, the label "narcissist" is being used interchangeably with the word asshole. (No shade whatsoever to those whose ex-whatevers are, indeed, narcissists. If that's the case, you know as well as I do that an asshole is not the same as a narcissist.)

All narcissists are assholes, but not all assholes are narcissists.

An asshole can have narcissistic traits, yet not meet the criteria for narcissistic personality disorder, which is the official diagnosis for a true narcissist. The biggest asshole in your life can be self-serving, hurtful, and rude. That same asshole can choose not to be. The average asshole can reflect, be accountable and make amends. They may not want to, but it's not out of the realm of possibilities for an asshole to commit to personal growth, to feel remorse, and shift their way of being. True reflecting, growing, and shifting are not possible for a true narcissist.

More significantly, an asshole is capable of feeling intimacy and empathy. Both are key to interpersonal relationships. A narcissist is not capable of feeling either. In fact, the hallmark traits of a narcissist are grandiosity, lack of empathy, superficiality, and a sense of entitlement.

At this point, you're probably thinking: That sounds like an asshole. And you'd be right. But, in my experience, if you pointed out these specific behaviors and attitudes to a narcissist, he would, without a moment's hesitation, confirm your assessment in some way, and wonder why you have a problem with it. An asshole, on the other hand, would at least pause for a moment to contemplate the possibility of being an asshole before moving on. Test it out! The next time you run across an asshole, ask the question: "Do you realize that you're acting like an asshole?" If that feels too aggressive, ask: "Do you realize that your behavior is hurtful … condescending … mean?" See what happens. The asshole in your life is likely to downshift, in some way. The narcissist will likely rage and make everything that is happening *your* fault.

In short, an asshole is able to reflect, see the problem they are causing, have empathy and choose to make amends and behave differently. The narcissist cannot and will not, unless the goal is to manipulate a person or situation.

More specifically, a person with narcissistic personality disorder is defined by The Mayo Clinic as "a mental health condition in which people have an unreasonably high sense of their own importance. They need and seek too much attention and want people to admire them. People with this disorder may lack the ability to understand or care about the feelings of others. But behind this mask of extreme confidence, they are not sure of their self-worth and are easily upset by the slightest criticism." To this I would add that other resources defining NPD emphasize a lack of empathy as a hallmark indicator of the disorder. In working with targets of narcissistic abuse, I have yet to hear of a person with NPD who doesn't show a tremendous lack of empathy. When the target expresses their pain and confusion, and pleads for understanding, the narcissist in their life is disinterested, angered, and often minimizes their point of view. It's also important to know that a person being diagnosed with narcissistic personality disorder must meet five of nine criteria listed in the DSM-5-TR (Diagnostic and Statistical Manual of Mental Disorders, Fifth Edition, Text Revision). There, NPD is defined as a pervasive pattern of grandiosity, need for admiration, and lack of empathy, with interpersonal entitlement, exploitativeness, arrogance, and envy.

***

The first time I heard the term narcissist regarding my husband was shortly after the birth of our youngest child. The second and third times quickly followed. The problem with those early diagnoses is that the information provided by the therapists was vague and limited. In three decades, not one of the therapists told me that I was in danger and should walk away. In fact, the first therapist who diagnosed my husband with narcissistic personality disorder simply said, "It's really nothing to worry about. It simply means that he has a rockstar mentality."

This therapist said that the diagnosis meant I needed to make a big deal about my husband's efforts. "Give him lots of praise," he advised. "Even for the small things! Thank him for a job well done. Laugh at his jokes. Make him feel important. You'll figure out what he responds to." That same therapist also suggested that I "throw on a sexy number once in a while and show him a good time."

This was coming from a therapist who led an eight-week long parenting class that Colin signed us up to attend. It was during what I now know to be a "love bomb phase." At the time, Colin was making promises of becoming an equal partner by getting more involved in parenting our boys. I fell for it. I wholeheartedly believed my husband wanted to fully participate in parenting our boys, and that once he learned how to contribute in this way, he would make the needed changes. I wanted nothing more than to have someone on my side, someone in the arena with me. However, half-way through the parenting course and after meeting with the head therapist, who thought it important enough to call me back to his office for a private conversation, I came out with more tasks and responsibilities than before. This therapist spoke as if dealing with a person who has a personality disorder was as simple as taking penicillin for strep throat.

The second therapist, a colleague of the first, agreed that I was indeed married to a narcissist. She added the additional strategy of playing the damsel in distress. She explained that it was essential for my husband to feel important, needed, and sexually desired. Just like the previous therapist, she also gave examples: "Ask him to kill a spider, to open a jar, to get items out of your reach." She urged me to get creative. She reminded me that it didn't matter if I could do the tasks on my own.

She said, "The important thing is to make your partner feel as if he is your knight in shining armor." Believe it or not, at the time, I actually found her recommendations more helpful than alarming. I knew what to do. I was grateful for the timely reminder. I realized that I had watched my mother do those same things with my father for years. *If only I knew then what I know now.*

The third therapist was someone my husband sought out to replace the therapists who declared him a narcissist. He still wanted to become a better partner, a husband that I could count on, and someone I would admire—or so he said. Therapist number three asked for a private session with me. She wanted to gather more information on the relationship dynamic. In the end, she explained that I was married to a marshmallow man. "He has no core sense of self. No backbone," she said. She went on to remind me that I had never been able to count on him to act any particular way in any given situation. It was as if she had been spying on my private life. She explained that it was because he was self-centered and without conscience. She expressed her sympathy for me, but being a Christian woman and counselor, she said that she was against divorce. Her strongest advice was for me to pray for my marriage. So, I did.

Each time I spoke with a mental health professional, I set out to do as instructed. I required very little of my husband and threw him the emotional equivalent of a parade each time he walked through the door. I fed his ego by laughing at his attempts at humor. (This part was easy because he had a funny side.) I feigned incompetence and pretended to be someone in great need of rescue. I thanked him repeatedly each time he saved the day. I taught our sons to run to the door cheering when their daddy came home from work. I taught them to thank him for every pair of new shoes and for each new toy that I bought. There was extra emphasis placed on each new video game that I purchased for the three of them to play together.

It wasn't until years after my marriage ended that I connected this to my mother teaching me how to pour my daddy's beer into a frosted mug slightly tilted so that very little foam was created. My mother was also the one who showed me how to polish my daddy's shoes, and how to make a Reuben sandwich just the way he liked it. I believe this was all to help her to provide my daddy with the narcissistic supply he craved. (Narcissistic Supply refers to the constant stream of attention and admiration needed by a narcissist. According to an article in PsychologyToday.com on narcissistic supply, "Pleasing a narcissist is thankless, like filling a bottomless pit.")[3] I understand why my mother needed help. Clearly, I did too.

I struggled greatly with the idea that my husband had no true sense of self. The concept was foreign to me. While I still do not understand how such a thing is possible, *I do accept it*. Back then, I had only to observe my husband's behavior to see that the therapist was right.

There has never been a situation, hypothetical or otherwise, where I could say with conviction, "He would never do such a thing! That doesn't sound like him! He doesn't act that way." The truth of the matter was that my husband was often someone new. He was whoever he needed to be in order to meet his own needs.

When it was explained that people with narcissistic personality disorder likely suffered an abusive and traumatic childhood, I thought it would be cruel to leave someone with such a diagnosis. I likened it to someone who, through no fault of their own, was stricken with cancer. *You wouldn't leave him if he had cancer, would you?* I'd ask myself that question on repeat. I seemed to be in a constant state of prayer,

---

[3] "The Concept of Narcissistic Supply." 2021. Psychology Today. 2021. https://www.psychologytoday.com/ca/blog/toxic-relationships/202108/the-concept-narcissistic-supply.

beseeching the heavens for faith. Evidently, on some level, I put all of my faith in the idea that "love conquers all."

For a long time, I thought a true narcissist was someone with an official diagnosis of NPD, someone who had a traumatic childhood that left them cold and aloof, unable to connect or even love fully, someone who projected a rock-star mentality to cover up the vulnerability and pain that they suffered as a child, someone who simply needed to be loved. While that may all be true, the past trauma and emotional pain of a narcissist isn't the only consideration. The big chunk that was missing was how the people living with and loving the narcissist were impacted.

Looking back over thirty years, the advice I received from mental health professionals was demeaning, disempowering, and flat-out emotionally exhausting. The therapists I looked to for support woefully misrepresented the insidious nature of narcissism, and no one came close to defining the full picture of what being enmeshed with a covert narcissist was truly like. The worst part was that the advice from those particular therapists made *me* responsible for the narcissist's happiness. I assume that's because narcissists' deficient self and inner resources make them dependent on other people to affirm their impaired self-esteem and fragile ego.[4] But that overlooked any needs that the boys or I had. It was Colin before me. Before us. Always. As a result, I became his willing and dedicated source of narcissistic supply, his proof of relevance. In trying to do what I thought was Christian and the role of a loving wife, I became complicit in my own abuse.

* * *

While the information regarding overt narcissists has become readily available, the resources regarding the covert narcissist (officially referred to as a vulnerable narcissist) are still in relatively short supply. In my

---

4   "The Concept of Narcissistic Supply." 2021. Psychology Today. 2021. https://www.psychologytoday.com/ca/blog/toxic-relationships/202108/the-concept-narcissistic-supply.

experience, the clinical descriptions of a covert narcissist's behavior don't explain how life with one actually plays out in the real world.

With a stroke of good fortune, maybe a mental health professional or two will come across this book and share the specific behaviors of the covert narcissist with the hurt and confused client sitting in their office. It's essential to know that the covert narcissist doesn't show up in the same way that the classic overt narcissist does. That's the trickiest part. The cover-up works.

Nowadays, I choose not to become bogged down with official diagnoses or the words of mental health therapists of the past. Instead, I trust the evidence of my experiences. I look for patterns and take steps to protect myself. I do my best to look objectively. I do not justify, nor tolerate, anyone's toxic behavior. Once the pattern is noticed, I adjust the person's access to me accordingly. Not all interested parties get to be part of my inner circle—family included. I have learned this out of the necessity to live life peacefully, safely, and on my own terms.

You get to do the same.

EXERCISES

Exercise 1: A Narcissist or Copycat?

The purpose of this exercise is to start identifying the less-than-supportive people in your life. Remember, it's not to bash anyone. It's a step toward protecting yourself from further harm. Reflect on the following questions: What's your understanding of the labels "asshole" and "narcissist"? What has been your experience of the possible narcissist in your life? Write about the good and the bad.

Exercise 2: Red Flags

Consider the relationships that came to mind in Exercise 1 above. Dive a little deeper. Make note of at least three of the signs of a toxic relationship shared below. Be mindful of their presence in your life. Write about anything you notice. For each relationship in question, tally any sign that shows up repeatedly.

- You are not quite sure where you stand in the relationship. *It is unclear to you whether this is a person that you can count on to have your back or someone who would "throw you under the bus" for personal gain.* There is no relationship security. *You find that you keep quiet about your concerns for fear that upsetting the person may cause a break-up or argument.*
- Your opinions, experiences, and preferences are often discounted, dismissed, or redefined for you. *The key is to notice when your voice is silenced.*
- When around this person, you behave in ways that are out of character for you. *In essence, you find that you are on guard and have a need to protect yourself.*
- You feel drained mentally, emotionally, spiritually, and physically after being in the person's presence. *Notice, too, any gut reactions you have when the person enters a room; do you*

instinctively hesitate, sigh, or have any other body signals when you think about being, or make plans to be, in the person's company? These are important body clues. Your body knows before your head!
- You are finding that your time, schedule, and energy revolve around meeting the other person's needs and interests, at the expense of your own. *Be especially alert as to whether or not your self-care is suffering (e.g., sleep).*

CHAPTER 2

WHAT THE DSM-5-TR SAYS AND DOESN'T SAY

All the research that I've completed thus far regarding emotionally and psychologically toxic relationships states that it is best for the victim to cut ties with the abuser. This is especially the case for narcissistically abusive relationships. However, not all narcissistically abusive relationships can be easily terminated. Fortunately, there is still a way to protect yourself. The first line of defense is to know and understand what you are dealing with.

Before I share the strategies I have learned, it's important to take a closer look at how mental health professionals understand narcissistic personality disorder. The criteria referenced here are in the DSM-5-TR, officially known as the Diagnostic and Statistical Manual of Mental Disorders, Fifth Edition, Text Revision. The DSM-5-TR is published by the American Psychiatric Association, and it is used by mental health professionals in the United States to diagnose mental health disorders.

Narcissistic Personality Disorder

Diagnostic Criteria

A pervasive pattern of grandiosity (in fantasy or behavior), need for admiration, and a lack of empathy, beginning by early adulthood and present in a variety of contexts, as indicated by five (or more) of the following:

1. Has a grandiose sense of self-importance (e.g., exaggerates achievements and talents, expects to be recognized as superior without commensurate achievements).
2. Is preoccupied with fantasies of unlimited success, power, brilliance, beauty, or ideal love.
3. Believes that he or she is "special" and unique and can only be understood by, or should associate with, other special or high-status people (or institutions).
4. Requires excessive admiration.
5. Has a sense of entitlement (i.e., unreasonable expectations of especially favorable treatment or automatic compliance with his or her expectations).
6. Is interpersonally exploitative (i.e., takes advantage of others to achieve his or her own ends).
7. Lacks empathy: is unwilling to recognize or identify with the feelings and needs of others.
8. Is often envious of others or believes that others are envious of him or her.
9. Shows arrogant, haughty behaviors or attitudes.[5]

It is important to understand that we can all have moments of narcissistic traits, such as feelings of entitlement, selfishness, or attention-seeking behavior. Yep! This includes those nights out with the girls when you've had a shot, or two, of liquid courage, and acted on a dare! Those moments, for most people, are not dominating character traits and do not indicate narcissism. In fact, most people feel embarrassed after highly narcissistic moments and will make needed amends.

---

5   Reprinted with permission from the Diagnostic and Statistical Manual of Mental Disorders, Fifth Edition, Text Revision (Copyright © 2022). American Psychiatric Association. All Rights Reserved.

Some people may consistently display several, but not all, of the traits noted in the DSM-5-TR. Such people would be considered to have traits of pathological narcissism, but they would not be diagnosed with narcissistic personality disorder. This can be the coworker who constantly one-ups you with every story you share, but also treats you to lunch or notices when you're feeling down. Maybe, it's the roommate who borrows your clothes without asking. With both, you're left wondering how to define the relationship—friend, or foe? You likely know people like this. They indeed have some toxic traits but are not full-blown narcissists. A heart-to-heart or a heated confrontation with such a person, where you set a few boundaries, may do the trick in getting the relationship on a healthier, more equitable track.

A diagnosed narcissist, or a person with highly narcissistic traits, has an exaggerated sense of self-importance, a lack of empathy, a constant need for attention and praise, and a strong sense of entitlement. They have narcissistic fantasies about power and an established history of exploiting others for personal gain. The true narcissist yearns to feel superior. It is extremely difficult or impossible for them to admit when they are wrong. These traits are consistent across time, present in most situations and relationships.

I've also spoken with therapists who say that to meet the criteria for diagnosis, the behaviors and patterns listed in the DSM-5-TR must be problematic in interpersonal relationships. I am baffled by this because the problems seem to be for those enmeshed with the narcissist, not for the narcissists themselves. In other words, narcissists make life hell for everyone around them. They manipulate and threaten others to get their way and punish those who do not comply.

***

The world heard the word *narcissistic* quite a bit during the highly publicized defamation lawsuit between actor Johnny Depp and actress and model Amber Heard.

Throughout the lawsuit, accusations of narcissism were hurled back and forth between opposing legal teams. Both Johnny Depp and Amber Heard accused the other of having narcissistic traits.

When I heard news reports of Amber Heard being a target of abuse, I felt demoralized. I've been a fan of Johnny Depp since the movies *What's Eating Gilbert Grape* (1993) and *Benny & Joon* (1993). I couldn't believe that a woman would lie about such a thing. But then I watched the trial.

I had a visceral reaction when Depp took the witness stand and said, "In the beginning my relationship with Miss Heard … from what I recall … what I remember, she was too good to be true. She was attentive. She was loving. She was smart. She was kind. She was funny. She was understanding … We had many things in common … Blues music, literature, and things of that nature. For that year or year-and-a-half, it was … it was amazing." Depp's description of Heard's early behavior reminded me of the idealizing (love-bombing) phase of every narcissistically abusive relationship. I could have spoken the exact same words about my relationship with Colin.

Depp goes on to explain how Heard was so attentive to him that they had a routine where he would come home after a long day on set and sit on the couch. Afterward, she would take off his boots, set them aside, and get him a glass of wine. Depp's voice wavered as he explained, "I'd never experienced anything like that in my life."

But then things changed. Depp described a time when he came home to find Heard preoccupied with something, so he removed his own boots. He goes on to explain how she had appeared visibly shaken, upset that he removed his own boots. She scolded him for doing her job, but then seemed to pull herself out of it … Something about the interaction had him saying, "The hairs on the back of my neck stood." For me, that was the point when the narcissist's mask fell off. However, when Heard pulled herself together and went on to get him the wine, something he had already associated with an act of love, Johnny momentarily dismissed the red flag.

Like millions of people, I was surprised to hear the recordings of

Heard in what sounded, to me, like emotional battering of Depp. In my opinion, the following exchange is an example of narcissistic invalidation and gaslighting. Listen in:

> AH: I'm sorry that I didn't uh … uh … hit you across the face in a proper slap.
> JD: You … uh … punched me.
> AH: I was hitting you. I wasn't punching you. Babe, you're not punched.
> JD: Don't tell me what it feels like to be punched.
> AH: You know … You've been in a lot of fights. You've been around a long time. I know.
> JD: No … When you fucking have a closed fist.
> AH: You didn't get punched. You got hit. I'm sorry I hit you like this, but I did not punch you. I did not fucking deck you. I fucking was hitting you. I don't know what the motion of my hand was. But you're fine. I did not hurt you. I did not punch you. I was hitting you.

Heard tried to alter Depp's perception of reality to match her own narrative. That is a concrete display of gaslighting. In the above recording, which aired during the trial, Heard dismisses Depp's experience. She insists that she *hit* him, and did not *punch* him, making semantics, *not her violence*, the issue. She further insists that Depp is fine and that she didn't hurt him. Her tone is dismissive and condescending, designed to make him question his own reality and intelligence for thinking that the matter was serious at all.

During the case, experts referred to psychological tests and findings, debating back and forth as to who was or wasn't afflicted with a mental health condition that would either condemn or justify behaviors.

Overt vs Covert Narcissists

There is no detailed distinction in the DSM-5-TR between the classic (overt) narcissist and the vulnerable (covert) narcissist. But what we do know is that a person showing at least five of the nine traits mentioned is considered to have narcissistic personality disorder. Such narcissism can show up overtly or covertly. Both expressions require constant attention and praise. Both lack empathy for others. Both are exploitative and have a great sense of entitlement.

My personal experience confirms that the classic (overt) narcissist and the vulnerable (covert) narcissist share many of the exact same traits. However, they present those traits in different ways. This distinction was the missing puzzle piece for me. Back when I first heard the diagnosis, all the information available to me seemed not to fit Colin. I was led to believe that the diagnosis was off.

The covert narcissist has a consistent pattern of appearing meek, humble, soft-spoken. They appear to most as if they are simply *a good guy—Mr. Nice Guy*. The covert narcissist also appears socially awkward, lacking in charisma, shy, introverted, sullen, and self-deprecating. These traits make many people—including you and me—feel the need to protect or even rescue the covert narcissist. It's the nice guy, underdog persona that makes us want to believe the covert narcissist's lies. In fact, we subconsciously look for ways to fill in the holes of their excuses, just to make it make sense. The thing to know is that all of those Mr. Nice Guy traits are distractors from the red flags that are hiding just beneath the surface.

It's the inner rage of the covert narcissist that I found most surprising. Covert narcissists are full of resentment and rage for not being recognized for their greatness. Or worse, they rage against the real-life evidence that they are not the person they imagined themselves to be. A covert has a very negative self-image. While they dream of being a high-powered, charismatic, well-known, admired, and wealthy person, in reality, they lack the confidence to achieve those things. You hear them using *if only* excuses: If only I had rich parents to pay for my college education, I would make a lot more money than I do now. If only people would stop holding me back with their jealousy and insecurities. If only others took the time to notice my unique gifts and perspective, instead of ignoring them and dismissing me. In short, the sentiment is: If only the world saw me for how truly great I am, then I would be. In their minds, covert narcissists believe themselves to be the victim of a world that does not recognize their fabulousness—in essence, *the world just doesn't get it*. If you are a close loved one of a covert narcissist, you are often the one to be punished for the world's lack of understanding. It's your job to reassure them that they are right, and good, and that everyone else is wrong. You are their narcissistic supply. And that's a big job. Trust that you will fall short. Don't blame yourself.

Another unexpected twist is that as you do your best to prop up the covert narcissist's self-image, you may be the target of their passive-aggressive rage. In other words, if you acknowledge their lack of confidence and fear by becoming their best cheerleader, who cheers them on toward a declared goal, the covert narcissist will likely grow to resent you. The same will result if you try to assure the narcissist that feelings of inadequacy are normal, and that with consistent efforts they will eventually be successful. Because they actually believe that they are superior to ordinary folks, the covert narcissist resents you for seeing their weaknesses and still loving them. It's as if they see you as a liar because deep down, they don't see themselves as capable of achieving the great heights you see them reaching. This is an example of what I mean when I say that you can't win with a covert narcissist.

Inner rage is the exact opposite of what others see when encountering covert narcissists. I didn't see it—at first. It doesn't fit the temper-tantrum behavior of the overt narcissists. Take a closer look at the possible covert narcissist in your life. The rage comes out in passive-aggressive ways: invalidation, dismissiveness, devaluation, silent treatment, never being satisfied (you can never do enough), condescending comments, not following through on commitments or promises (because it's beneath them, and you shouldn't have asked in the first place). All of it is disguised as being forgetful, distracted, or confused. At times you will see an overt burst of rage from the covert narcissist. This is purposeful. It conditions you to walk on eggshells as you try to figure out what happened and what you did wrong. This is all so you don't upset the facade of the covert narcissist being a sweet, humble Mr. Nice Guy!

I wish that the DSM-5-TR, or any other textbook, informed mental health students about what personality disorders look like in real life. That has not been my experience. In fact, when I spoke with therapists who have joined the field in the last five to ten years, they said that their studies do not include a deep dive into specific personality disorders. Not one has reported having targets of narcissists as guest speakers who share about their relationships with a character-disordered person. I wish that the therapists, whom I looked to for help, knew what possible childhood traumas to address with me, traumas that left me wide open for narcissistic abuse. That would have been extremely helpful.

CHAPTER 3

EXPERIENCING THE COVERT NARCISSIST

In my experience, personally and as a recovery coach, a covert narcissist presents as a harmless, humble, charming, shy, nice person who wants to do the right thing. And I fell for it, "hook, line, and sinker" as the saying goes. It seems that most people do. Grandiosity, exploitation, entitlement, and lack of empathy are not apparent—unless you know what to look for.

The Beginning of the End

In 2015, months before I allowed my marriage to implode by not feeding Colin's ego anymore, the therapist that he and I were seeing together and individually said that she could and would teach him empathy. At the time, part of me was intrigued and hopeful because no other therapist had made such a bold claim. Plus, she had already spotted Colin to be a narcissist, which he found hysterical after his first session with her. He laughed when he told me what she said. When I met with her, she added, "I want you to know that Colin truly loves you. He really wants your marriage to work. That should bring you some comfort." I don't know if it brought me comfort, but it did soften me and open me again to wishful thinking and toxic hope. It made me hopeful that the Colin I first fell in love with would return. As it turns out, research shows the exact opposite to be true. Empathy cannot be taught to a full-grown narcissist, nor are they capable of genuine love. A narcissist's love is transactional. It's self-serving and highly conditional.

This was the same therapist who believed Colin to be on the far-right end of the narcissist-sociopath-psychopath continuum, but who could not say that he was a full-blown psychopath because she hadn't seen any signs of violence. Had she truly understood the disorder, it seems that she would have known that psychopaths cannot be taught empathy, at least not in the sense that she meant it, not in a way that would improve my marriage. Psychopaths have a strong understanding of empathy and how to use it to torture and manipulate.

She hadn't seen the violence, but I had experienced it and I told her so. Yet, she never addressed it.

The therapist hadn't seen the violent parts of Colin because a covert narcissist presents as Mr. Nice Guy. For most people on the outside looking in, he was a perfect partner. Instead of asking me for more details about violence, she reassured me that Colin indeed loved me and wanted our marriage to work. She assured me that the work she was doing with Colin required him to make a contract with himself to be more accountable for his actions and responsibilities. I thought about how absurd this idea was for a person without a conscience. I was wondering, "What personal code of ethics would bind him to this contract?" Then I was distracted by the words that came afterward, where she explained that she would have to bill my medical insurance for treatment of attention deficit disorder, which she believed Colin also had, because narcissistic personality disorder (NPD) is not covered by medical insurance. According to the powers-that-be in the medical field, NPD is deemed untreatable. Therefore, counseling sessions for NPD are not covered by insurance.

My head swam in confusion as I tried to connect the facts: Narcissists are manipulative, and incapable of true empathy, and NPD is considered untreatable. Yet this mental health professional, a person in a position of authority, a person who supposedly identified Colin as a narcissist, assured me that Colin did indeed love me and that a remedy was available. What had Colin said that made her ignore the research and present me with reasons to hope? What had he said that prevented this therapist from saying to me: "There are so many variables. None of them are likely to work out in your favor. You are possibly in danger. Create an exit strategy."?

Those weren't the words I heard from her or any of the earlier therapists.

My Misconceptions of Narcissism

Immediately following the first diagnosis, I made a sincere effort to understand narcissistic personality disorder. I did the recommended reading. At that time, an area of concern that mental healthcare practitioners assessed was impairment in self-functioning. I didn't think that applied to Colin because he was self-motivated to do well in school and to set other goals, to get out of bed and go to work, and to maintain good hygiene. I understood this to mean that he *was* self-functioning, which would be contrary to a diagnosis of NPD. *I was so wrong!* Self-functioning in this context means being self-aware, being able to reflect on your behaviors and goals, having a sense of self, to become self-actualized. In short, it means not needing or allowing others to define who you are and how you will behave, more often than not. It means not having vacillating values, goals, and an identity that fluctuates depending on who is standing in front of you. Colin was not able to do that. He was not self-functioning.

Over the years, I came to realize that what Colin would say and do depended on the person standing in front of him, and whether he felt superior or inferior in comparison. Colin had proven to me repeatedly over the years that his choices, actions, words, and behavior depended on one factor, and one factor only: Will I get a hit of narcissistic supply, or won't I? If the answer was YES, then it was a GO! If not, then it was a NO! Colin's self-worth depended on it.

This has proven to be true despite any previous conversations or agreements, regardless of the resulting financial damage, and despite repercussions to our relationship. Nothing outside of narcissistic supply, in the present moment, mattered when it came to Colin's behavior. His need for the approval of the person in front of him at that moment was more important to him than me, our marriage, or our kids. I experienced this again and again and was left to sort through the fallout.

One example that comes to mind took place months after our honeymoon. Colin was a groomsman at a friend's wedding. As expected, he sat with the bridal party for the dinner and toasting portion of the reception. No big deal. The trouble began when Colin and the bridesmaid that he was paired with remained at the head table. They continued sitting together, long after all the other members of the bridal party dispersed to mingle, dance, or sit with their families. Colin must have been in rare form. He must have been charming, amusing, and flattering, because the bridesmaid was laughing, leaning in so that her Rachel Green haircut would fall in her face in such a way that required several movie star hair flips. An hour passed. For part of that time, I sat at my table alone. Then I walked the halls of the venue and participated in a few line dances. Another hour passed. It was when the bridesmaid's laugh could be heard over the music that I thought to myself, *Colin is funny, but he isn't that damn funny!*

I approached the bridal table and said to Colin, "Excuse me, but I'd like you to spend some time with your *wife* now."

The poor woman's smile fell in horror as she looked at me and then Colin. She turned red, made an audible inhale, held her breath, and shot daggers at Colin with her eyes. Clearly, she had wasted her best moves working him—all for naught.

As Colin and I walked away, he put his hand in mine and said, "Thanks for saving me, babe. I thought she'd never shut up. I didn't know how to get away." I knew Colin holding my hand was meant to comfort me, but every cell in my body screamed *DANGER!* Unfortunately, at the time, I didn't know what to do with the information my body was sending me. When I explained my frustration to Colin, he whined about how stuck he felt. He said he didn't want to hurt the poor girl's feelings and that he thought as a groomsman he was supposed to stay with his counterpart at a wedding. I wasn't able to decipher the conflict that I felt in my body. On one hand, something felt *off*. On the other hand, I knew Colin to be shy and socially awkward, in which case, his excuse made sense. In my mind, this was not a reason to throw in the towel so early in our marriage. I missed the red flag.

In this situation and others, I explained to Colin how his choice made me feel and what I'd rather he'd done in a given situation and why. I made up *what-if* scenarios to demonstrate how he'd feel if the roles were reversed. But Colin seemed incapable of learning from his mistakes and transferring the information from one situation to the next. Over and over again, I was dismissed in some way or another, so that he could win the adoration and approval of whichever family member, friend, or complete stranger happened to be in the room. The situations usually played out where the reflective, responsible and more supportive choice was ignored, all so that Colin could get his fix.

This didn't change with the arrival of our boys. Instead, they were simply folded into the mix. For instance, Colin agreed to babysit for a friend whose kid mistreated our youngest son. He did this after I had already told her no. I had explained that childcare was no longer part of our friendship and why. This woman dropped her son off with a smirk saying, "Colin said he'd watch him."

Colin's excuse was that he just wanted to help! Evidently, my boundary and our son's emotional and physical well-being were not a concern. On that particular day, my youngest son spent the next three hours at my side in order to feel safe in his own home. Despite my explanation and the welfare of our son, Colin chose the hit of narcissistic supply that he got in those moments of being the hero—Mr. Nice Guy. He didn't see how he undermined me and my boundary of not providing childcare for a supposed friend who didn't keep our son safe. To me, the boundary seemed obvious, necessary, clear.

Over the years, there were other situations in which Colin undermined the agreements that bound us as a couple. It didn't matter whether the source of narcissistic supply was male or female, young or old; Colin needed constant boosts to his ego. Each boost was his proof that he was a good guy.

More than once, it had been suggested to me that Colin's behavior was just typical male behavior. It's certainly what I grew up witnessing. However, for me, the difference is that with the Colins of the world, they know the damage that their behavior is causing, and they do it anyway.

Each time I explained the sense of betrayal that I felt in specific situations, Colin seemed to get it, to empathize, to understand. He made promises to choose differently. There were even a few times that he did choose differently. I praised him for it. Yet too often whenever the opportunity arose to choose me, to choose us, at the expense of disappointing someone that he admired, or wanted to impress, he did not. He could not. What Colin chose was the hit of narcissistic supply. Over the years, the label "marshmallow man" made more and more sense, and the man that I thought I married faded away.

The Slip of The Mask

All of the videos I watched, along with the books and articles that I read, kept leading me back to the idea that narcissists are mean, grandiose, attention-seeking assholes. This simply wasn't Colin. That's because covert narcissists play a different game. They fly under the radar as a socially awkward wallflower. So much so, I had compassion for him, maybe even pity at times. Little did I know that those alluring and non-threatening traits masked the sullen, apathetic, self-indulgent, rage-filled, and self-loathing truth.

I've learned that the covert narcissist is not the boastful center of attention and life of the party, like his overt counterpart. The covert narcissists definitely crave attention and admiration, but, as the name implies, they have this sneaky way of demanding it without saying a word. Throughout our marriage, Colin covertly demanded compliance by stonewalling, projecting his faults onto me, lying, gaslighting, and giving me the silent treatment, all while presenting himself as the confused and dutiful husband and maintaining the Mr. Nice Guy facade. That way, he would still have people, including me, feeding his desperate need to feel worthy.

One-on-one, the covert narcissist can be charismatic. However, they lack the self-confidence and charisma of the classic overt narcissist. The covert wants to be the center of attention and to be worshiped. He feels entitled to such treatment, just as the overt narcissist does, but he can't pull it off as easily. Often, this ignites the hidden inner rage that the covert feels toward the world for not recognizing his brilliance. When this happens, the covert is the person who finds his *in* by pointing fingers at others who are stealing the spotlight, asking *Who is that buffoon?* Believe it or not, this tactic often works because at any given social event, there's a point where enough people are indeed thinking that the overt narcissist, who is one hundred percent talking and laughing above everyone, *is* a buffoon. And just like that, the covert narcissist has the attention he craves. He's the hero, who said what others couldn't.

When covert narcissists aren't able to make themselves the center of attention in a social situation, it's common for them to pick a fight. I've come to know that picking a fight allows the Colin in your life to release some of the pent-up anger that surfaces and intensifies when they're not in the spotlight. The fight is designed to make the covert look like a victim in the situation.

No matter the scenario, this fight will be someone else's fault. Most likely yours.

Perhaps you will fail to respond appropriately to a comment or forget to laugh hard enough at a joke the narcissist makes. Or, instead, it could be you questioning the way the covert is looking at or flirting with another person, purposefully invalidating you. You will be accused of having an overactive imagination, or of being too sensitive, or of always starting a fight, and never being happy. *You are the reason that they want to go home!* The covert narcissist has successfully escaped the frustration of not being the center of attention. And now, they get to release their rage on you.

I lived through such events repeatedly with Colin.

The first time it happened, we were at a friend's housewarming party. I was having a good time chatting with other women about makeup, and then a new mom about the best children's books to add to her baby's library. As I had been groomed to do, I went to check on Colin who had been sitting alone for a short time—fifteen minutes or so. I was prepared to sit with him, if he was still alone.

He watched me as I made my way over, then said, "Don't wear those pants again. They make you look fat."

The comment was mean and meant to hurt. Mission accomplished! There was no way to talk his way out of that one.

Colin wanted me to feel self-conscious so that I would want to leave the party, making me his excuse for leaving. For covert narcissists, that's far better than feeling inadequate by admitting their own need to escape because they feel inferior and rageful.

I was about to tell him that his comment was uncalled for and would have been more helpful twenty minutes before we left our apartment. There was no need. Our friend had heard Colin's comment. This friend let him know exactly what she thought about his words and assured me that I looked great. To soften the blow, she teased that Colin deserved to sleep in the doghouse.

This was a wound to Colin's ego. Someone else saw who he really was—that he was not really Mr. Nice Guy. Colin tried to backpedal. "Well! I thought she'd want to know," he said.

Our friend didn't buy it, instantly earning herself the title "the world's biggest bitch" as far as Colin was concerned. *Time to go!*

My punishment was the silent treatment during the drive home and for the rest of the evening. However, the next day, he acted as if nothing happened. When I tried to get some closure on the event, and express my feelings about his insulting comment, Colin's response was, "That party was so lame. Plus, I can't believe Heather is paying that much for a tiny condo." Colin said this while walking away, so as to avoid taking any accountability for his behavior. By the way, this walking away was not only a power play to avoid accountability, but it also set me up to be the aggressor—and Colin the victim—if I had followed him demanding an explanation or some sort of accountability.

Isolation and Exploitation

The covert narcissist's tendencies play out in another subtle way. They have a way of isolating you from your family and friends. I am not sure if this is due to the narcissist's need for control, their feeling of superiority, or their sense of entitlement, but one thing is for sure: your social life and support systems will gradually become non-existent the longer you're with a narcissist.

You'll start noticing your calendar slowly clearing up. It could be because someone had the guts to call the narcissist out for their bullshit, and that sparked the covert's passive-aggressive rage. Or perhaps the narcissist feels inferior in some way—be it intelligence, finances, looks—and their ego can't tolerate that person's presence. Or maybe it's all about control, which provides the validation that the narcissist craves.

Look for a pattern. I promise you, it's there.

For me, the isolation started innocently enough. I began skipping much-needed Friday night happy-hour events with my fellow teachers. I was new and felt that getting to know my workmates outside of the school building was essential for me to fit in and create friendships.

With kisses and puppy-dog eyes, Colin would suggest, "Let's stay home tonight! Just you and me ... I've missed you all week."

Occasionally, he changed up his tactic and threw in a classic line, "I'm so tired. Clinics have been brutal. I just want to stay here and watch the game. But you can go!"

Ugh! The defeated tone in his voice would make me feel guilty, so I often ended up staying home with him. And when I did, Colin would shower me with kisses and gratitude, saying, "I'm so glad you stayed home with me. I like it when it's just us."

When I did go out for the night without him, Colin would act sullen and dejected when I returned home, making comments like, "It wasn't the same without you."

I fell for the *I want you all to myself* sentiments. I believed it was all part of our honeymoon phase. It took me years to see the pattern, especially when it happened during one of Colin's love-bombing episodes, showering me with the adoration, affection, and attention that I subconsciously needed and wanted. I hated the energy of the sullen and dejected Colin and wanted to avoid his presence.

If you're reading this, I am guessing that you've probably fallen for something similar yourself. It's uncanny that the narcissists know exactly how to pull on your heartstrings!

But here's the reality: If Colin felt superior to others at an event, we'd get to stay. But the moment he didn't feel like the smartest person in the room, we'd magically find a reason to leave early—or simply not show up at all.

It's all about control. The covert plays the Mr. Nice Guy role, gaslighting you by telling you their actions are not malicious, and that it's just that they love you so much. The behavior is non-threatening, low-key, and can feel like love, or pleading. You want the narcissist to feel loved, and you want to be loved, so the red flags are dismissed. In contrast, the overt narcissist is more likely to act like a dictator, forbidding you from going out or demanding constant check-ins. That wouldn't have worked on me—at least not at the time.

It's important to know that the covert narcissist wants to keep their true nature hidden from others. They don't want witnesses to the charade, so the fewer people observing the better. The covert will go through great effort to prevent blowing their cover.

The more sinister result of a relationship with a covert narcissist is that when needed, when you are questioning your sanity, or wanting someone to talk to, there is no one there. You've lost connections with friends and family. Reaching out becomes hard, so you don't. As time passes, you adjust your behavior to maintain the last relationship standing—the one with the narcissist.

There's another level to the social aspects of being in a relationship with a covert narcissist. It is one that caught me by surprise. I first noticed this a few months before my marriage imploded. The backstory is that I rarely feel inadequate in the company of others. It's not that I feel superior, or even super confident in my wit, looks, or accomplishments. I'm simply excited to meet people.

I'm the sort of person who asks, "So, how did you find yourself working in a crystal shop in Sedona, Arizona?" I'm interested in people's life stories. And on the whole, people are willing to share. Some a little. Some a lot. A few, not at all.

My questions were often met with a smile and the raising of eyebrows. For the most part, people are surprised and warmed by my curiosity. That's the me that caught Colin's eye back in college. In fact, it's one of the reasons he asked me out on a date.

Little did I know, there was more to it. It turned out that Colin had a hidden agenda from the beginning. He would invite me to meet his classmates, and later to his staff functions, only to serve as a go-between. I was the warm-up act until Colin felt confident enough to shine on his own. I seemed to be the personal bridge connecting Colin with other people. For all narcissists, others only exist to serve a role, and this was mine.

At the time, I thought that I was doing my part as a wife, a team player, and a good friend by using my strengths to support my husband and strengthen our marriage. My attitude was, "Yeah, I got this!" Little did I know that behind the scenes, Colin was secretly resenting me for being … well, me!

Many narcissists admire what they can't have and then resent others for having it—whatever "it" is! I was naïve enough to believe Colin was introducing me to the people in his life because he loved me and wanted others to know me—to know us.

That was not the case—at all. Looking back, I can't help but laugh at my utter blindness.

Colin didn't have an ounce of love for me. He proved that in the end.

Hidden Resentment

What I know now is that the covert narcissist lives vicariously through those that they admire, until their own inadequacies become too much to bear. When that happens, all those traits that they claimed to love about you suddenly become the target of their hate. You're suddenly too much for them, and they want to punish you for it. You must pay the price for their pain!

I believe that we are all wounded in some way. That's the human condition. For much of our marriage, I believed that where I was weak, Colin was strong, and vice-versa. I thought we were fortunate to find one another. This was not by mistake. Colin, just like all narcissists, presented himself as one way when he was quite the opposite. It became apparent that Colin showed very little strength in navigating life—except within his profession, which allowed him to feel superior to others. When this became evident, I felt true empathy for Colin. Over the years, that empathy shifted into sympathy, an obligation to stay, and then guilt for wanting to leave a person who was unwell. It was during the final hoover that I saw Colin's wounding and resentment clearly. (Hoover is the term commonly used when referring to the narcissist's attempt to suck you back into the toxic relationship.)

For whatever reason, Colin had become consumed with karaoke. He went to karaoke bars several nights a week. He did this on weeknights, often coming home after midnight, and this had been a factor in why I asked for a separation. His karaoke obsession intensified to the point where Colin started going to bars nightly. After being hoovered, I accompanied Colin to karaoke. I wanted to go for several reasons. One was because Colin had brought it up in our pretend therapy sessions, where he cited my lack of interest in karaoke as a disconnect in our relationship. (He hadn't mentioned the fact that he had never invited me, or that he had been going on a weeknight, knowing that I worked the next morning. He simply shifted the blame to me, and the therapist never called him on that. But that's another chapter.) The second reason was that Colin had seemed more confident, less brooding and depressed. He said that he was happy to get back into singing and that he had forgotten how good he was at it. I genuinely wanted to support him.

During the karaoke events I saw the covert grandiosity, the over-inflated sense of importance, reveal itself. Colin had bragged that his best song was "Come Together" by The Beatles. It was Halloween night, or at least Colin wore a costume. It was a purposefully cheesy blue and white plaid tuxedo jacket and a cheap afro wig. During the song Colin pulled the wig from his head and tapped his knee with it as he sang something about having *hair down to his knees*. Colin had bragged about this stunt and was excited to do it. Supposedly, it had gone over big at one of his other Halloween events. This particular night, it failed. Personally, I didn't find it surprising or amusing because I knew it was coming and was waiting for it.

Perhaps the other patrons in the bar thought Colin's act was gimmicky or cheesy. At the end of his song, there was the obligatory hand clapping. By obligatory, I mean clapping because the DJ says, "Let's give him a hand," so you clap. You clap as you continue your conversation, even though you didn't watch the performance.

When Colin got back to our table, I could feel the shift in energy. He was not happy.

"How did I do?" he asked.

I knew immediately that it was my duty to make him feel good about the performance, so I said, "You looked like you had fun!"

He said, "This crowd sucks. They didn't even watch."

I remained silent. If this reconciliation was to really work, I had to resist the habit of building up and protecting Colin's ego. I wanted to build something different with Colin—something better than what we had.

"Probably all drunk," he said.

I remained silent.

Colin continued to brood. His next song, sans bad afro wig, was "Sweet Caroline" by Neil Diamond. The crowd sang along. I even sang quietly. It's that kind of song. Colin beamed when he was finished.

"How about that one? How did I do?" he asked.

"You definitely got the crowd going! They were so loud, I couldn't hear you. I'm sure you did fine." All true facts as I saw them.

"Pfff! What do you know?" Colin muttered. His tone was biting. "You don't know anything about singing." Colin was pissed and was taking it out on me. However, true to form, when I gave him the raised eyebrow look, Colin sought to justify his comment with, "Well, you *don't*. You studied art, not music. Right?"

Truth is, Colin had suffered a narcissistic "injury," and it was my job, as his wife, to soothe his pain. But I had already quit my job of bolstering his ego.

Colin responded with passive aggression, which is typical for covert narcissists, so that the action can be dismissed with an *All I said was ...* or *Well, isn't it true?* The covert narcissist's insults and attacks are rarely blatantly cruel. They are stated in a way that allows them to feign ignorance and confusion. Colin was correct. My talents do fall in the realm of visual arts, not music. However, his intent was clear. He meant to put me in my place, to insult me, to question the validity of my experience or opinion. These are the types of attacks that you feel in your body before they register in your mind as the insults they are. Still, more often than not, your mind will question it with the thought, *Did he just say what I think he said?* until you realize exactly what type of person you are dealing with.

But this time I refused to accept ownership of the problem. I did *not* take responsibility for making Colin feel better about himself.

Instead, I made a mental note of the message that my body was sending me: *Danger!* THAT'S what I started paying attention to.

On another karaoke night, there was a young Black woman who I assumed to be twenty-one considering she was in a bar. However, I would not have been shocked to learn that she had a fake ID. She could have easily passed for a sixteen-year-old girl. This young woman appeared shy. She had a round face, and the way she held her arms protectively folded across her belly suggested that she was self-conscious about her body. She wore her hair naturally, a small afro with a thick, blue, patterned headband. She wore a miniskirt with tights and short boots. I noticed her quick smile when a friend at her table said to her, "You're on the list!"

When Colin saw me looking in the direction of the woman and her friends, he said that they were regulars. He insinuated that he knew them.

The next time I saw this young Black woman, she looked quite different. She stood on the stage. Confident. Powerful. She belted out Adele's song "Rolling In The Deep" as if she were Adele herself. She sang with her eyes closed and her arms spread wide. The energy she radiated filled the room and bounced off the walls. There was thunderous applause and the drumming of tables. When the Black Adele exited the stage, she became the young Black woman I saw before—shy and wishing she was invisible. She hurried to get to her friends.

The only thing standing in her way was Colin. There he was in her narrow path with his arm stretched out for a congratulatory palm slap. The girl made moves to go around him. Colin adjusted his position—still intending the palm slap! The girl's face looked panicked. She quickly slapped Colin's palm, realizing it was the only way to get him to move. Colin did the same with the next twenty-something, young female, singer from the bunch. This one scrunched her face in distress as she made her way back to the table.

The exchange reminded me of adults who show physical affection (a back rub, a hug, or a kiss) to children without permission. The power differential is obvious. I felt bad for the young woman who simply wanted a fun night out singing karaoke, yet her agency and power were compromised. She was essentially forced to allow Colin into her personal and mental space. I felt like I should apologize to the young women.

At the same time, I felt embarrassed and responsible for Colin. He was the creepy, fifty-year-old barfly, desperate to be cool, but didn't realize it. The notion that he was not "one of the gang" was not an option for Colin. The covert narcissist has grandiose delusions just as the overt narcissist does. Pointing out anything that contradicts those delusions will result in passive-aggressive payback. When I asked Colin if he was sure that the young Black Adele remembered him, his response was, "Of course! Why wouldn't she? I'm here every week!"

My gut raised the alarm: Pay attention!

* * *

When enmeshed with a covert narcissist you end up living in a constant state of high alert, burdened by physical and mental exhaustion. There is a slow steady change in your focus and behavior until one day you discover that all of your thoughts and actions are in effort to keep the covert narcissist happy or, at the very least, from acting out. You likely won't be able to put your finger on just what it is that has you feeling out-of-sorts, you will simply know that, after being with said person, you are *off* in some way. After all, you have belief and hope that the covert narcissist *is* Mr. Nice Guy. You don't want to believe that someone you love is sucking you dry.

It wasn't until I went **no contact** (a term meaning to cut off all communication) with Colin that the healing and true understanding of my experience began.

Being a true crime fan, I can't help but liken my time with Colin to the type of cases where the unassuming, seemingly devoted wife is poisoning her husband (and sometimes her children) with regular doses of arsenic, or ethylene glycol. At first the victim has a headache that can be explained by fatigue, or stress. Then there's a stomachache and vomiting that is, in the victim's mind, *surely* a flu, or gastrointestinal bug. There are other system breakdowns of the body. These are all explained away as other possibilities—that is, until someone notices that the victim improves when in the hospital and away from the dutiful wife and mother. Sometimes the culprit is caught on security cameras, or with some sting operation. Most times, however, the poisoning isn't discovered until an autopsy. Then it becomes a case of whodunit.

Life with a covert narcissist is like drinking a daily dose of arsenic, or ethylene glycol. The longer the exposure the greater the damage. The only way to recover from poisoning and narcissistic abuse is to end your exposure so that you can heal. Otherwise, the result is death.

At the start of the separation from Colin, the first thing I noticed was just how exhausting life with him had been—mentally, emotionally, and physically. So much space opened up in my body. I felt less constricted and woke up rested and energized. Looking back, the changes were so profound. Life felt so positive and full of possibility. I knew I felt better. It was as if more alone time was all that I needed—time to sleep in, practice self-care, and put my interests first. Of course, Colin was in full love-bomb phase. Therefore, it hadn't occurred to me then that being away from Colin was the reason I'd felt better.

I was no longer receiving daily doses of poison.

Going fully no contact (physically, emotionally, mentally, and energetically) after my divorce opened my eyes to more changes that occurred within months. First of all, my asthma improved. I wasn't shutting down while walking through the cleaning supply isles and I was able to walk through freshly cut grass. Second, I noticed that I no longer had migraines (other than those that were traced back to the food additive, MSG). Migraine-free days gave me more opportunities to be fully engaged in my life. Third, I joined Facebook and was surprised to see that I had a genuine smile on my face when tagged in group selfies. In fact, in most of the shots, I was actually giggling, in sheer joy.

Before, when Colin was taking pictures and posting on Facebook, my smile was not genuine. I hated taking selfies with him because I knew that for the 40–60 minutes following the post, he would be consumed with checking people's responses. Colin's mood for the rest of the curated occasion would be determined by the number of likes his post received. Facebook became a narcissistic supply for Colin. I hated it!

After a year of being fully no contact from Colin, I began to recognize that I was entwined in relationships with other covert narcissists: two family members and a boss. For me, it shows up as physical exhaustion, a headache, an unexplained sadness, or mental numbness as if I had taken Benadryl. When I look back on it, and after seeing a pattern in my coaching clients, I would attribute this to the "victim energy" that the covert narcissists have.

Without having to say a word, the covert seems to beg for recognition and validation. There have been times when Colin seemed to radiate resentment toward me. It's those times when the covert is with you and they appear more down, more subdued, than usual. But, when you ask, "What's wrong?" the answer is "Nothing!" Yet, there's no conversation. Just sighs or stares in your direction. The energy between you is heavy and tense. You know that something is wrong, and you wrack your nerves trying to figure it out. You do this partly because you care, and partly because you know that you will likely pay later for not doing, or saying, the right thing. Maybe you've experienced the same with someone else. Next time, notice how exhausted you feel.

Once you are no longer subjected to daily doses of the covert narcissist, and you've learned to listen to your body cues, you may find that other covert narcissists in your life will reveal themselves and become more apparent to you. Be sure to make mental notes when you are in the company of a person who you suspect is toxic for you. Notice how your body responds. Don't be shocked if you find that you have been surrounded by quite a few narcissistic people. They exist, and you may be serving as Grade A narcissistic supply.

We're gonna find out and fix that!

* * *

The dynamics of a relationship with a covert narcissist are not the same as one with a mentally healthy person. In trying to provide the narcissist with validation and admiration, we get lost. We cross our own boundaries for the sake of peace. Due to time constraints and exhaustion, self-care seems to be the first to go. Eventually, our friendships and other factors that connect us to other people start to fade away. Before we realize it, we are impacted in large and small ways.

The trauma goes deeper. Like a reflex, the targets of narcissists find themselves apologizing and taking full responsibility for the narcissist's mistakes and troublesome situations. I firmly believe that you can't be with a covert narcissist without quickly becoming a participant in your own abuse. In other words, just like me, you will start adjusting yourself—a little at first, because that's what relationships are all about. However, the changes that you make are never enough. The narcissist will continue to insist on more, either in subtle or overt ways. *Slowly but surely, you are systematically erased, and you are complicit.*

Worse still, you never really know where you stand in a relationship with a covert narcissist because conflicts between you are never fully resolved. Narcissists repeat poor behavior because they are unable to accept responsibility, reflect, and therefore learn from their infractions.

* * *

Believe me when I say that chipping away at yourself takes its toll. You become someone you don't recognize. Just a month after going fully no contact, I realized that I didn't know myself anymore. My entire identity had become the woman who put out Colin's fires; the woman who talked him down off the ledge; the woman who sang his praises and put his needs first.

Being in a relationship with a covert narcissist leaves you feeling that you are to blame for the turbulence in the relationship. After all, he is a "Mr. Nice Guy," and people in your inner circle often tell you so, going so far as to even adopt the narcissist's point of view. With so many people speaking against your reality, you feel that the problems in the relationship must be your fault. I actually felt guilty for calling Colin out on his bullshit.

My therapist, my girlfriends, and family were saying, "You're too hard on him!"

When I shared the back story of my frustration and anger, they dismissed me, saying things like, "You must have misunderstood his intentions!", "I'm sure he didn't mean it that way," and "Maybe, you're just tired. When was the last time you got away?" My father even added the Bible scriptures: "Pride is before a crash, and a haughty spirit before stumbling" (Proverbs 16:18). In other words, not only was I being gaslighted by the narcissist, but everyone who saw Colin as Mr. Nice Guy also had me questioning my reality.

* * *

I want you to know your truth. I want you to begin discovering it by completing the exercises below. They will help you document your experience. That way, when the confusion and exhaustion set in—and they will—you will have your notes. Eventually, you will see a pattern, one that I missed, or dismissed, for far too long.

EXERCISES

Exercise 1: You're Not Insane. You're Being Gaslighted

Keep track of the behaviors and comments of the suspected narcissist. Keep the details on your phone. Record them as they happen, or soon after. Use a special shorthand or code that only you would understand; that way, you will be free to write the details of the event.

Note any and all evidence of:

- "Poor me. I'm so misunderstood."
- The inner rage. Sometimes expressed openly, but most often in passive-aggressive comments and actions. This also shows up as anger for not being appreciated, admired, and celebrated. (This is covert grandiosity.)
- Having to bolster the narcissist's ego and confirm their brilliance.

Keep this information for future reference as you read this book and gather more information regarding the antics of the covert narcissist.

Exercise 2: Manipulation vs Love

Remembering that you deserve happy, healthy, and supportive relationships, get very honest with yourself.

Ask yourself: Do I really love (insert name), or do I feel sympathy and obligation, a sense of responsibility? *Remember playing the victim, the misunderstood underdog, is a manipulation of the covert narcissist. They are so sure that they could reach their full potential, if only they had someone like you by their side. Soon you won't be good enough. Then, in their mind it will become: So-and-so (you), is holding me back. I could reach my full potential, if only I had someone new, someone who gets me. The problem is that the cost is quite high for you.*

- What is the relationship costing you now?

- What has it cost you already?
- What could it cost you in the future?

Exercise 3: The Love List

Too often we know what we don't want, but we aren't clear on what we DO WANT. We simply know when something feels icky, yet we can't identify what personal boundary it crosses. Creating a list gets you half-way there.

Make a list of what you want in your dream partner. No matter how ridiculous, picky, or arrogant each desire may sound, write it down. You can edit it later.

- What DO you want in a relationship?
- What are the deal breakers?
- How do you want to feel?
- How does your ideal person handle conflicts?
- Is accountability important to you?
- Do you resent having to point out repeated transgressions?
- How do you want to be seen?

CHAPTER 4

IDEALIZING. DEVALUING. DISCARDING.

Idealizing, devaluing, and discarding are tactics used by both overt and covert narcissists. These three words describe the abuse cycle that both types of narcissists deploy against their targets. I have yet to encounter a single target of narcissistic abuse who hasn't been caught in this abuse cycle.

Once it's explained and understood, mixed feelings may ensue. The recognition often brings surprise, anger, and self-blame for being so gullible. I can't tell you how often I've heard the words "I feel so stupid" from clients. I strongly caution against self-blame because the covert narcissist's abuse cycle is so insidious and subtle that the phases often look like the ups and downs of a typical relationship. Most of us grow up believing that relationships are hard, so we soldier on.

Before I go into details, see if this sounds and feels familiar: At the beginning of the relationship, you two seemed to just fit together. You were put on a pedestal and showered with attention, affection, and adoration. You gave as good as you got. Then, without warning or clear cause, you picked up on subtle—or not-so-subtle—shifts in the relationship. Comments and actions left you feeling humiliated, confused, and insecure in the relationship.

When you asked for clarification, as mature, non-disordered people do, you were dismissed with "Wow! I didn't realize you were so sensitive!" or "What are you talking about?" or "All I said was … You took it the wrong way!"

Perhaps you made a move to show physical affection, but you are shut down. Maybe he pulled his hand away when you reached for it with a sudden need to search for something in his pocket or make a call. Maybe he stopped opening the doors for you (something he made a great display of in the beginning). Each of these examples is a subtle maneuver meant to humiliate you and sow seeds of self-doubt and insecurity, and they are usually the result of one or two reasons: narcissistic injury, or projection. In the case of narcissistic injury, you have unknowingly insulted the narcissist's ego or failed to feed it sufficiently. Projection is the narcissist punishing you for an action that they are guilty of. However, you have no way of knowing these vital details in the relationship. Note that, as you continue to receive this punishment, in the narcissist's eyes you are discarded temporarily, or semi-permanently, as they move on to seek narcissistic supply elsewhere before circling back to you.

This cycle can end in several different ways: (1) the narcissist decides you have been punished sufficiently and begins once again showering you with love and affection, (2) you take the blame and don't hold the narcissist accountable, or (3) you feed the narcissist's ego. Then the abuse cycle starts all over again.

With a covert narcissist, this abuse cycle can play out in subtle ways, on repeat, for decades.

Idealization

Idealization is the clinical term for the love-bombing phase of the abuse cycle, also sometimes referred to as "the honeymoon phase." All new relationships experience this. It's when you use all the manners your momma and grandma taught you, and you're less demanding and more willing to compromise. Most of all, it's when you *hide your crazy!* Putting your best face forward is expected.

This time is yummy, full of giggles and energy. Often, there's sexual tension, which is quite exciting whether you indulge or not. It feels as if you don't have a care in the world. Your previous worries appear trivial. You do very little thinking and become consumed by a lot of positive emotions. Life feels fantastic. At times, it feels like you can live on love alone because very little sleep and food are needed. You know the feeling—especially if you've been with a narcissist.

It's called the love-bombing phase because when the narcissist learns that you really like roses, they send you enough to fill a room. You are the envy of every woman at work. You feel appreciated and adored. But be warned, for the narcissist love-bombing is a manipulation tactic. It creates a strong emotional bond quickly. It's used to control or manipulate your feelings.

With an overt narcissist, the idealization phase is often so over the top that most people will see the behavior and events as too much. Whether they choose to ignore them or not, many people see lavish gifts, costly trips, and around-the-clock attention early in a relationship as red flags. Others may see it as a dream come true and jump into the deep end.

It's important to know that the narcissist's goal is to get the target emotionally invested. As a manipulator, the narcissist will adjust their behavior accordingly, ramping up the attention, affection, and adoration, or pulling back to ensure that the target feels safe and grounded or just uneasy enough to feel that she may lose out if she doesn't leap, heart first. Logic goes out the window.

The narcissist is very attuned to how others respond to their tactics and adjust along the way. The idealization phase with a covert is more low-key and subtle when compared with an overt narcissist. Here the covert appears to be shy, yet willing to be vulnerable and even self-deprecating; bright, adventurous, yet socially awkward; humble, a good listener, looking directly into your eyes as you tell your story; and most of all, the covert narcissist feels safe, not only safe but in need of saving. As a result, the red flags are missed.

***

As you probably guessed, Colin did not extend his hand and say, "Hello! I am charming. I will make you laugh. I will take care of you.

I will make you feel safe. I will profess my love often. I will comfort you when you are in pain. I will be someone you can count on to be there when you need me. BUT don't be fooled, I am an asshole. So, the above will become sporadic and eventually disappear altogether and you'll be to blame … Wanna go out with me?"

Instead, he was nervous and sweet.

Colin and I met in college during the summer quarter. He had been nervous and asked a friend to lay the groundwork.

The friend asked, "If Colin asked you out, what would you say?"

My immediate response was laughter.

Colin, as a love interest, was so off my radar. He was not the sort of man that usually caught my eye. But I found Colin's efforts amusing. I saw him as non-threatening and safe—I discovered later that this met a subconscious need of mine. The fact that this exchange took place in our college dining hall added to the fun. Back and forth, his friend relayed flirty messages, as we watched for each other's reactions. The only thing missing was a handwritten note that read: Will you go out with me? Check YES or NO. Years later, I'd witness similar shenanigans during second and third grade lunch duty. It made me giggle.

My rationalization at the time was, *He has zero game. How dangerous could he be?*

Our first date was to a local movie theater. It had the musty smell of a haunted basement, stale beer, and pepperoni pizza. *I loved it!* This was the first theater I'd been to that offered more than the usual popcorn, soda, and candy. They offered beer, subs, and pizza. On top of that, the theater had old-fashioned candy jars. I could get scoops of peanut M&M's, chunks of red licorice, or malted chocolate balls in a small, white paper bag. The walls were dark, and my sneakers stuck to the floor as I walked. Many of the chairs were in disrepair. Most had duct tape to cover the holes in the vinyl. This place was a jolting contrast from the multiplex cinemas where I had spent many Saturdays growing up. Movie hopping, as my mother called it, was my way of getting away from my father. Movies were my way of coping. I was in heaven.

Colin had gotten the times for the movie wrong, so we arrived an hour early. Not wanting to risk losing what was clearly a prime parking spot by leaving and coming back later, he suggested that we walk around the neighborhood. I was grateful for something to do. Walking would calm my nerves.

I wasn't sure why I felt off, or why my senses were heightened. I brushed it off as first-date jitters.

Colin chatted about the small family dog back home. I'm not certain how the topic came up. I hated small dogs. I listened as best I could while trying to calm the pit in my stomach and the burning in my chest. Apparently, the family dog was named Pippin. And Pippin had a fondness for pantyhose and eating things he shouldn't as payback for being left alone. He also liked sleeping in bed with his humans, and doing tricks at the sound of, "Who's a good boy? Pippin's a good boy!"

I was both curious and irritated with Colin's incessant talking. I was curious because he was clearly embarrassed about getting the movie times wrong and was trying to compensate for the mistake. Irritated because I didn't want to hear about Pippin. Pippin sounded like a spoiled pain in the ass. (My thoughts about Pippin never changed.)

Ironically, the thing that stopped Colin's narrated documentary about small dogs was that a not-small dog charged at us. I was in the line of fire, the focus of the dog's intimidating growl. Its fur was bristled, and its tail high. Without a moment's hesitation, in one superbly executed move, Colin scooped me back and positioned himself between me and the charging mass. Almost immediately, I heard the sound of two dogs barking: one that was running toward me, and another that, by the sound of its bark, was a much larger dog, one that I could hear but not see. The dog that was clear on his intent to shred me to bits for having dared to walk down its street suddenly made an about-face and retreated, head low and tail between its legs. As I thanked my lucky stars, I looked around for the larger dog and couldn't find one. Until I realized he was right in front of me.

The larger dog turned out to be Colin. He had barked and advanced toward the attack dog, scaring it away. I remember thinking *This boy is crazy!* and *Damn that was brave!*

I had been taught to not run from a dog, and that a charging dog would chomp on the first thing you hand it. I had never heard of, nor imagined, making oneself bigger and mimicking the bark of a much larger dog. But, it worked, Colin standing there in front of me, arms arched out, making himself look bigger, while also growling from somewhere deep and low.

I couldn't help but laugh out loud. "Wow! Where did you learn that trick?" was all I could get out.

"I don't know," Colin said laughing himself. "I didn't know what else to do. Are you okay? I didn't push you too hard, did I?"

"I'm fine. My heart is still beating out of my chest. But I'm good. Thank you."

We decided to return to the theater for a beer. We watched *Romancing the Stone* (1984) starring Micheal Douglas, Danny Devito, and Kathleen Turner. That night I became an instant Kathleen Turner fan. It was her voice that got me. I also found the movie to be very funny. I laughed more than I had in a long time.

I decided that Colin had earned himself a second date.

***

Colin and I had fun together during the remaining weeks between our jobs at freshman summer orientation and the start of the fall quarter. Most of our time was spent in the Drake student union listening to music while Colin drank and smoked cigarettes and I played with the hot wax from the red or white votive candles that burned at each table. Colin did most of the talking, which I appreciated.

There was a particular night that I cherished for years. Later, when I wondered what had become of the Colin I fell in love with, it was this night that I often remembered. Life was easy. Our connection was genuine. The night had started with dinner being whatever they were serving in the dining hall. Then we set out to walk across campus to High Street, the destination being United Dairy Farmers. We were broke college students, so splurging on ice cream was a big deal.

As we walked past the Horseshoe stadium, Colin told me of his dream to be a walk-on kicker for the Ohio State Buckeyes. His voice cracked when he shared this with me, which I interpreted as sincerity.

"All I have to do is increase the length of my kick. I know I can do it with practice. I definitely could be better than Spangler."

I didn't follow football at the time, so I didn't know the feasibility of Colin being a walk-on kicker. All I knew of Spangler was that he had a rare soccer-style kick. None of that mattered. What mattered was that Colin had a secret dream and he was sharing it with me.

Later, I would help Colin practice his kicks by retrieving the ball and throwing it back to him—well, not to him but in his vicinity. My football-throwing skills were laughable.

At the UDF we each got double dips of our favorite ice cream. I got butter pecan, Colin got chocolate almond, each on a sugar cone. With about a quarter of our ice cream left, we switched cones. It was Colin's idea. "It will be like having a second ice cream." It made no sense. But that became our routine. Instead of getting a double-scoop, one of each kind, we would simply switch cones.

We ended up at the Drake Union again that night. Colin confided in me with a story of when he ran over his neighbor's cat. As he told the story, he bit his bottom lip and shook his head in sadness.

"Well, I'm driving down the street. Probably going too fast, and the damn cat comes out of nowhere. I see the orange and white tail in my peripheral vision. As soon as I do, I slam on the brakes ... but it was too late! I hear a Rrrrrl sound....and, then I feel the thump under my tires."

I gasped and put my hand to my mouth. I was not a cat lover, but

I certainly wouldn't want to have run one over. I was fully invested in his tragic tale.

Colin makes a face like he is going to vomit. "So, I was on the road, and it was dark. I didn't know if the cat was dead. I decided to pull over to look for it. When I did, that's when I felt the thump under my back tire again. I thought, 'It's certainly dead now.' So, I decided the only decent thing to do is to go up and confess to my neighbor. I took a deep breath and walked up the sidewalk to their house. I rang the doorbell, hoping that they wouldn't answer. But they did."

"Of course, they did," I said with a giggle.

Colin continues: "I introduced myself as a neighbor living a few blocks down. 'I think I hit your cat,' I said. 'I'm afraid it's dead.' Then they asked, 'Well, how do you know it's our cat?'" Colin lets out an exasperated sigh at this part, then says, "By this time, the woman was all hysterical. She was coming out onto the porch. Then she asked, 'What did the cat look like?' and I said, 'I don't know. Like this, I guess!'"

Without missing a beat, Colin tilted his head to the right, stuck out his tongue, rolled his eyes up and back into their sockets, and posed his arms and hands like immobile limbs.

With that, I realized that I had been had! I closed my eyes and tried to hold back a laugh. "You are such an asshole," I said and punched him in the arm for emphasis. But I was laughing so hard my abs got a workout. We both were.

"You're so much fun," Colin said at that point, adding, "I really want to kiss you!"

"Well, you are going to have to stop smoking cigarettes for that to ever happen," I said.

"Done!" he says. "I was only doing it to look cool."

We don't kiss.

* * *

The next night, he held my hand for the first time as I pretended to not be afraid watching *An American Werewolf in London*. As a rule, I avoided such movies because my imagination always kicked into overdrive later—when I was alone in the dark.

The currents of electricity that coursed through my body when our hands touched shifted my focus. I was surprised by my body's reaction. I hadn't found Colin attractive when I first met him. However, to this day, I do not recall any specific scenes from the movie American Werewolf in London. I don't even remember the plot.

That night, Colin asked for permission to kiss me, and I said, "YES!"

We were sitting on my tiny sofa bed in my dorm room. Colin leaned toward me. As he did, I could see the nervous excitement in his eyes. Clearly, he had not expected me to say "YES!" He lifted my chin with his index finger. The kiss was a gentle peck on my lips. Then another, and another. Soft and tender.

He kissed my nose and whispered, "I really love your nose."

Before I could say anything, Colin's mouth was on mine again. This time, he parted my lips with his tongue. It was when our tongues met that I realized that I had been holding my breath. I exhaled. All at once the pent-up energy rippled through my body. I felt it mostly in my nipples, and my panties.

I regained my composure and pushed Colin away. "Well, aren't you just the cat's pajamas!" was all I could say.

"What?" he asked laughing. "What does that mean?"

Like the three nights previous we talked until the wee hours, starting first with the meaning of the cat's pajamas! I had to prove that I hadn't just made it up. Then we talked about music. I was excited about Tina Turner making a comeback. He loved Elton John most of all. We discovered that we enjoyed the same off-campus bars along South High Street. However, he usually left around 10:00 p.m. which was about the time I arrived. We both found it kismet that we were finally meeting considering the many times our paths had likely crossed.

We laughed about life as college dorm RAs, about the pot plant growing in his room, and how he was sure he would be busted when his resident supervisor stopped by for no particular reason. We admitted that we both wanted to smack the people who found it funny to make the elevators inoperable by using a smashed beer can to keep the doors from closing. This meant that the RA on duty had to get out of bed—usually at 2:30 a.m.—to release the door. Neither of us could figure out why the night security staff couldn't handle it. After all, they were already up and working. Of course, we talked about movies.

Colin slept over that night. Fully clothed. No pressure for sex. I felt seen. Understood. Safe.

In my heart and mind, I had likened Colin to my own Detective Columbo—a smart, bumbling, socially awkward, brilliant man. It never occurred to me then that, just like Columbo, the fictional character, Colin was also acting a part.

Colin was nothing like the men I had dated previously. He wasn't a jock. He wasn't physically gorgeous. He wasn't loud, or the life of the party. Nor was he trying to immediately get into my pants. Simply put, Colin presented himself as kind, smart, generous, humble, shy, and above all safe. He seemed to be a wounded bird who just wanted the opportunity to love and be loved.

It's exactly what I wanted, too.

Colin seemed to appreciate everything about me. He even loved the way I dressed, the way I presented myself.

At one point, he wore my red ball cap and my favorite Chicago Yacht Club sweatshirt more often than I did. Back then, he presented this as having some memento of me with him always. When he wasn't wearing my clothes, he'd spritz himself with my perfume. This was often followed by a moan, and "I can't wait to see you again later tonight."

Back then it was over-the-top flattery. It made me laugh. It endeared him to me. Within months, Colin and I had become inseparable. Whenever we weren't in class, we were together. Why wouldn't we be? It seemed that we could talk about anything, and we made each other laugh.

Colin and I had even had conversations about religion. He grew up as a Methodist, with his primary experience being summer youth camps, where the unsupervised agenda was fornicating and smoking cigarettes and weed. Colin didn't know any Bible scriptures or God's name. This was in stark contrast to my strict religious upbringing as a Jehovah's Witness.

I not only knew Bible scriptures, but I was expected to recite them for my own condemnation and to sanction the physical beatings I got with my father's belt or a switch from the forsythia bush in our yard.

Colin was visibly shaken by the idea of me being physically punished.

I sarcastically assured him that it was not only fine but sanctioned by the Lord. I paraphrased the scripture in Proverbs 13:24: "The one holding back his rod is hating his daughter, but the one loving her, beats her ass on a regular basis."

We both sighed.

I shared with Colin how Jehovah's Witnesses are not permitted to go to college, but I was determined to not be stuck with a man like my father or the elders in our congregation. (*And yes, I am well aware that I failed in my efforts. I married my father, just like Freud said I would.*)

I shared with Colin that the one time my father drove me from Cincinnati to Columbus, he lectured me the entire way about storing up treasures in heaven rather than on earth, and how when we finally arrived, he pointed to Morrill and Lincoln Towers and said, "You are going to die right there in Sodom and Gomorrah." Morrill Tower is where we were both living at the time, so we had a good laugh.

Colin didn't need to know the Bible story of Lot's wife to grasp the gravity of the situation. He was impressed by my resolve.

Because of my questioning and defiant nature regarding my religious upbringing, I had a somewhat tumultuous relationship with my father. It just so happened that Colin had a difficult relationship with his mother. As he explained, she simply didn't understand or appreciate him. Colin recounted the time he got a C in a chemistry class, and instead of acknowledging his hard work, his mother remarked how a former high school classmate of his had earned an A in the same class. There were tears in his eyes when Colin explained how he simply couldn't please her, and how nothing ever seemed to be good enough.

He told me about how his mother had abandoned him when he was quite young. Without explanation, she was simply gone, and his Aunt Sophie was in her place. Although she did return, Colin says that he never knew the story behind what happened.

In my thirty years with Colin, I came to believe that his early stories about his mother were likely half-truths. The only thing I know for sure is that he had great resentment for her, yet also craved her love and attention.

＊＊＊

Colin and I seemed to just fit! We shared the same goals in life and had the same ideas about the meaning of family—one differing from what we individually had experienced thus far.

Having both grown up in dysfunctional homes, we each claimed that if we ever got married, divorce was not an option and that we'd commit to making it work.

Besides a visit to Niagara Falls, I had never been out of the country. Colin had already traveled to Canada and Europe. He wanted to show me the world. I wanted to see it—especially Italy.

Colin understood my strong will and drive. He seemed to admire my tenacity and tell-it-like-it-is attitude. He respected my boundaries. We laughed at the same jokes. We had the same work ethic and career goals. He was different from other men I'd dated. Yet, we seemed made for each other.

The problem is that it was all a lie. Colin was merely pretending.

I asked Colin once, "What made you pursue me and go through all the trouble of getting your friend to set us up? Why did you marry me?"

His response, years later, was quite revealing. He said, "I thought you were quite beautiful. You were smart and funny. I thought that it would be amazing to have someone like you in my life!"

On the surface, it seemed complimentary. But, if you listened closely, it's clear that his motive was all about himself. His status and image. I was an exotic prize. As I would learn later, I was also to be a thorn that Colin used to torture his mother.

*   *   *

During this idealization phase, manipulating the target isn't the only goal. Narcissists use flattery and attention to meet a need within themselves. Recipients equate these feelings with love and romance, then joy and connection. They, therefore, reciprocate the admiration, attention, and affection. *That is the key.* That reciprocation is what narcissists seek all along. The supply of admiration, attention, and affection validates the narcissist's very being. It makes them feel valued and worthy. It dissipates the self-loathing and shame that hides in the very core of all narcissists. The covert looks for narcissistic supply to quiet the feelings of self-loathing, unworthiness, and shame. For the overt narcissist, narcissistic supply seems to confirm the self-confident image they have concocted for themselves—devoid of self-hatred, unworthiness, and shame.

When I showered Colin with thanks and kisses, bought him gifts, laughed at his jokes, asked about his adventures abroad, sided with him against the poor treatment he supposedly suffered at the hands of his mother, all of it validated his very existence. Once I no longer provided this validation and kept his self-worth afloat, my usefulness was gone. What I thought had been love and connection between us was replaced with resentment. Eventually, someone, or many someones, came along to become his source of narcissistic supply.

It's important to note that for the non-disordered person, the slowing of this fast-paced honeymoon period is normal, and the natural progression of a maturing relationship develops. As real-life problems and conflicts are navigated, connection and trust develop between the two lovebirds. Again, for the non-disordered person, this is a good thing. It's empowering to feel grounded, safe, and secure, and to have your person—your life partner—by your side. However, for the narcissist, this is devastating. The everyday fluctuations of life—routines, kids, jobs, and the like—means that attention is directed away from the narcissist. Real life is intolerable for the narcissist. Drama must ensue.

Devaluation

With the covert narcissist, the abuse cycle of idealization, devaluation, and discarding can repeat itself for years, with the targets being none the wiser. The abused person attributes relationship difficulties to stress, married life, misunderstandings, and the like. This same empathetic and committed partner interprets most, if not all, glitches in the relationship as a cue to adjust their thoughts, behavior, and general way of being.

He's tired … He's stressed … The traffic was bad … I picked the wrong time to bring this up … Perhaps I am too sensitive … Maybe I need a nap. I told myself all these things and more. It's how I became conditioned to a marriage of walking on eggshells.

Following the idealization phase, devaluation begins subtly with a whispered insult or off-colored remark. Your body responds to the narcissist's true intent. But then the questionable comment is explained away as harmless teasing. You decide to squash any doubt and accept the explanation. Maybe you accept the narcissist's explanation because you truly weren't bothered by the comment at the time. Maybe it's because the alternative is unbearable. You'd rather hold on to the facade you've come to believe about the narcissist. After all, the facade is far better than the pain of admitting that you are just a pawn in a narcissistic game. It's rather easy to rationalize the behavior and recommit to the facade because the narcissist is the person who claims to love you.

The problem comes into play with those moments of cognitive dissonance where you are caught between what you desperately want to be true and what your intuition and body are telling you is true. It's those times when you thought everything was fine, given all the idealizing and love-bombing happening, and you're suddenly thrown for a loop by a dismissive gesture or insulting comment. You may or may not speak up. If you do, you are met with invalidating comments like, "Calm down," or "You're so sensitive." Either way, you are not sure of what to say or do. You don't want to appear petty. You don't want to ruin a potentially good thing by escalating the situation, so you dismiss the behavior.

It was these moments, these in-between moments when I felt my spirit diminish, when I felt unsafe, and taken for granted. It's important to acknowledge these moments, even if they are mere seconds, because they have tremendous impact, mentally and physically.

As those seemingly insignificant moments pile up, you begin to undermine yourself. You accept blame that's not yours. You begin questioning all you thought you knew and loved about yourself. Those moments become more significant and impactful. They begin to chip away at your sanity, your perception of reality, your self-love, confidence, and respect. You may start to feel tired and depressed and can't figure out why.

Now that I have perspective regarding the abuse cycle, I see that I was living that cycle on repeat from the very beginning of the relationship. For me, it felt familiar and normal considering I was raised by a narcissistic father, and I was filled with obligation, guilt, and toxic hope.

**

With Colin, an act of devaluation that had the greatest impact on me and our marriage involved his mother. I distinctly remember feeling *something is very wrong here*. During the first three or four years of our marriage, for reasons that baffled me at the time, we would make monthly two-and-a-half-hour treks to have dinner with Colin's mother and stepfather. Once there, we would all enjoy a lovely meal where everyone sat at a formally set table, one complete with a salad fork and dessert spoons. (This was something Colin often made fun of regarding his family.)

Over dinner, Colin and his mother would exchange the same pleasantries of "How's school?" and "Are you still on schedule to graduate?" Colin would relay some witty anecdotes about his experience at school or my job. This was followed by questions from the other dinner guests.

I always likened the conversations between Colin and his family to the kind of chit-chat that you'd have with a complete stranger on a bus. The exchange is entertaining and helps pass the time, but there's no true connection or depth created.

After dinner, Colin and I would essentially be ignored as his mother and her company would sit around discussing church events and what was happening in the lives of other people. Then shortly after that, she and Colin's stepfather would head off to bed. Colin and I would stay up watching TV before heading to bed ourselves. The next day, the small talk and niceties would begin again.

After a full year of long travels and late dinners, I overheard a conversation between Colin and his mother. We had arrived at our usual time.

"Finally!" His mother said. "Now we can eat. I hope it's not dried out."

Colin said, "I'm sorry we are always late. Monica had to handle some last-minute things—again. You know how she is!"

What? My body froze in disbelief. Colin was blaming our tardiness on me, and it sounded like it wasn't the first time. My stomach began to burn and bubble. I was not able to eat much that night, which of course made matters worse in his mother's eyes. She had once again prepared this childhood casserole dinner, complete with Colin's favorite dessert, Death by Chocolate, and I was insulting her by not eating it.

All through dinner, I searched in my memory for instances when I was the reason for our not leaving Columbus in time to make the two-and-a-half-hour drive. Not one time had I been the cause of our late arrival for dinner. I was always packed and waiting for Colin to get home from school. He was the one with late clinic hours. My workday ended at 4 p.m. His day ended at 6 p.m. It was never going to be possible to make a two-and-a-half-hour trip from point A to point B in the allotted 1.5 hours. Colin's cowardice and need to be liked, cherished, and adored made it easy for him to agree to a 7:30 p.m. dinner, knowing full well that he could not embark on the journey until 6:00 p.m. This meant an 8:30 or 8:45 p.m. arrival each time. No matter how many ways I looked at the situation, we were always going to be late for dinner, and I was not to blame.

When I confronted Colin about this, his response should have sent me running for the hills long ago.

With tears in his eyes, he said, "I didn't mean to make you look bad. It's just that I didn't want her on my back with a guilt trip. I knew she wouldn't say anything to you. Thanks for taking the hit for me. We are in this together, right?" Then he pulled me into his arms, gave me that sheepish smile from the idealization phase, and kissed me.

I explained to Colin how I was bothered by his behavior and how my relationship with his mother had been damaged by his blaming me. I asked Colin to simply admit to his mother that his schedule conflicted with a 7:30 p.m. dinner.

He promised that he would. That promise was a lie.

Colin never came clean about his deceit. That became apparent with the cutting remarks his mother made about another dinner drying out in the oven as they waited on us. She looked right at me while saying this.

I had to tell his mother myself! "I'm not sure why you and Colin keep agreeing to a 7:30 dinner time. He doesn't get home until 6 p.m. The drive is two-and-a-half hours. We will never be here by 7:30 p.m."

She looked at him in disbelief. Colin said nothing. What could he say?

From that point on, Colin's mother would no longer hold dinner for us (and no longer be pissed at me for being late). It was agreed that getting there by dessert time would be a more reasonable goal.

I now understand that Colin's repeated charade served several purposes. First, it allowed him to maintain his "good son" image, which he desperately needed to do. Second, it allowed him to devalue me in the process. Both actions fed Colin's ego, and his sense of power.

It seems that the narcissist will pathologically lie, without remorse, simply to preserve the perfection of the false self. Maintaining this image is the highest priority. My choice to call Colin out on his narcissistic shenanigans had ramifications—namely, the covert discard.

Discarding

Discarding is the third phase of the abuse cycle. *Note that I did not say final phase. That's because for the narcissist the relationship is never truly over.* It simply means that you are no longer the primary source of narcissistic supply. It is important to realize that for the narcissist—covert and overt—your relationship never held the same value and meaning as it did, or perhaps still does, for you. The personality disorder allows the narcissist to see you as a tool to use, or put away, for his benefit. A true final discard only happens when the non-disordered person draws a hard line in the sand, ending the relationship, and insisting on no contact.

In the abuse cycle, this phase is called the discard phase due to the abruptness and disregard that the narcissist demonstrates toward the victim. For the victim, it looks and feels like cruelty and abandonment. In many cases, the victim is completely blindsided. She is going about life as usual just to come home and find that her partner has packed up and moved in with another woman. Little to no explanation is given.

When seeking an explanation, the victim is met with hostility and blame from the narcissist.

I struggled with the idea of Colin seeing me and the love I felt for him as nothing more than a tool to use and put away at his discretion. That is until I dug through my closet for an old pair of sneakers. Then it clicked for me. Think about it this way: The relationship and the love that a narcissist has for their target is like your feelings toward an old pair of sneakers. There's nothing wrong with the sneakers. They are not in disrepair in any way. No holes. No tears. They are worn in and no longer pinch. The tread has plenty of life, and the color has held up despite several washings. You simply caught a sale and splurged on a new pair of sneakers. The new sneakers are your size, just like the old ones. The color and design of the new sneakers are just your style. They make you feel and look fabulous, just like the old ones once did. Since your old sneakers are perfectly fine, you don't throw them out. That would be silly. You simply put them in the closet or slide them under the bed. You wear your new sneakers as often as you can. Your friends compliment them. You beam.

But now it's a Saturday morning. You have errands to run and a number of tough household projects to tackle. Comfort and speed are the top priorities. You look for your old sneakers. Just like your sneakers, for the narcissist, your relationship simply serves a functional purpose. There is no deep connection and love between you and a pair of sneakers. You felt no guilt for relegating your old sneakers to the back of the closet while you pranced around in your new sneakers. You did not find a need to empathize with your old sneakers. You definitely felt no shame when you retrieved them to carry you through a day of errands.

In the same way, the narcissist will feel no emotional turmoil when discarding you and your relationship, and no shame or guilt when returning to you when there is an inclination to do so. Remember that the primary need for all narcissists is to be praised and admired. When the need for narcissistic supply is unmet, all narcissists will circle back to former sources. This move to hoover you back into the relationship does not mean that the narcissist considers you special or has recommitted to your relationship. No matter what's said, the narcissist is only concerned about having their needs met—period. There has been no epiphany about what they lost by discarding you.

In a relationship with a covert narcissist, the discard phase is significantly different. It's this variance that makes the covert so dangerous. With a covert narcissist, the discard phases within the cycle are subtle and frequent. Remember that at his core the covert narcissist is a coward and must present as Mr. Nice Guy. But like all narcissists, the covert has a sense of entitlement and superiority, and when that sensibility is crossed, the narcissist responds with rage. The rage and the Mr. Nice Guy persona are at cross purposes. Therefore, the discard phase must be disguised. This is what makes the abuse cycle with a covert very difficult to detect. Since the target of narcissistic abuse does not know exactly what to look for, relationships with covert narcissists can last for years, with the target questioning herself and taking responsibility for the dysfunction.

That drama involving weekend dinners with Colin's mother led to a covert discard because Colin never came clean with his mother regarding his schedule and her dinner plans. This left Colin feeling angry and embarrassed. He resented me for sticking up for myself.

Colin looked to be full of shame and frustration with the disappointed look his mother gave him after realizing that I was not the reason we were always late for dinner, but he was. As a result, I was given the silent treatment for several days. Colin kept to himself and avoided being in the same room with me. There had been no chatting as we got ready for the morning. Colin went to bed before me without saying a word. Each time our eyes met, he'd look away. To any on-looker, it would appear that Colin was remorseful and too ashamed to speak about the matter. This was my initial thought as well. It took some time to see his pattern. Although I couldn't quite explain what was happening, there was no denying the tension between us.

Finally, I asked, "How long are you going to keep sulking and ignoring me?" I reminded him that I had asked him to clear matters up with his mother and that my relationship with her was important to me. I explained that by blaming me for our late arrivals, he had created a wedge between his mother and me.

Colin stared blankly at me for a moment, then said, "I've just been waiting for you to tell me that you're leaving." This was a lie.

The behavior that Colin had been displaying and the energy that oozed from him were not of remorse, reflection, or regret. Yet, that's what his tears and pleas of forgiveness were supposed to represent.

He began to verbally berate himself. He questioned why I was with him. In short order, I was comforting the person who had mistreated me, betrayed my trust, and sought to damage an important relationship. The next few days were filled with hugs, kisses, and expressions of gratitude for putting up with him, and for not leaving.

I was led to believe that the covert discard—the silent treatment and the sulking—wasn't him punishing me, but Colin punishing himself.

This became our pattern. Our dance.

I now know that it's the dance of the covert narcissist. All of the covert narcissists of the world use this form of emotional manipulation, or a variation of it. Their goal is to appear as Mr. Nice Guy, the misunderstood victim, the social misfit—the guy who prostrates himself on the floor, literally or figuratively, so that you feel obligated to forgive and to support.

The pattern of repeated discarding by the covert narcissist can take many forms. In my experience, the most common forms are stonewalling, silent treatment, withdrawal of physical affection, feigning exhaustion or sickness to avoid intimacy, blame-shifting, and gaslighting. When using these tactics, the covert narcissist will always, *always* present himself as innocent, confused, and as simply trying to get along—as *the good guy*.

When the covert narcissist uses tactics more often employed by the overt, such as a smear campaign (maligning your name to anyone who will listen), the covert narcissist will appear to be the dutiful partner who is misunderstood, under-appreciated, and trying to do their best to meet your impossible expectations. They will beseech advice from your closest friends and family under the guise of how best to please you. (Note! This is a very powerful move when the covert has appeared shy and private with your family or friends in the past.) In short, the covert narcissist plays the victim!

The drama of the silent treatment or other passive-aggressive behaviors from the covert narcissist is always followed by an idealizing, love-bombing phase. It looks like love, like a new beginning. It looks as if the covert narcissist is really trying to mend the pain inflicted. You will likely experience many of the same behaviors and flirtations that were so endearing at the beginning of the relationship. It's meant to get you reinvested in the relationship, in the facade.

For me, Colin would become more demonstrative of his feelings. Kisses on the forehead. Love notes. Bakery treats. He showered me with platitudes of "I don't know what's wrong with me," or "Why do you put up with me?" He would become very animated while recalling past experiences we'd shared. He would plan future events, like trips or date nights.

I would believe that my old Colin had returned. I'd convince myself that he truly was remorseful. I'd give him credit for trying. I'd forgive large transgressions. However, the reflection, remorse, mending of thinking and behavior—none of it was real! Instead, what was actually happening was that I was being reprogrammed, and that Colin was being granted another opportunity to hone his skills. He learned how to not let the mask slip in quite the same way next time. There were times when he'd add phrases like, *Let me come clean on this ... I know I messed up here ... You're probably sick of having to remind me about ... I handled that situation a lot better than last time, right?* These were all manipulations to look like personal growth and progress.

This cycle of offense and feigned remorse kept me in my abusive marriage for longer than I should have been. It kept me operating in a fog of confusion, guilt, and toxic hope. I didn't understand why Colin was behaving in such immature, manipulative ways. There were times I had wanted to leave out of sheer exhaustion. Then, I'd feel guilty over wanting to leave my poor husband, who had been abandoned by his mother. I'd feel ashamed for being so angry and hurt about Colin's behavior. I would ask myself, *Who are you to judge?* And I would stay.

It's critical for you to realize here that my behavior and thinking were also fueled by religious indoctrination, expectations of my narcissistic father, and my subconscious belief that I needed to hustle hard to earn love and safety. Remember, this was the wisdom of my traumatized five-year-old self. Like everyone, my early interpretations of the world became my filter through which to navigate adulthood as well.

I hoped that Colin would actually make the changes he promised to make. The relationship for me was real, founded on love, compassion, loyalty, connection, and empathy. I wanted the marriage to work. Colin apparently never was invested. He had been showing me this repeatedly in his behavior, but I hadn't recognized it. In the end, Colin told me that he never loved me and that he only married me to upset his mother.

Apparently, all those years of forgiving, believing, and recommitting were for nothing! Be warned.

* * *

I invite you to take another close look at your relationship. But this inventory will be different in that you will check in with your body to see what it has to say about your relationship. In situations like ours, we can overthink, minimize, and talk ourselves into and out of situations. In short, we can lie to ourselves. However, our bodies never lie. Identify the truths your body wants to share by completing the exercises below.

EXERCISES

Exercise 1: Tuning Into Your Body

REFLECTION:

Do you feel that you have experienced the abusive cycle of *idealization, devaluation, discard* in your relationship(s)?

Allow yourself 20–30 minutes. Grab your journal or your tablet to keep notes. Sit quietly. Think of a person whom you love and respect. Hold their image in your mind. Place both of your hands over your heart. Breathe in the love that you feel for that special person in your mind's eye.

- How does that love feel in your body?
- Record how love (a.k.a. truth) feels in your body.

NEXT:

Say out loud: I feel loved, valued, and respected in my relationship with (insert name). How did your body respond? Does the affirmation feel true? How and where did the answer appear in your body? Was it a pain? A burning? A cold spot?

Whatever your body's response: focus on that point. Resting your hand there may help.

Ask: What is this (pain, burning, cold, etc.) about?

Journal your body's answer to the question.

Do not question or censor your answers. TRUST your body.

Afterward, thank your body for its wisdom.

You do not have to do anything with the answer at this time. Keep reading. Keep asking your questions. Notice any energy shifts. Notice how your body responds. Check in with your body daily. Notice how fear, curiosity, happiness, love, safety, and belonging feels in your body.

Exercise 2: Noticing What Comes Up

Ask yourself the following questions. Spend a day or two on each question, gathering objective evidence. See what comes up. After several days, journal your answer. What patterns do you recognize? What are the themes?

1. Are my needs being met in this relationship?
2. Do I feel safe and grounded in this relationship?
3. Do I feel safe sharing my concerns?
4. Do I feel safe sharing my dreams?
5. What happens when I disagree with my partner?
6. Do my needs and wants really matter?
7. Do I feel seen and heard in this relationship?

Exercise 3: Documenting Your Experience

Make a note of any evidence of the abuse cycle: idealizing, devaluing, and discarding. This can be as simple as a list on your phone. Make a heading for each phase. Add a check mark emoji each time you have the feeling you are being love-bombed; Note each time you wonder, *What the heck just happened? Did I hear what I think I heard?* Note each time you are ignored or given a backhanded compliment. This is especially important if you are asking for clarity or accountability from the person. Also, keep track of the times the suspected narcissist feigns ignorance, or plays the victim. Remember, the covert discard can look like attending to an emergency with the promise of getting back to you later. If it feels like a blow-off, it likely is.

Look for patterns. Adding context to your notes will make the pattern clearer. Recognize when you are in the abuse pattern. This is critical insight into your relationship. Share your concerns with a trusted friend, therapist, or coach.

I strongly recommend not mentioning your record-keeping. This will be used against you when the narcissist is in victim mode.

CHAPTER 5

INVALIDATION

Validation is something that we all hope to receive in a close relationship. We want to feel seen and valued, not just for the things we do, but for the person we are. Of course, the opposite of that is invalidation, where you feel that the things you do, or even your very existence, are inconsequential in your partner's life; you may as well not even be there, at that moment or ever. In my experience, that is the perfect description of a relationship with a covert narcissist. Invalidating seems to be the covert narcissist's default move against a target.

Colin invalidated me in ways that were so covert I didn't recognize them until years later. I did not see them as efforts to deprive me of effective or continued existence. They were so subtle and seemed so innocent. Yet they were damaging and also present from the very start of our relationship.

In the dating phase, I was so caught up in the love-bombing that I automatically interpreted Colin's invalidating comments and actions as teasing or forgetfulness. The grace that I extended was reinforced when Colin also justified his behavior in the same way. As you likely figured, going to the movies quickly became our thing. However, more than once, I arrived at the theater to find that we were seeing a movie that I specifically did not want to see, but he did.

He would dramatically explain, "Oh, I misunderstood. I don't know what's wrong with me ... I can't believe I did it again!" Because he seemed genuinely embarrassed, I accepted them as truth.

In different situations, my preferences would be overlooked. This happened often enough that in a short time, Colin had established himself in our relationship as a loving, adorable goofball. He even coined the phrase "I pulled a Colin," referring to the times that my preferences were *forgotten*. He appeared able to laugh and poke fun at himself for what seemed to be a regrettable character flaw. He would pretend to be apologetic and give the appearance of making amends by putting reminders on his mirror, pointing out his desire to get better, asking for feedback. I saw this behavior as good intent, as a dedication to change and progress. What it was in actuality was a distraction and manipulation. My attention was diverted to notice what appeared to be remorse and efforts to be supportive and loving. It's what I thought about as the invalidating behavior continued. *He's working on it* is what I told myself. This was easier to believe when Colin would make comments like, *Shoot! I even put that on my mirror. How could I forget?* And of course, there were stretches of time when I did feel seen and heard.

There was an event that occurred within the first year of our marriage. I call this *The Sleep Incident*. Looking back, I see that this single event had all of the warning signs. Every red flag was present—flags that I totally misinterpreted. The dynamics in this event became a recurring theme in my marriage. Although some days it varied, the main ingredients were always there: invalidation and some form of DARVO: Deny, Attack, Reverse, Victim, Offender (more on this in chapter six).

Whatever was happening at the time, my life as a new teacher had me exhausted and sleep deprived. One night, I said, "Babe! I am going to be up really late again doing schoolwork. So, please don't wake me in the morning when you leave. I really need some sleep!"

Colin made all the right sounds and nodded appropriately. It was agreed that I would sleep in.

But, the next morning, he woke me up to say goodbye. I was

stumped. And awake. Once I was awake for the day, there was no going back to sleep.

That night, I made the same request again. "Please don't wake me in the morning. I need to sleep in." Admittedly this was a break in our routine. However, once again Colin nodded and said the words that suggested he understood.

The next morning…. You guessed it! He woke me up again.

This time he was nibbling on my neck and whispering in my ear. I remembered going to bed hoping for maybe four hours of sleep *if* I slept in. Yet, there I was, awake, two hours before I needed to be.

Holding back tears I said, "Babe, you said you were going to let me sleep in!" I was confused and hurt.

He said, "Oh no! I forgot." He then winced as if to say, "Shit! I really F'd-up here!"

I thought: *How could he forget? How does someone forget something like this?*

Then he started tickling me, saying, "It's just that I won't see you all day, and I miss you already. Don't be mad!"

I was laughing and pleading with him to stop.

He said, "No! Not until you tell me that you love me."

I fell for it! Giggling I yelled, "*Okay.* Okay. I love you!"

Colin stopped tickling me. I was grateful to be loved so deeply.

That night, events repeat themselves again. Same request. Same explanation. Same universal indications of understanding from Colin.

The next morning, he did it again. The third time in a row. I was stunned. It felt surreal. Nausea came over me—that sour-tasting, burning sensation at the back of my throat. I forced a smile and blew him a kiss goodbye. As Colin left, I heard myself say, "I love you too."

It didn't make any sense to me.

On the third night, while he was watching TV, and I was sitting on the floor doing teacher stuff, I asked him, "Um, Babe! So can you tell me why you keep waking me up in the morning when I've asked you to let me sleep in?" I admit that there was a tone to my voice. But not a fight-starting tone that warranted the response I got.

Colin jumped up from the couch, threw the TV remote in my direction, and yelled, "Well, excuse the hell out of me for loving my wife so much that I want to kiss her goodbye in the morning!"

He continued, "Gawd Monica! Some women would love to have a husband like me. But I can't seem to do anything right in your eyes!" He had a laundry list of evidence of my alleged haughtiness, my lack of appreciation, and my insistence on seeing him through "shit-colored glasses"! Then as suddenly as it started, the storm was over. He went to bed and was snoring within ten minutes. I, on the other hand, was wide awake.

Sleep never came to me that night. Instead, I spent the night trying to make sense of what happened. I questioned if I was indeed an ungrateful and demanding wife. *If so, then am I going to lose the love of my life?*

I replayed the four previous days in my head. I looked for something that I missed, something that I had done to warrant his anger. I tried to make sense of his words and reconcile them with the feelings in my stomach.

Colin said that he couldn't let me sleep because he loved me too much! But that didn't sound or feel like love! It seemed to me that if he loved me, he'd let me sleep. I found myself mumbling and dizzy. I climbed in bed next to him just to stop the room from spinning. I had nothing but hope—hope that everything would be better in the morning.

In this incident, Colin invalidated my wishes and needs. My very real human need for sleep was dismissed. It didn't matter. His excuse at the time was, "I forgot!" That was partly true simply because another person's needs are not a concern for a person with narcissistic traits. My needs simply didn't register in his mind. His narcissistic need for attention and adulation in the morning trumped my need for sleep. Period.

Invalidating a person's requests, boundaries, rights, and well-being is textbook behavior for all narcissists. What makes the covert different is the set-up and the Mr. Nice-Guy excuses: *I forgot … I'm going to miss you … I miss you already.* The act of forgetting is understandable. It's human. We all forget at times. But Colin didn't really forget. My needs didn't matter.

Now, imagine if I had said, "Forgetting is not an excuse. I asked you three nights in a row." Imagine if I'd pushed him away forcibly and yelled, "STOP!" through gritted teeth, instead of giggling and trying to catch my breath, as he tickled me and professed his love. Imagine if I had thrown the remote back at him. I'd look like a royal bitch. And again, Colin would appear as Mr. Nice Guy who simply woke his wife up to say goodbye. Just another example of a situation in which the target loses no matter what they choose to do or say. Even sadder, in this situation, I was conditioned to question what I had done wrong. I questioned whether or not I was being unreasonable.

* * *

Colin disguised his repeated disregard for *my wants and needs* as innocent oversight. However, the intended message eventually became crystal clear: Your thoughts, wishes, concerns, and boundaries do not matter. *You* do not matter. My needs are more important!

It bears repeating: A covert narcissist is concerned about one thing and one thing only—narcissistic supply. Our morning routine was just another means to an end for Colin. Showering me with love and attention in the morning before he left for work was like fueling his narcissistic engine before he hit the road. It was his way of feeling on top of the world, all pumped up and ready to go. And me? I played my part by feeding his ego, unknowingly becoming a narcissistic supply source.

In truth, I was no one special to Colin. It wasn't that he loved me so deeply that he needed to start his day showering me with kisses. Anyone could have filled the role. Anyone who was willing to give Colin the attention and admiration that he craved could have taken my place.

I know what you're thinking: *Well shit!* I know because I thought the same thing when I realized this fact.

* * *

The covert narcissist also has a talent for invalidating you by squashing your joy and diverting any attention focused on you. This tactic is common. Any attention on me had to either stay on me or quickly shift to Colin, depending on his mood or needs. When I was to serve as the warm-up act or the connector between Colin and someone he wanted to impress, then attention on me was allowed. But if there was no personal benefit to him, the attention needed to be swiftly diverted.

Looking back, my one and only birthday bash is the perfect example. Being a former Jehovah's Witness, I had never experienced an official birthday party. Up to that point, celebrating birthdays had been worthy of being destroyed by Almighty God at Armageddon. Forget presents and the idea of having a good time! When we left the organization, it was very important to me that my boys feel free to celebrate their birthdays. To show them that it was safe, it seemed that I should go first. So, I did.

I invited nearly 100 people, and let me say, blushing, they showed up! The party went on for twelve hours, with some guests arriving late and staying until the wee hours of the morning. It was an epic event. At one point, my almost ten-year-old son whined, "When will this party end? I'm so sleepy."

I assured him that he was free to go to bed.

His response was, "No! I might miss something." All I could do was laugh.

People from different corners of my life came together to celebrate me. I received presents left and right, despite the words "No Presents Necessary" written on their invitations.

While everyone was busy celebrating and showing their love, Colin couldn't help but focus on the number of guests who showed up. He kept going on and on—and on—about how he was afraid to throw a fortieth birthday party for himself because no one would show up. Plus, Colin had invited my heroine and mentor, Oprah Winfrey, because *Why not?* I'm all about dreaming big! But instead of letting me bask in the spotlight as the birthday girl, tend to my guests, and show our boys that birthday parties can be fun, he kept lamenting about how Oprah didn't respond to his letters and calls. So, instead of fully embracing my special day, I ended up spending my time comforting and reassuring Colin that it was okay that Oprah couldn't make it and that his fortieth birthday party would be just as spectacular.

The day became more about him than me. I felt emotionally depleted. I hid in the bathroom more than once.

* * *

Colin's signature move for invalidation is what I started calling "A Cup Of Tea." It was a combination of invalidation and gaslighting. Colin wanted to project his Mr. Nice Guy image, so he'd ask me about my workday. He would do so to appear thoughtful and caring, but in reality, there was no sincere interest or empathy behind his question. When he was really laying it on thick, he would even ask about a specific person or event, connecting bits of information that he managed to remember. Mundane chit-chat between us was tolerated because it didn't require much energy or effort for Colin to listen and catch a few key details. But whenever I required too much energy or time, whenever I had real issues at work to talk about, he'd go to the kitchen to make tea.

When he returned, *if he returned*, Colin would change the topic of conversation and divert the attention away from my concerns. This invalidating action was hard to spot for several reasons. First of all, Colin and I shared a love of Constant Comment Tea during our college days, so I initially saw the gesture as sincere. Secondly, I wasn't aware of covert narcissists at the time, and making a cup of tea didn't fit with what I'd read about the classic overt narcissist. On the surface, it is a very empathetic gesture.

Colin began to use this tactic whenever I expressed concerns about his behavior, our relationship, or money—basically anything for which he lacked interest or refused accountability.

I was shut down by a cup of tea!

Eventually, I stopped sharing any significant events of my workday, my dreams, or my fears. It became clear that what mattered most to me was of no interest to Colin. There was *never* tea made when Colin himself needed to talk about how to undo the upset he had caused with his staff by a comment he'd made, or a new policy he wanted to implement. On the contrary, he had my full attention as I explained what his employees were likely thinking and feeling. I often scripted the conversation he should have the following day, or as an email.

Just so you know, Colin made me quite a bit of tea when my mother died! In other words, I was not welcome to process my pain and sadness about my mother. Colin has yet to hear the full story of how my mother died in my arms. I wanted to tell him how frightening, yet beautiful, it was. I wanted to tell him how she had motioned for me to sit at the head of her hospital bed and how she lifted herself up until she was resting in my arms with her head laying on my chest. I wanted to explain how my mother asked me to massage her scalp by taking my hand and plopping it on top of her head, then slowly moving my fingers. Most of all, I wanted to tell Colin about the *death rattle* that I had heard about but never thought I'd experience. There was so much I wanted to share. But he made it clear that he had no interest in holding space for me, not then, not ever. Over the years, there had been so many times that I wanted Colin to just listen, or to just hold me. But unfortunately, he preferred making me tea. After all, isn't that what a Mr. Nice Guy would do?

***

At some point, I had had enough tea for a lifetime. That's when I began to insist that we start addressing the herd of elephants in the room. That's when Colin started to stonewall me by flat-out refusing to cooperate or communicate. He would pretend to be surprised or confused whenever I pushed for some accountability. If that didn't work, he would just sit in silence, staring at the floor. Sometimes, he would act afraid, as if my anger and frustration were some kind of supernatural force.

It was infuriating. Anyone in this position would be tempted to scream, "Answer me, you bastard!" But please don't because that's exactly what the narcissist wants. They want you to lose your cool so that such reactive behavior can be used as evidence against you.

The whole point of invalidation is to slowly chip away at your self-esteem, self-confidence, and self-love. As if that wasn't bad enough, your frustrated responses to their invalidation tactics become a source of narcissistic supply. *You read that right.* Whether it's a negative or positive, an emotional outburst from you fuels their sense of power and significance.

Both the covert and overt narcissists are experts at using invalidation to manipulate you and twist situations to their advantage. The biggest difference is that the covert narcissist is a toxic chameleon, cloaked in confusion, innocence, fake concern, humility, self-deprecation, and fragility. They want you to overlook their toxic behavior or make you feel guilty or ashamed for even questioning it. That's their game plan—they do not want to be called out or exposed.

My invitation to you is to promise yourself that you will stay alert and don't let the covert narcissist's manipulation tactics go unnoticed. Find out if you, your needs, desires, and well-being really matter to the person in question. The following exercises will help you to focus your attention on key areas. When completing these exercises, notice how your body responds, as introduced in the previous chapter. Notice if you feel safe, heard, and/or loved.

EXERCISES

Exercise 1: Being Invalidated

Just notice! Spend this week noticing how often your words, feelings, preferences, and requests are honored or dismissed when interacting with the could-be covert narcissist. Notice if you are greeted when the person enters the room, or if your greeting is returned. This is an easy tell of the narcissist's mood or motivation. Notice if you are interrupted repeatedly in conversations.

Notice if you are "one-upped" when sharing about your day or an accomplishment. Do they respond to your story, or do they reply with one that is bigger, and more dramatic?

Keep an actual tally sheet. It may happen so often that you lose count. Remember, it's often subtle; it often looks innocent and helpful. Yet, the end result is the same. You are silenced and deemed insignificant! A few covert examples include feigning an important call, interrupting you to urgently tell you something that they have been *supposedly* waiting all day to tell you, offering to get you a beverage, and, of course, having to use the restroom, only to never return to the conversation.

Keep track of the times you aren't quite sure about. Those times are the situations you'll want to take a closer look at. For instance, maybe your thoughts, feelings, and wishes are being ignored to impress a specific person—a parent, boss, a new supply. Maybe it's a passive-aggressive payback toward you for a narcissistic injury that you inadvertently caused. Just notice!

Exercise 2: Is Invalidation the Norm?

Now that you've noticed when your words, feelings, preferences, and requests are being invalidated, tap into how this makes you feel.

Ask yourself a few important, revealing questions:

- Am I more often honored or invalidated in this relationship?
- How long has this invalidation been going on? You may have noticed some patterns that you didn't recognize as invalidation. For me, this was like Colin always making me tea. At one time, I misinterpreted it as a sign of love and support after a long day. I had never suspected that it was really a way to leave the conversation when it suited him, until the evidence was staring me right in the face, leading me to test it out. Undeniable.
- Did you notice the invalidation right away? If so, what was your body cue or indicator? Did you feel it in your stomach or a squeeze in your chest?
- Was this feeling familiar? If so, when else in your life did you notice the same feeling? With whom were you interacting? How old were you? Get specific about your feelings. Journal them out. How is your relationship with the previous person these days?
- Why do you think you're just noticing the patterns of invalidation? What will you be on the lookout for in the future?

Exercise 3: Taking Up Space and Standing Up for Your Right

Challenge the suspected Colin in your life! Take a look at what you've noticed over the past week. What was the most hurtful or surprising? Script out an interrupter, a chance to take your power back. Or at the very least, put the narcissist on notice that you are aware of the behavior.

The pattern interrupter could go something like this:

- I've noticed how you often interrupt me when I am telling you about ____. I'm just wondering why you do that. Do you know?
- You interrupted me. I'd like a chance to finish my thought.
- I feel like you don't value me or our relationship when you do XYZ.

- Why do you ask me my opinion and then not let me finish? Or then tell me how wrong my opinion is?

The responses to the pattern interrupter will be very revealing as to the other party's intentions and motivation. Is an acknowledgment forthcoming? Or a justification? Does the person get angry? Or do they apologize and make an attempt to repair the damage? Are you mocked? Are you accused of being too sensitive? Keep interrupting! Stick up for yourself. Notice the responses.

CHAPTER 6

DARVO

As I introduced in the previous chapter, DARVO is an acronym for **Deny/Deflect, Attack, Reverse Victim and Offender**. It's like a toxic person's escape hatch whenever it comes to taking accountability for their actions. Their first step is to deny or deflect any wrongdoing, followed by launching an attack on the person who dares to seek accountability or clarification for any poor behavior.

As it turns out, this was Colin's immediate response whenever something threatened to shatter his perfect self-image. He couldn't bear the thought of being at fault or responsible for anything that might tarnish his facade, even if it was something trivial and laughable—altogether human.

Go back to *The Sleep Incident*, for example. Remember, I asked Colin why he kept waking me up early despite my plea to sleep in. He didn't reflect on his choices, take responsibility, or apologize. Instead, he threw our TV remote at me and yelled, "Well, excuse the hell out of me for loving my wife so much that I want to kiss her goodbye in the morning!" Then he added, "*Gawd*, Monica! Some women would *love* to have a husband like me. But I can't seem to do anything right in your eyes."

He made it all about himself and accused me of being ungrateful. It was a perfect deflect-and-attack combo! Colin blamed me and my supposed lack of gratitude. Not only was my question a threat to Colin's facade, but my request for an explanation and attempt at enforcing a boundary was deemed inappropriate behavior in his eyes. This made me the enemy, worthy of punishment.

Any outsider looking in on the situation objectively would question Colin's intention and wonder why he refused to let me sleep. Most importantly, Colin saw his own actions as questionable. In his own mind, he saw himself as the bad guy ... as NOT Mr. Nice Guy. His ego and grandiose self-image couldn't handle it. So, what did he do? The next best thing—he shifted the attention away from himself and put the blame on me. There I sat, stupefied! Another way to look at this situation is that I was the one who forced Colin to look at his behavior, so I was the enemy. Wrath is a common response when narcissists, covert and overt, are forced to look at their behavior.

Colin yelled, threw something, and accused me of being demanding and haughty.

Growing up with a narcissistic father, I had an automatic response to his attack-and-deflect treatment, and that was to take responsibility for things that weren't mine to own. I started questioning myself and wondering if I was wrong. Of course, this played right into Colin's hands. And that hint of physical violence—jumping up from the sofa, yelling, making absurd accusations—was all part of his conditioning strategy to make me think twice about questioning or asking him to take accountability in the future.

It worked.

Back then, that is. But not anymore.

Colin's behavior really caught me off guard. It was like he did a complete 180-degree turn from the charming guy he pretended to be during the love-bombing phase of dating. We had only been married a year. This was the first outburst I had experienced from Colin. It left me bewildered, and I wanted answers. We all want to feel some sense of control and safety in our relationships. I needed to find out what went wrong and how I could avoid it happening again. This had been my default strategy as a child in efforts to stay safe. As an adult, living on my own, married, I subconsciously fell right into that childhood pattern when the familiar problem arose.

By attacking me and setting himself up as the husband who loves his wife so much that it gets him into trouble, Colin became the victim, and I became the offender. I am the bitch of a wife attacking her husband whose only crime is wanting to kiss her goodbye in the morning.

In Colin's mind, this preposterous reversal was enough to reestablish himself as Mr. Nice Guy. For me the result was emotional conflict in my mind and body. This was a familiar but misinterpreted sensation at the time. Was Colin indeed the threat, the offender? Or did I need to question my own behavior to see if there was any truth to his accusations?

I certainly didn't sleep well that night.

Colin, however, just walked away, closed the door to our bedroom, climbed into bed, and was asleep within ten minutes. *In essence, he unloaded all of his shame and guilt onto me, leaving me to pick up the pieces.* Meanwhile, I spent hours dissecting every little detail, searching for any evidence of my alleged haughtiness and lack of gratitude.

The next day, Colin didn't wake me up. Not because he wanted to let me sleep as I had asked, but as a form of punishment. When I got up on my own and greeted him, he didn't say, "Good morning, babe!" Instead, he left without a word.

That night at dinner all I got were grunts and shrugs. No interest in my day, no conversation when I asked about his day. I ended up watching our Friday night movie by myself. This was further punishment.

The silent treatment continued into the next day. There were no phone calls, no sweet messages from his weekend gig saying, "Hey, just thinking of you! Want me to bring home something for lunch?" All those little connections that used to be part of our routine vanished into thin air.

Later that afternoon, when I heard his keys in the door my

stomach churned with nervousness. I considered escaping to the bathroom to buy some time and gather my thoughts, but it was too late. The door swung open, and our eyes met.

"Hello," I said.

Colin put his hand on his chest, directly over his heart and said, "Thank goodness! You're finally speaking to me. You aren't mad at me?" He even looked like he was about to cry.

I was taken aback. Frozen. The events of the previous four days flashed through my mind. His behavior and the events as I knew them to be didn't match the Colin standing before me.

I started to explain myself, mostly to verify the facts in my head. I wanted to explain how I was staying up late each night to work, which left me exhausted. I had more to say, but before I could continue, Colin dropped to the floor, grabbed my hand, and started claiming he understood.

"I know! I know! Please don't be mad at me. I am such a loser. I don't know what's wrong with me …" He stood up. While still holding my hand, he directed us to our bed. I sat down. It sounded like he was crying, though I couldn't be sure.

Colin rested his head on my lap. "You have every right to want to sleep in. You're the one working hard. I'm still in school. You need to sleep."

I didn't know what to say. And Colin was undone. With tears now clearly streaming down his face, he pleaded with me not to leave him.

He sobbed, and asked, "Why do you put up with me?"

But that was the manipulation. Not once had I threatened to leave. Colin planted that thought between us to make me the bad guy.

At first, I ignored the comment because it came out of left field but then he repeated the plea. "Please don't leave me!" This time with pronounced sobs and quivering lips, as he tried to hold it together. Almost immediately, I started feeling guilty—like I was the *actual* offender, the person planning to abandon her partner. I was focused on defending my good name, needing to convince the narcissist (the true offender) that I was not the sort of woman who would leave her partner when he's hurting. I wanted to ease his pain.

Just like that, Colin had completely deflected my attention, attacked me, and reversed our positions as victim and offender. I became the offender. I became the one needing to clarify my intentions, to apologize, to provide comfort and repair the damage.

In the fog of emotional abuse, it's hard to pinpoint what's really happening. Projecting our own empathy and values makes it harder to believe that someone who supposedly loves you is purposefully manipulating you to avoid accountability. So, we try to come up with explanations that better fit our image of a shy, humble, generous, and kind "nice" guy. We want to believe this despite the truth staring us in the face—the covert narcissist is not who he claimed to be.

* * *

Not wanting to look like the bad guy is understandable. Most people would say it's quite normal. Who wants to admit that they sometimes suck as a friend, or at behaving as a decent human being in general? Admitting mistakes and owning our flaws, even the small ones, takes courage, self-awareness, and integrity. Being able to do so is considered a benchmark of emotional maturity and intelligence. Not being able to do so is an indicator of toxic behavior and several personality disorders.

The covert narcissist's inability to admit his mistakes and be accountable is a clear sign of emotional immaturity and toxicity. DARVO takes it to a whole new level. Not only does the covert avoid responsibility, but he deflects and denies the behavior, attacks, and reverses the blame onto you. With the overt narcissists, DARVO is full of bravado, arrogance, and insults. With the Colins of the world, DARVO includes whining, pseudo-apologies, tears, and pleading. It's mind-boggling and can leave you guilt-ridden, especially when you want to scream, "Stop crying … Man up … Take responsibility!"

* * *

It's important to establish boundaries to minimize the effectiveness of DARVO. But beware, narcissists will up the ante and try to unsettle you with a raised voice and insults. Their goal is to rattle you just enough that you won't know how to respond appropriately. You read how I responded in the sleep incident. I was silent. Stuck. Frozen.

To be clear, your goal is not to change the narcissist's behavior, because let's face it, you can't. That's a lost cause. Your goal is to stay strong and not let the DARVO behavior rattle you to the point where you blame yourself for the narcissist's behavior.

First things first, you need to recognize when the narcissist is deflecting. Once you notice the deflection, call it out for what it is. Do whatever it takes to stay calm. I recommend a technique called "4 x 4 Box Breathing." It is reportedly used by the US Marines to stay calm and levelheaded. I thought, if it works for them, it can work for me too. So, I gave it a shot. Turns out, it's very effective. It has helped me deal with frustrated parents upset about report cards, lousy customer service from my internet provider, and even a narcissistic boss. The method works like a charm. It is said that the breath-holding part of the technique balances the chemicals in your nervous system. Plus, focusing on breathing and counting takes your mind off the narcissist's antics.

Here's how it's done. I picture a square in my mind. Then, starting in the bottom right-hand corner, I mentally trace the square as I count and breathe. Up the side, inhaling for four counts. Across the top, holding for four counts. Down the left side, exhaling through my nose to a count of four. Across the bottom, holding my breath for four counts. Repeat. Inhale. Hold. Exhale. Hold. Try it. Continue until you feel your body calm and your head clear. Box Breathing takes practice.

Another strategy is to ground yourself by naming random things that you see around you, like a blue chair or a red coffee mug. Naming things around you brings you to the present moment. It takes you out of the story that is playing in your subconscious. It helps calm your nerves and engage your frontal lobe so that you can think.

A technique to calm the narcissist and prevent the situation from escalating is to avoid responding to the narcissist. If you do respond, then do your best to keep it flat and detached. Say something like, "Yes. I hear you. That's not what I said, I remember it differently." Say whatever is necessary to appease the narcissist for the moment. The goal is to not lose sight of the truth and fall victim to the DARVO nonsense that the narcissist is throwing your way. If you are with a narcissist whose rage will grow when you are not giving the emotional response he wants, then *act* the part. Your safety is paramount. Keep sight of your intention, which is to stay safe, not to get the narcissist to see their behavior clearly.

Over the years, encountering various versions of the DARVO move left me feeling confused, defeated, angry, or just plain exhausted. Sometimes all at once. At other times, I foolishly believed that if I explained things one more time louder, softer, slower, or faster, Colin would see that I was not the enemy, that he would finally understand the damage he was causing to our marriage and change his ways. It never happened. Don't expect it.

I encourage you to see if DARVO is wreaking havoc in your relationship. Take stock of your situation. I want to remind you that you are not keeping score, as in holding a grudge. Far from it. You are simply gathering information. Think of it as collecting puzzle pieces to get a true picture of your relationship. It's time to put the pieces together and see the bigger picture.

EXERCISES

Exercise 1: DARVO Reflection

Take a few minutes to think about your interactions with the possible narcissist. Can you identify times when you found yourself apologizing for something you didn't do or taking responsibility for a task that wasn't yours? These are the moments when you find yourself thinking, "He shat on my head. Why am *I* the one apologizing?"

In hopes of keeping a semblance of peace, have you ever chosen to not challenge the false accusations of the narcissist? These could be large or small accusations where blame or responsibility for an event is unfairly shifted to you.

Exercise 2: Standing Your Ground

Start a collection of responses that you can give when the narcissist is using DARVO against you. Visualize yourself using the phrases. Practice speaking them out loud, so that you sound firm in your resolve. Some examples are:

- I hear what you are saying. I simply disagree.
- Let's table this until tomorrow. How about at 12:30, during lunch?
- Tempers seem to be high. We both should take a moment.

Remember the goal is to stand your ground while not inciting the narcissist's rage.

Exercise 3: Groundhog Day

Start a list of the events, issues, or plans that never seem to be resolved in your relationship. For me, one of the issues that showed up over and over again was Colin's decision to sacrifice my wishes, well-being, or needs if honoring them meant losing favor in someone else's eyes. This included complete strangers.

CHAPTER 7

PLAYING THE VICTIM

Rejection and exposure are the greatest fears of covert narcissists. In my opinion, when you couple a distorted self-image with a desperate need to maintain a Mr. Nice Guy facade and then add a touch of delusion on top, you're on your way to understanding why the covert narcissist behaves the way they do.

Covert narcissists cannot handle taking responsibility for their questionable actions. The dysfunctional nature of NPD does not allow for that. The narcissist believes the world should and does see him as nothing short of miraculous. He works hard to keep this facade alive.

Playing the victim seems to be a multi-purpose manipulation tactic. It's used to garner pity, to get narcissistic supply, to exercise power and control, and of course, to avoid accountability. The tactic is effective.

Playing the Victim to Garner Pity

While very subtle, playing the victim to garnish pity is also very effective. It's often a first date tactic the covert narcissist uses to ensnare the target. The purpose is to groom you to feel safe and connected to the narcissist, which leaves you primed for manipulation later.

Consider this example. Once you read it, I bet it will sound familiar—either from a movie you've seen, a book you've read, or the very moves used on you. The narcissist will start with a compliment saying something like, "I can't believe how much fun you are! You're so different from other women I've gone out with. My last girlfriend was such a bummer and wouldn't even watch the Super Bowl with me."

Can you spot the manipulation here? He's tapped into your subconscious desire for approval and connection, along with your empathy, to make you feel special and valued above others. You might wonder how someone could mistreat him. It also sets the stage for you to always want to watch football with him in the future, even if it's not really your thing. In this situation, he may, or may not, apologize for bringing up his last girlfriend. You don't set a boundary because it's the first date. He notices. He has just laid the groundwork to bemoan his past relationships, with more details next time, sucking you in further.

At first, you may think that sharing about yourselves is a natural part of getting to know each other. And that's true for you! But for the narcissist, it's a way to gather information and test your reactions. So, down the road, if you ever oppose or express a desire not to go to his buddy's house to watch football for the third time that month, the likely response will be something like, "Oh! I thought you liked football. You seemed to have a great time last game. My bad!"

You respond by saying, "I did, and I do. I just don't want to go tonight."

Then you might hear an audible sigh followed by them saying, "Fine! What do you want to do?" You ignore the manipulative sighing and hope for a cozy evening filled with connection and intimacy. However, you find yourself asking, "Are you okay? You're very quiet!" You also have to deal with moments when he checks the score and quickly texts a friend about the game. In the end, the evening doesn't turn out as you had hoped.

Score one for the covert narcissist. He has gathered more information and further groomed you. Next time, you'll likely find yourself choosing to go to the game just to please him, or at the very least to *not* be like his last girlfriend. She was a bummer!

Playing the Victim to Get Narcissistic Supply

Continuing with the goal to manipulate, the covert narcissist plays the victim to get narcissistic supply. Just as a reminder, narcissistic supply is essential for a narcissist since it serves to validate their intelligence, desirability, superiority, charm, physical appearance, etc. Playing the victim to get narcissistic supply looks and feels a lot like someone fishing for compliments. Here the covert narcissist may pretend to feel disappointed and frustrated with their personal limitations. This dramatic scenario unfolds with the narcissist saying something like, "I'm really bummed that I couldn't do more for so-and-so. When she asked for help, the best I could do was to pay her rent for the month."

As the listener, you are then expected to shower the narcissist with adoration and reassurance, praising their generosity and assuring them that they have done enough. In this charade, the narcissist claims that their hands are tied by factors beyond their control like company policy, budget constraints, the scale of the problem, or time limitations. The accolades pour in, fueling the narcissist's ego and providing assurance that they have done everything they could. Praise abounds, reinforcing the narcissist's self-importance and providing a hit of Grade A narcissistic supply.

Playing the Victim to Protect Image

Because covert narcissists are terrified of being seen as the toxic person they truly are, they will engage in smear campaigns to protect their Mr. Nice Guy image. By playing the victim in this context, the goal is to manipulate perceptions and to control the narrative, ensuring that others see them as innocent, misunderstood, or unjustly targeted.

In a workplace environment, this could play out as the narcissists spreading rumors that colleagues are unfairly targeting them due to jealousy and personal vendettas. To play up the victimhood, the narcissists would appear worried, or even fearful of workplace bullying and discrimination.

In a romantic relationship, this could look like seeking advice from family and friends because they have "been trying so hard" but you simply don't appreciate them. Of course, there will be selective storytelling where the narcissists will downplay their own words and actions, and amplify yours to suggest that you're too sensitive, volatile, or insecure. It's all part of their grand plan to be seen as the ultimate good guy, even if it means rewriting history, cherry-picking facts, or straight-up lying to look like the innocent victim.

Playing the Victim to Hurt and Devalue You

Playing the victim here includes triangulating you with another person. This means that a covert narcissist will bring a third party to bear the burden of ill feelings or unkind comments against you. This third party may be someone you know, or a complete stranger, depending on the narcissist's goal. They'll say things like, "I was so upset about what you said that I spoke to your brother. He totally disagreed with you. In fact, he said you've been acting like this since you were in diapers. So, maybe it's not me after all." Or he may claim, "I talked to everyone at work, and not one single person thinks I act selfishly. They all think I'm the most thoughtful person around. Not to brag, but most of the women on the team said they wish their husbands were as great as me!"

You are left feeling vulnerable, exposed, judged, and betrayed. Meanwhile, the narcissist has established, or reinforced, a network of sympathy and an image of innocence. By default, you are left in a defensive position. To add insult to injury, there is another layer of abuse added to this tactic. You begin to doubt that what you are experiencing is abuse. After all, other people see the narcissist as a nice guy. You begin to question your perception of reality. Worst of all, your self-esteem and sense of security take major blows.

Playing the Victim to Transfer Accountability

By casting themselves as the victim, a covert narcissist can deflect blame, elicit sympathy and manipulate others into taking responsibility for the narcissist's poor behavior.

Imagine the narcissist being confronted because they made a rude, hurtful, or inappropriate comment during a social gathering. Instead of acknowledging the transgression, the covert narcissist may respond with, "I can't believe you are attacking me like this. All I said was (fill in the blank). I was just expressing my honest opinion. Now, you're making me out to be the bad guy. Am I not allowed to speak my mind?"

Such a situation would escalate into the narcissist saying something like, "Well, if I'm not allowed to speak my mind, I'll just leave. Clearly, I'm not wanted here." The goal here is to have the person who confronted the narcissist, and others present at the gathering, to side with the narcissist and to ask them to stay. As a result, their questionable behavior is whitewashed and minimized, to de-escalate the situation. Alternately, the covert narcissist is just as likely to stay at the event and sulk, drawing others into inquiring about their well-being, or making attempts to comfort the narcissist. This tactic is similar to DARVO. However, it involves a number of people taking responsibility for the narcissist's drama.

Another way the covert narcissist avoids accountability for their actions is with the non-apology apology. In their quest to appear as Mr. Nice Guy, the covert narcissist will speak words that mimic an apology but are in no way acknowledging the hurtful behavior. Instead, they twist the story and reinterpret the transgression to make someone else the one with the problem. The would-be apology usually sounds like, "I'm sorry you took it that way!" Although the words, *I'm sorry* are spoken, the blame is turned back on you, suggesting that it's your faulty interpretation or reaction that is the issue.

The fact that most people would react similarly is completely disregarded. Never mind the fact that the narcissist may have crossed a personal boundary where your interpretation is all that matters. Never mind that your feelings and boundaries should be respected. The narcissist's behavior remains unchanged. In the end, you are left hurt and confused. Somehow you were the one who was wronged, yet you are also expected to apologize or defend and justify your reaction and feelings.

Playing the Victim to Extract Something from You

This strategy is the one that is often portrayed in real-crime documentaries, where the gullible woman is swindled out of large amounts of money by a charming, down-on-their-luck Casanova. From the comfort of your sofa, it's easy to spot the manipulation. But real life isn't edited like those documentaries. There are nuances that pull on the woman's heartstrings and make her more susceptible to the charms of a covert narcissist. Most notably, she assumes that the covert narcissist has the same moral compass that she does. After all, he has put forth great effort to give her that impression from day one—pretending to be open and transparent with no hidden motives.

When the target and the covert narcissist meet, she becomes the focus of his attention and adoration. Often buying lavish gifts for her with the money he swindled off his last mark. He swears that he is the luckiest man alive to have met her. He pretends to be everything the target ever dreamed of. He shares a little about his goals and dreams. Because she is empathetic and feels seen and heard in the relationship, she is happy for him and cheers him on. The love-bombing continues. He forgets his wallet on one of their big outings. "That's okay," she says. "Surely, I can pay. You've paid for nearly everything up until now." Little does the woman know, this is all a production to test her malleability and to set her up for the narcissist's big win.

In the end, the drama often plays out this way: The narcissist comes home clearly distraught over something that happened where they were misunderstood, treated unfairly, or left powerless with the risk of losing something significant. Often this reported event is a complete lie, or some portion is true but is exaggerated in order to serve its purpose of exploiting the target emotionally—with requests for action or monetary contributions to come later. In any case, her job is to side with the narcissist. She is to confirm that the narcissist was completely misrepresented or mistreated. In this drama, there may or may not be tears or anger. This actually depends more on the target!

Does she need extra convincing? Does she respond in soft tones of indignation on the narcissist's behalf? Does she try to build him up or distract him to focus on something more pleasant? Or does she cuss-up-a-storm and join in a strategizing plan to recover his image or to get revenge? The narcissist adjusts his behavior and the details of his victimhood accordingly.

It's this dynamic that allows smart, loyal, supportive women all over the world to eventually fork over their life savings to a manipulative narcissist in hopes of helping him to see and reach his full potential—a man that the women thought was a committed partner.

So, how would you respond? The key is to notice that the narcissist is putting on a performance for you. The safe bet is to remain neutral. Be the observer. Show support by saying something like, "You're smart. I'm sure you'll figure it out." Or "Wow! What's your plan?" As a rule of thumb, never ever give or loan more than you can afford to lose.

* * *

Playing the victim is a common and natural move for the covert narcissist because they truly see themselves as the victim in the world. Grandiosity convinces the covert narcissist that their struggles would end, if only the world acknowledged their magnificence. But the most nerve-racking part of the covert narcissist playing the victim is that it can turn your everyday life into unnecessary drama. Their constant need to play the victim can rob you of your daily joy and peace of mind.

During my time with Colin, his consistent first response to any question, or clarification regarding his behavior, was along the lines of "Nuh-uh, no, I didn't! I didn't say that! I didn't do that." No matter the subject or situation, if he felt he was being cast in a negative light or was somehow in error, denial was the default response. He immediately saw himself as the victim of my *false* accusations. I eventually learned to walk away. But, before that lesson was learned, I fell into the trap of explaining the facts, again and again. I thought surely if I lay the evidence out calmly, systematically, logically, and if I repeated myself just one more time, slower this time, then Colin would see that he was not a victim, nor was he being falsely accused.

Colin's playing the victim shadowed our daily lives. It was difficult to predict what would trigger a downward spiral. There was no sure way to de-escalate the drama. At some point walking away no longer worked. Colin's playing the victim grew to be days-long, exhausting, mind boggling events, complete with gaslighting and triangulation. I stood by helplessly as I watched our boys being manipulated to see Colin as the good guy. My speaking against the manipulation turned into more fodder for Colin to declare, "See! I can't do anything right in your eyes." More victimhood.

Ignoring Colin to the best of my ability or accepting his non-apologies as a form of accountability registered as self-betrayal in my mind, body and spirit. Ironically, it also became a source of resentment toward me on Colin's part. Deep down he knew that his behavior was damaging. He resented me for calling him out on it *and* for the times I ignored it.

Below, I share a seemingly benign incident that is representative of everyday life that becomes a source of chaos and emotional turmoil. With Colin's inability to be imperfect or mistaken about anything, such events became more and more common. From my vantage point, there was simply no way to reason with Colin or stay true to myself. Mole hills grew into mountains. Looking back, due to DARVO and the covert's need to play the victim, most conflicts went unresolved in our marriage.

The Facebook Incident

"Fuuuddge! Laurissa just played a 52-point word on me!" I said. "I thought for sure I was going to win this game."

"It's probably all those margaritas she's been drinking on the beach," Colin said.

"What do you mean?" I asked. "How do you know Laurissa is on a beach drinking margaritas?"

"I saw it on Facebook! She's in Miami. She has been there all week," Colin answered with a giggle.

His words caught me off guard. I didn't know what to say. I didn't know he knew Laurissa like that. I decided I needed more information.

"You're Facebook friends with Laurissa? *My* friend from work?"

"No. Nuh-uh!" He answered immediately, sounding defensive.

"Then how do you know what she's up to over spring break?" I had no idea that the two were connected. Or that they even knew one another directly.

"Because of Facebook!" He said, with a *duh* tone in his voice. "But it's not like I read her posts."

"Well, clearly you do," I pointed out. "What made you send her a Friend Request?"

"I didn't!" Colin says. His voice was suddenly filled with rage. "You just don't understand how Facebook works."

I laughed—which had become an involuntary response for the times when conversations with Colin had me questioning my sanity or my understanding of the English language. On the one hand, he was correct. Up to that point I had not been a Facebook user. On the other hand, I was fairly certain of how Facebook worked, and I understood logic!

Without further prompting from me, Colin mansplained, "They send you messages in your feed that say, 'You May Also Know …' Her name and picture were in my feed." From that point Colin mentioned the name of two other workmates. He boasted that when Facebook recommended their names his response was, "Fuck No!"

All I could do was continue to look at my phone, pretending to think of a word to play. I checked in with my body, remembering my promise to no longer betray myself for the sake of Colin's ego. I asked myself, *Did he just say what I think he said?*

Trusting my body cues, I called him on the contradiction, "So you *did* choose to friend Laurissa. But you passed on Lucy and Lorraine. It's fine, I'm just surprised."

Colin was not going to give an inch. "No! I did not," he insisted, clearly pissed off. "Like I said, you just don't understand Facebook. Why do *you* always have to make *me* out to be an asshole?"

He stomped away.

Around year fifteen in our marriage, stomping away had become one of Colin's signature moves to use whenever he felt threatened or realized he had been caught. This pattern was introduced into our relationship by Colin who claimed that he needed the time to cool off and get his thoughts together. I once believed that such behavior may have been helpful because Colin was awkward in conversations and seemed triggered whenever there was a conflict of any kind. Over time I came to realize that his exit was more about finding time to formulate a better lie than creating space to allow for cooler heads. The narrative in the end was often the same: Colin was the victim, and I was the attacker.

* * *

In the Facebook incident above, Colin returned hours later with the following explanation: "I can see why you think I *friended* her. But I didn't plan to read her posts. Ever. I'm not interested in her. She's too skinny for me, and her husband … ugh!" I made note of the fact that Colin tried to distract me by suggesting that my curiosity stemmed from suspicions of a romantic interest in Laurissa. I didn't take the bait.

This explanation still made zero sense to me. It was like signing up for email newsletters or subscribing to magazines that you never planned to read. Besides that, he must have been reading her posts in order to know about the beach and the margaritas. I have to admit that these are the kind of situations that supported my idea that Colin had some other mental deficiency, one where he lacked critical thinking skills. There was a part of me that could not reconcile that Colin could be brilliant enough to become a doctor yet lack common sense. I also had feelings of obligation to give the benefit of the doubt, to help Colin to understand, and to forgive. It was times like this when the scripture that admonishes us to *forgive your brother seventy-seven times* shamed me into silence. I also felt guilty for thinking that my husband was mentally deficient.

Colin continued, "I know you don't believe me, but it's true. I'm not the ass you keep making me out to be."

For several minutes, I said nothing. I was very aware that this incident was happening during Colin's last hoover, a time of our relationship where we had committed to repairing the damage and doing things differently. It all felt familiar. I knew that this was just part of Colin's routine. When repeated attempts at denial failed, explanations followed—nonsensical explanations and projections. (I wasn't worried that he and Laurissa were having an affair.) However, at the time, I didn't have the labels and current understanding that I have now regarding the tactics of the covert narcissist. Nor did I know that this was all part of an insidious abuse cycle of grooming and conditioning—a cycle that I had grown up with in dealing with my father.

But in my mind, I had *fixed things* in the past, so, my strategy was to see how I could truly understand his side, be heard, and fix this.

Colin went on as before with his nonsensical explanations, blaming me for not understanding how Facebook worked. I sat numb, trying hard not to betray myself. I had foolishly hoped that Colin would come clean and be accountable. (Doing so was part of the contract he made with himself and the therapist mentioned in chapter 3.) That wasn't going to happen. Numbness is often the reported response from other targets of abuse when having a conversation filled with excuses and stories that are *so* absurd that you convince yourself that *you* must be failing to understand a key factor. As a child, I went somewhere else in my mind. It's possible that I did the same at times while married to Colin.

I remember asking, "So, you believe the goal of Facebook is to friend people that you know, but you don't intend to communicate or keep up with them. If I decided to get a Facebook page and friend Mick (another doctor in his field), would you be okay with that?"

Colin fumed in anger.

"No! It's not the same." Notice the hypocrisy.

My eyes started to well up with tears. I was just *so* frustrated. It felt like Colin was intent on killing our marriage. It was as if he was willfully blind to the damage he was causing with his lies and hypocrisy. As silent tears spilled over and ran down my face, Colin walked away, seething in anger and self-pity. He ignored me for the rest of the night.

In the Facebook Incident, when my sons noticed my sadness and low energy, they asked Colin what was wrong with me.

He responded with exasperation and feigned concern, "I don't know … I guess I messed up again. Your mom is so sensitive. She feels things so passionately. I keep forgetting." He whispered to play up his agony. Then he went on, "Let's let her sleep. Hopefully, she'll feel better after she gets some rest."

My insides screamed.

He portrayed himself as the victim. He was the poor husband and father who was just doing the best he could. After all, who can blame him for forgetting? Everyone forgets sometimes.

Far too often, I was portrayed as the Wicked Witch of the West to my children. Unfortunately, and understandably, in this incident and others, my empathetic sons fell for their father's manipulations. They pleaded, "Please don't be mad at Daddy."

This result was just what Colin wanted, because he remained Mr. Nice Guy and World's Greatest Dad. From an early age, the lens through which my kids saw me was tainted.

Targets of covert narcissists eventually end up betraying themselves by asking less of their partners. It becomes easier to go without having their needs met in the relationships than to expect more from the narcissist. For years, I deluded myself in toxic hope thinking that Colin had shifted his behavior when, in reality, I had simply softened my standards and expectations.

EXERCISES

Complete the following exercises. Be as objective as possible. If you must lean one way or another, err in your favor. This will balance the tables some since it is highly likely that you have started adjusting your behaviors, thoughts, and plans to accommodate the covert narcissist.

Exercise 1: Taking Inventory

Think of the conflicts you've had with the narcissist in your life. Consider how many times you have found yourself defending your very normal, very justified feelings and responses to insults and invalidation coming from the person-in-question. You are not to blame for speaking up for yourself. You have been put in the position of defending yourself against the one person in your life who is supposed to be safe. If you have been treated as if you are unhinged or crazy, I want you to know that you're not.

You just want (and deserve) more. As you take inventory, look for patterns. Does your partner always seem to be the victim? More importantly, notice the frequency of such events. Once we are accustomed to something, we barely notice it. Like polluted air. It becomes part of our everyday life. This includes toxic interactions with people, especially family.

Exercise 2: Acknowledgment

How many times this week/month have you been required to betray yourself for the benefit of the narcissist? How many times have you denied your truth or silenced your voice to make another person feel comfortable?

This is your opportunity to acknowledge that each time you silence yourself, you betray your own needs. It's time to make amends with yourself and stop giving pieces of yourself to the narcissist, no matter how much you love them. This is also the time for you to look back at your childhood dynamics. What beliefs, teachings, circumstances, and events shaped the way you handle conflict? Are you programmed to be a people pleaser? To be the fixer? Were you taught that love meant sacrifice? Do you believe that relationships are hard? Are you repeating thinking and behavior patterns that you saw as a child?

Exercise 3: Preserving Your Personal Integrity

It can seem impossible to avoid sacrificing personal integrity for peace, but there may be some techniques that turn the tables and help take back your power. When transgressions against you inevitably occur, in small or large ways, try saying the following:

- "That's not the way I remember it."
- "We will have to agree to disagree."
- "I'm not willing to do that."
- "That doesn't feel right. Let me think about it."
- "We talked about that. The answer is still no!"

You may be faced with reactions of rage, sulking, retreat, or passive-aggression. Whatever the case, I recommend that you incorporate this exercise for at least three days into your weekly routine. This is one small step that prevents you from having any part in your own abuse. The goal is to quietly and firmly stand your ground.

Exercise 4: This Is What I Know

When the narcissist is playing the victim, it's important that you not fall for the performance yourself. That's the point where many of us lose ourselves. The covert's performance is so elaborate or dramatic that we convince ourselves we must have done something wrong. Otherwise, why would they be so adamant, so upset?

We spend a great deal of mental energy trying to figure out what we are "not seeing" or are "misunderstanding." Stop! Instead, write down a summation of what you believed really happened. Date it.

As you continue this practice, look for patterns, look for signs of playing the victim, and look for the others in the situation (triangulation). Note when those others are manipulated into siding with the narcissist.

CHAPTER 8

GASLIGHTING

The term comes from the movie Gaslight, a 1944 film starring Ingrid Bergman and Charles Boyer. In the film, Ingrid Bergman plays Paula, an heiress to a fortune left to her by her murdered aunt. Charles Boyer plays Gregory, the man Paula is manipulated into marrying following a quick, intense romance. It is slowly revealed that Paula's new husband is also her aunt's murderer. Gregory had targeted Paula from the beginning with the sole purpose of getting his hands on the jewels that he failed to get during the botched robbery. After marrying her, Gregory seeks to undermine Paula's sense of self and her sanity. His plan is to have her committed to an asylum, gaining power of attorney of all her belongings, namely the aunt's precious jewels. Gregory's evil strategies include moving items in Paula's environment and pretending that conversations and events happened that have not. The act that lends the movie its title is convincing Paula that she is imagining a change in the lighting, and a darkening of the gaslights in the house. (Before electricity became commonly used for lighting in homes, most homes had gaslights.) Gregory denies any change in the lighting, knowing full well that he is responsible for the dimming gaslights. He then suggests that Paula is losing her mind. It's all just part of his plan to systematically drive his wife insane.

I watched this movie with my mother when I was just a kid. It was one of our favorites, along with every Alfred Hitchcock movie ever made. Imagine my surprise to find out later that I was raised by a covert narcissist, married one, and that the term gaslighting originated from this movie. Life is so funny. I wonder if my mother ever made the connection.

Gaslighting is a tactic often used by toxic individuals seeking to manipulate you. Gaslighting makes it easier to maintain control. It allows a person to avoid accountability, deflect responsibility, or to just simply win (whatever winning looks like to the toxic person). They will say or do things to make you question your memory, perceptions, or even your sanity. It's a sneaky way of making you feel like you're going a bit crazy or that your thoughts and feelings aren't valid.

Remember with covert narcissists, gaslighting is cloaked in victimhood, or the facade of Mr. Nice Guy. It's important to recognize that gaslighting is *not always* a straightforward disagreement or lie. Instead, it's an action, statement or point of view that leaves you feeling confused, questioning your reactions, and condemning yourself. Colin's tendency to "forget" is an example. How can I prove for certain that he didn't indeed forget?

The end of The Sleep Incident is another perfect example. I did say that there were many red flags in this single event. Recall that the Sleep Incident started as an example of Colin invalidating my requests and need for sleep. He also moved into using DARVO. In that chapter, we ended with Colin coming home from school, feigning shock and relief when I spoke to him, pretending that I had been the one giving him the silent treatment. He was gaslighting me. But it got worse when Colin started begging, "Please don't leave!" Not once had I mentioned leaving. His comment triggered shame and guilt in me—shame and guilt that lived deep inside me from events that had nothing to do with the situation got ignited and played its part in Colin's gaslighting. Colin knew about the care-taking role I played in my family. He played on my empathy. The narcissists know just what to say or do. They know which buttons to push, and how to push them.

When Colin started bemoaning, "I am such a loser. Why do you put up with me? Please don't leave me!" As if I were born for the sole purpose of bolstering Colin's self-esteem, I began doing exactly that.

"*You* are *not* a loser!" I said, with just the right inflections. I held Colin. I rubbed his back. I repeated my reassurances. I got him a tissue, water, and later the bathroom trash can. Colin accused me of always being disappointed in him, and of acting as if I didn't want to be married any more. He was so emphatic that I began to question my past actions. For days later, I chose my words carefully and I worked hard to keep my facial expressions neutral. "Of course, I'm not leaving." I said. At the time, I was not aware that I was fully participating in maintaining Colin's nice guy facade. At the time, I wasn't even aware of the term narcissist. I was definitely aware of feeling nauseous, and that my head hurt. I felt confused and fearful. I now know that I was being molded like clay by Colin.

The Sleep Incident ended with Colin laying on our bed and pulling me in to join him. As I lay next to him, Colin snuggled in and spooned me. Draping his long arm over me, Colin took my hand and kissed the back of it, followed by each of my fingers.

"I ... love ... you ... so ... much," he said, one word for each finger. Afterward, he softly sang a song in French— a song whose melody I recognized but couldn't recall the meaning. It was a song that I liked.

I was filled with obligation to meet Colin's needs. I remember the guilt I felt for not feeling grateful or joyful about our apparent reunion. My confusion and question of *What the f*ck just happened?* continued to flood my mind. My thoughts were pushed deep inside. They lay dormant until the next time.

And just like that, my understanding of the dynamic between Colin and me was altered forever. My perception eventually became permanently skewed in Colin's favor—him the victim, me the aggressor. The Sleep Incident was a milestone event that set a course and precedent for a lifetime's worth of narcissistic abuse.

* * *

The damage caused by continued gaslighting permeates your entire being and can last for years after the relationship has ended. I misinterpreted the signs of narcissistic abuse. Accepting my husband's explanations and pleas to reunite felt like the right thing to do for the man I loved, especially when he was displaying clear signs of distress. Beyond that, my chaotic upbringing with a narcissistic father had me pre-conditioned to fawn in those situations. *I had learned early in life that the best way to get through emotional situations that made zero sense was to play nice until the storm passed.* My default was to accept any glimpse of an apology as a sign of safety. I didn't recognize narcissistic behavior as toxic. I knew that it was not right. It made me feel anxious and *in trouble*, but as a child I didn't have the experience or language to make clear sense of my environment. My focus was on staying safe. Fawning worked for me.

I've learned that the long-term damage of gaslighting reveals itself in your inability to trust your own reasoning and judgment. It makes you feel anxious and insecure. You find yourself running most, if not all, of your decisions by others—*just to be sure*. Worse, you find yourself making the choice of indecision, which is a choice in itself. In the end, you lose all sense of power and control over your own mind, body, and life.

Signs and symptoms of continuous gaslighting:

- You start to second-guess yourself and your ability to make sound decisions.
- You find yourself seeking other people's opinions to validate your own.
- You avoid having to make even mundane choices.
- Emotional and mental exhaustion become your new normal without a clear reason why. *I liken it to someone following you around all day, tapping you in the back of the head with a plastic bat. Just imagine it. It doesn't hurt. It doesn't completely disrupt your life, but it sure takes a toll.*
- You make up excuses for the toxic person's behavior.
- You find yourself wishing that you had a recording of events

involving the narcissist as they tend to rewrite history in their favor.
- You don't trust your memory, nor your perception of events.

Being gaslighted seems to have an almost immediate physical effect. Next time it occurs, notice how you feel in your body immediately following the moment you doubt your reality. Notice if your energy wanes. Notice if your stomach feels queasy. Do the hairs on the back of your neck and arms seem to stand up? Your body knows and goes on high alert seeking more information. But, because the issue is never resolved, and solid proof never surfaces, your body stays on high alert.

Gaslighting steals your peace of mind and spills over into other relationships. For me, it was my relationship with my boys. As they grew up, my sons were deprived of the real me. Just recently, I learned from my youngest son that I was the one he remembered as standoffish and unapproachable. In the midst of our discussion, specific events stumbled into my memory. As if frozen in time, I relived the physical pain of knowing, yet not being able to verbalize, that I had been wronged, manipulated, and mistreated.

I spent decades suffering from emotional abuse. I knew something was amiss, but I couldn't prove it. In those moments, I was doing all I could to hold myself together. Sometimes I physically wrapped myself into a tight ball to keep from wailing. There were many times that I retreated to my bed, or left the house for a drive to cry, or to shop until I was numb. My sons were watching. They couldn't see it, but the truth is that I was trying desperately to hold onto my sanity—especially for their sakes.

Some days I wish that my sons could see what was happening back then. I regret that either of them had reason to doubt my love and devotion to them.

I had already suffered symptoms of C-PTSD with the gaslighting I experienced as a child. Gaslighting had been a major tactic in the religious indoctrination I experienced growing up as a Jehovah's Witness.

Add to that the cognitive dissonance experienced from my father's words and actions and it meant that by the time Colin entered my life, there had been some damage. He compounded it … exponentially.

What follows is one of many episodes with Colin that resulted in me doubting my sanity and considering ending it all. Had my boys not been born, I believe I would have followed through.

More Than a Cup of Tea

Colin didn't know I heard him on the phone. What he did know was my sexual history. He knew about the sexual trauma I experienced from multiple abusers who were my dad's friends or acquaintances—all members of the Jehovah's Witness congregation. He knew the resulting struggles I've had being comfortable in and with my own body and sexuality.

Yet, he said what he did.

I had made it clear that I didn't want to see my father, that I was not ready to talk about my anger and confusion. Nor was I able to pretend that all was well. Colin knew of my many attempts to talk to my father about the repeated sexual abuse. He knew about my father's refusal to acknowledge any responsibility and how my father painted himself as a victim who was powerless to keep the predators away. For those reasons, my father had to stay away. He was not welcome in our house. I needed space and time. Colin knew this.

When I realized that the elders, including my father, knew about the pedophiles in the congregation but did nothing to protect the children—the feelings of rejection and betrayal that I felt were the latest of the many layers that my therapist said needed to be processed. I explained to Colin, as my therapist had, that the process would take time. I needed time.

Colin was supposed to be on my side. He said he understood. He appeared to be empathetic. So, when I heard him say, "Sure Tom, come on up!" I froze in disbelief.

"I can really use your help moving the heavy stuff … Yep! We will be here ... see you then." These were the words Colin told my father, after promising me that he would tell him the opposite.

I heard him from the top of the stairs. Instead of protecting me and telling my father not to come—instead of telling him that he wasn't invited to help with the move, and that it wasn't a good time for me—Colin welcomed my father into our home.

Colin pretended to be frustrated as he said, "Your dad's coming. He'll be here in a few hours. He insisted. You know how he can be. He wouldn't listen to me about not coming up here."

I knew Colin was lying. I had heard his side of the conversation. But I pretended otherwise. The important thing was that my father was coming and would be there in a few hours.

I wasn't ready. Protecting myself was my main priority.

"I can't see him ... I'm not ready ... I can't." I tried not to sound angry or panicked. "I will just have to leave right before he gets here ... or I can go upstairs." As the words left my mouth, I knew that plan would not work. My father would simply wait for me to return home or would come upstairs to look for me. I needed Colin to keep my father away from me. So, I suggested a script for Colin, "You can tell him, 'Monica isn't able to see you. She's working through the things that she's talked to you about over the last few months. She needs more time.'" I went on explaining to Colin how he could protect me. I told him how much I needed him. I said, "When my daddy gets pushy you can be straight with him and tell him he needs to give me some space. You can remind him that I asked him not to come up here."

Colin promised again to say just that. He promised that he would keep my dad away from me. That he would protect my boundary. That I could count on him. It's exactly what I wanted to hear and what I *needed* to believe.

But that's not what happened. Once again, I had misplaced my trust.

My father came sooner than expected, catching us both off guard. Colin let him in without warning. I looked my father in the eyes, but he looked away. I went upstairs and listened from there.

I heard my father ask, irritated, "What's wrong with *her?*"

I wanted to yell, "I'll tell you what's wrong with me!" But I wasn't ready to talk. I was not ready to hear the excuses and denial. I knew there would be no resolution. No accountability.

So, I simply listened.

"Who knows? You know how she can be!" was Colin's answer. His one and only answer. I heard it and I crumbled inside. My chest felt as if it had caved in on itself. I couldn't catch my breath. My field of vision shrank and turned black. I felt dizzy. I fell to my knees and crawled to my bed.

That's where I stayed. Confused. Unable to name the familiar pain I felt. I wanted to understand Colin's betrayal.

Hours later, I heard the bedroom door open. It was Colin. I looked at the man I counted on to stand by me and protect me. I wanted to know why he didn't. I wanted to tell him I heard everything. I wanted to hear what he had to say. I wanted to understand. I said nothing.

Colin's lips were moving, but I couldn't comprehend anything he was saying. He brought me a cup of tea. Stroking my hair and my face, Colin said, "Drink your tea. It will make you feel better." I convinced myself that he had an explanation. One that would make the pain go away. One that would make this all make sense. I was curious. I looked into Colin's eyes. They looked tender and full of something I just couldn't put my finger on. In denial, I decided that it was remorse.

He loves me, I told myself. *He is going to make this right.* I waited.

Colin sighed and said, "I'm sorry that your dad is such an ass, babe!"

What? My mind screamed. The question echoed in my ears and head, but I couldn't get it to come out of my mouth. My head throbbed worse than before. My eyes burned. My breath caught in my throat. The tears began to flow, followed by a wail that came from deep down. I cried loud and hard. I wanted to be held. Rocked. I wanted to know that I was safe. That I was loved. That I was going to be okay.

Colin said nothing to comfort me. He simply walked away. The bedroom door opened and closed. I was alone!

* * *

The cognitive dissonance I felt was unreal. I didn't have the words for it, but my body knew. I now know that I left my body that day, just as I had many times before with each encounter of childhood sexual abuse by members of the so-called Christian congregations I grew up in.

From what I understand, I dissociated, which is a psychological defense mechanism that involves a disconnection or detachment from one's thoughts, feelings, memories, or sense of self. It can be a way for our minds to cope with overwhelming or conflicting emotions, stress, or trauma, including situations where cognitive dissonance occurs.

I was traumatized by the contrast between Colin's words, his sweet comforting voice, and the reality of what my body and mind knew to be true. My husband had shown himself to be a liar, a coward, and above all else, someone who was dangerous for me to be around and trust. This was more proof that I needed to watch out for the enemy who was living in the same house and sleeping in the same bed with me, who had access to my children, and who claimed to love me.

In other words, the very same person who was actively destroying me was also offering comfort. That's the hell of gaslighting—it plants poison and nurtures it to grow.

I have a sneaky suspicion that the target's tendency to dissociate, coupled with the covert narcissist's subtle tactics within the abuse cycle, is how such toxic relationships manage to last so long. I am certain that the psychological distress of not being able to reconcile who I was actually married to with who I kept pretending that I was married to played a huge part in the thirty years I endured. It played a bigger part in my divorce agreement.

* * *

Colin lied about this event when I asked him about it. He held onto the lie that he hadn't invited my father to our house until I picked up my phone to call him. I warned Colin that I planned to ask my father how he knew we would be home and that we were moving.

Deep down I had learned that Colin was less friend than foe. My body knew and sent me signs. I developed asthma, which continued to worsen until after the divorce. My migraines increased. My digestive issues got worse.

From that day forward, I stopped sharing my dreams and worries with Colin. We lived more as roommates than as loving partners. I felt extremely lonely.

***

If you are in a relationship with a covert narcissist that is affecting your health and wellbeing, my advice to you is this: Save yourself. Review the signs and symptoms of gaslighting listed earlier in the chapter. All of this will become more fodder to use against you. Don't let it happen.

Complete the following exercises with the goal of holding on to your perception of events and providing evidence to verify facts at a later date if needed. As always, notice all body cues as you experience the shifts.

EXERCISES

Exercise 1: Adopt This Mantra

A friend who had also been married to a narcissist taught me a grounding phrase. I'm not sure where she heard it. It goes: "I heard what I heard. I saw what I saw. I know what I know." Repeat the mantra whenever you find yourself silently asking, "What the hell just happened?" or "Why am I apologizing?"

Exercise 2: Refining Your Gut Check

If you haven't already, start keeping quick notes on your phone to keep track of the number of times you find yourself in a conversation or incident where you feel that something is off. Trust your gut.

Notice how often and with whom this feeling arises. Don't worry about the details. You are focusing on the number of gut/body cues you get with the suspected narcissist. You can start keeping more extensive notes later, if needed.

Do not minimize the power in simply acknowledging the connection between the covert narcissist's words and behavior, your interpretation of the situation, and your body's response. Simply saying to yourself, "I got the message," will have your body and intuition speaking louder. Keep checking. Keep confirming. The more often you exercise this connection, the stronger it will get.

Exercise 3: Decisions

Decide how you want to proceed in the relationship. Perhaps you want to distance yourself. At the very least, you will want to keep the above mantra in mind. Trust your gut. Validate your interpretation of events. DO NOT explain to the narcissist what you are doing or why. This will be used against you. Either the culprit in question will get better at gaslighting you, or they will taunt you with your valid suspicions. If you find that you are being gaslighted by an intimate partner, I strongly recommend that you plan an exit strategy. Distance yourself emotionally first, so that you can begin to think clearly again.

CHAPTER 9

ENTITLEMENT

Entitlement is someone believing that they deserve special treatment or privileges *just because*. Entitlement is one of the hallmark traits of all narcissists. They act as if the rules don't apply to them and expect to have their needs met regardless of the impact on others. It's akin to having a spoiled "me-first" attitude all the time. When Colin was first diagnosed, I thought narcissistic entitlement referred to the jerk who cuts to the front of a long line or who berates the server in a restaurant. This wasn't Colin. Yet, he did believe he was entitled—and to a great deal. All covert narcissists feel entitled. They simply don't broadcast it.

One day, when our flights from Chicago to Columbus were delayed due to a winter storm, there was a man demanding to be put on an alternate flight immediately. "I'm a doctor," he said. "I have patients to see, and I am a thousand percent sure there are other flights available. Find one." The doctor was loud and downright mean to the woman working at the desk. He insisted on speaking with someone more competent. This order was to happen immediately! No matter how often the customer service manager repeated the information, this man seemed unable to process that the issue was the weather, that *all* flights were delayed for hours, and that his flight was, in fact, canceled. He kept insisting that what she was reporting was unacceptable.

This is what hundreds of people witnessed at O'Hare International Airport that day. I can only imagine what they thought of that oh-so-important doctor's behavior. I know I thought, *That poor woman.*

What an asshole! What those hundreds of people didn't see, and what I didn't connect to covert entitlement, was Colin's behavior and attitude.

Colin complained about the ridiculousness of it, how crowded the airport was, and the incompetence of the airport staff. He made comments about his heavy caseload the next day, about how he needed to be in Columbus, not sitting on the floor at O'Hare.

I did my best to reassure Colin that his patients would understand and that everything was going to be okay. I brainstormed ways he could get word to his patients to have them rescheduled.

"They'll be pissed, and I'll probably lose half of them," he complained.

I thought of tokens of gratitude that he could offer patients in appreciation for their understanding and patience. He was insulted that I would suggest that he offer a bribe. I knew that Colin was seething on the inside. Looking back, I see that Colin was just as angry as the asshole making the scene, but he was hiding it better. Colin did not publicly reveal his outrage because it would fly in the face of the Mr. Nice Guy image that he projected at all costs.

Instead, I was his audience. And because I was not the audience that he needed, wanted, or thought he deserved, I was also punished.

When I asked Colin to hold our son so I could go to the airport bathroom, he ignored me. No eye contact, no shrug, no reaching for our baby. Nothing. So, I strapped our son into the baby harness and took him to the bathroom with me.

At the time, I still wondered if Colin was on the autism spectrum. I dismissed this behavior as being a coping strategy as he went off into his own world to deal with frustration. Of course, canceled flights are frustrating, even downright maddening. But I didn't connect the stonewalling and silent treatment to covert narcissistic entitlement until many years later.

When I returned from the bathroom, Colin acted surprised that I was gone. "Where were you?" he asked. "What if they had called our flight?" He sounded angry and bewildered. By then, I knew this was Colin's modus operandi for appearing innocent.

I didn't fall for the blame-shifting. I reminded him that I did indeed tell him I was going to the restroom, and that I had, in fact, asked him to hold our baby while I was gone. He said nothing.

The next day Colin behaved as if the previous events hadn't happened. There was no acknowledgment of his rude or unkind behavior. (This is a form of gaslighting.) I have since learned that Colin's behavior that day was about entitlement and outrage. Down the road, I found out that the fear of voicing his rage was because he was terrified of being ignored or mocked.

Could you imagine the narcissistic injury that would result if it were confirmed, in front of hundreds of people, that his rage was irrelevant and that his opinion didn't matter?

I find it interesting that Colin devalued and invalidated me by dismissing my words and feelings and making it clear that I didn't matter. Yet, being irrelevant and abandoned were his greatest fears.

* * *

There seemed to be a delusional aspect to Colin's entitlement. It was as if my words, my tears, or anything else about me mattered only in relation to his ego. The word "no" was never a definitive answer for Colin. He would coerce me into granting his wish by constant begging, using the silent treatment, or by flat-out ignoring my wishes and proceeding with his desires, despite the consequences.

During a joint session with Colin's last therapist—the one who insisted that Colin did indeed love me and wanted to be an equal partner—she insisted that I simply needed to make my requests and needs clearer. She insisted that I wasn't being as direct in my communications as I might think, and that I mistakenly saw Colin's failure to respond appropriately as combative. She indicated that she could show me how to improve. When this happened, I felt my energy wane, as I was once again being directed to adjust my actions in order to accommodate Colin's behavior.

This time I countered her claim: "I can assure you that I am very clear in my communications with Colin. Not only do I state my requests and demands clearly, more often than not I repeat them. It's an annoying habit I developed as a teacher."

Colin laughed out loud at my admission. This got the therapist's attention.

She asked him outright, "Do you understand Monica's requests and frustrations? Do you understand when and why she is often upset with your choices and lack of follow-through?"

Colin nodded.

The therapist was surprised by this answer. It was obvious that her lesson plan for this session had been shot to hell.

I giggled inside because I could relate to the expression on her face. Teacher's lesson plans seldom go exactly as expected. However, I didn't feel vindicated. I felt attacked. She wanted to prove me wrong, and that she was right about my not communicating clearly.

The therapist then redirected her line of questioning. "Colin, you say you want your marriage to work and that you want to be an equal partner." She took a long pause and added, "If so, once you understand Monica's needs and her frustrations in the marriage, what do you do with the information?"

Without a moment's hesitation, and with a smirk on his face, Colin flatly said, "Sometimes I forget, but mostly I just ignore her." There was silence in the room. I wanted to cry but refused to give Colin the satisfaction.

He continued, "It's always her way or the highway." His tone was angry and accusatory. He made his signature claw-like gesture with his right hand for emphasis.

The therapist asked for examples and Colin listed events that adversely impacted all four of us. These were events that I had protested, events when Colin chose to act in his own interests, and for which he later felt embarrassment and shame for the mess he'd caused. In Colin's mind, I was to blame for such times. As I sat there, I remembered a letter that Colin wrote me, actually putting into writing what he expected from me as his wife. He wanted to be needed, acknowledged, admired, respected, adored, and sexually satisfied. He wrote that he had worked too hard to become a doctor to be hassled by me about household chores. He informed me that other doctors didn't have household chores. He also let me know that I was not entitled to his income and that he was free to do whatever he wanted with his money. Back then Colin had recanted his demands when I reminded him that other doctors made enough money to hire support staff—nannies, housekeepers, and cooks. It was mean. I know.

Still, Colin's behavior that day in his therapist's office, and my memory of the letter, confirmed for me that I had a real problem on my hands.

Finally, accepting Colin to be a true narcissist filled in so many holes, and questions I had about our marriage.

Still, it took hindsight and distance for me to *truly see* the depth of his entitled behavior.

Not in the Mood

One night, about eighteen years into our marriage, Colin climbed into bed and immediately spooned against me. It was nice. It felt familiar and comfortable. It had been our thing, the way we fell asleep in the early days. Throughout the night we'd separate and find our way to each other again. Most mornings I'd wake up in his arms with my head on his chest. I felt loved. I felt safe.

On this particular night, I was surprised when Colin began nibbling on my ear and kissing the back of my neck. Hadn't he noticed that I wasn't feeling well? Hadn't he heard me tell him that several of the kids at school tested positive for strep throat and that I was afraid that I might have it since I had ringing ears, a sore throat, and a headache? I knew I told him. I knew he heard me because he made me a cup of tea. I decided to ignore his nibbling.

"Do you wanna fool around?" he asked.

"Definitely not! I feel like crap." I said. "Maybe in the morning." I had gotten accustomed to adding that last bit in hopes of protecting Colin's feelings. There was always passive-aggressive hell to pay when Colin felt small or rejected in any way. In truth, I did hope to feel better after a good night's sleep—however, it's because I had two boys to take care of and I didn't leave plans for a substitute teacher on my desk.

Like most women, despite being sick, I still had shit to get done.

Colin pressed himself against me. I could feel his hard penis against my lower back. He kissed my shoulders, then nibbled on my ear again.

I thrust my hips backward to get him off of me. "Unless you plan to finish that off yourself, you should stop." My tone was matter of fact and direct.

Colin scooted back a little. He began stroking his penis with his left hand and playing with my hair with his right. Stroke. Twirl. His breathing got heavier.

"Come on! I'll make it worth your while."

"No!" I said it louder than I meant to, but I was getting pissed at the thought of having to explain to him, for what felt like the hundredth time. My body was not a light switch that he could just turn off and on at his discretion. I didn't think I should have to explain why ringing ears, a sore throat, and a headache were not an aphrodisiac.

He put his hand down the back of my pajamas. "Wow! You have a nice ass," he said for the first time in a long time.

I was not flattered. My head was pounding by then and my eyes felt like they were burning (my fevers usually spike at night). I was just hopeful that my body would burn off whatever infection it was fighting by morning. I closed my eyes tighter.

"Please stop." I said and pulled away. I pushed the covers back to get up to leave. Colin caught me by the back of my pajama shirt. As I fell back, he swung his leg over me. Within seconds, I found myself flat on my back with Colin on top of me. I held the waist ties of my pajama bottoms, and as much of the fabric as possible, in my fists.

"Come on … it's been so long … I know that I can make you feel better." He said this while kissing my neck and running his tongue along the space between my boobs.

"GET OFF OF ME!" I yelled with as much volume as I could muster. My voice cracked. I knew that the tears were just blinks away. I wiggled my hips to free myself. It didn't work.

"I want you so much. I am about to burst!" Colin whined without moving. Whining had gotten me to change my mind about other things. I know now, it was just his way of excusing his own behavior and granting himself permission to proceed with his plans.

"So what!" I said. "I'm NOT interested."

At this point, his hurt feelings were the least of my worries. I pushed his shoulders and his head away. I wanted him off of me. The maneuver worked against me. Somehow it made it easy for Colin to get both my pajama bottoms and panties down.

Colin adjusted his body so that he was on his knees. He grabbed my wrists and pinned my hands above my head. My thighs and hips were immobile under his weight. Still straddling me, Colin bent over to kiss me. First my nose, then my forehead. He kissed my eyes. First the left, then the right. He licked his lips. I knew then that he could taste my tears.

I shook my head in protest and pleaded with him to stop. He ignored it all.

Suddenly, I was five years old again, in the basement of my babysitter's house. He was ignoring my noes and my tears back then, just the way Colin was. Both were touching me in places without permission. Both were guilty of sexual assault.

Holding my wrists above my head with his left hand, Colin puts the index and middle fingers of his right hand into his mouth. Once. Twice. Three times. After the third time, he put his fingers inside me. I cried out loud. I knew he could hear me. He said nothing. Instead, he used his pre-cum to wet his penis.

Within minutes he exploded inside me. Colin groaned and collapsed on top of me.

I cried harder, from deep inside. There was no sound, but my body trembled.

Colin laughed out loud. "Oh my gawd! See? I told you! I needed that. That felt *so* good." He then kissed me on my forehead and rolled off of me. He lay on his side with his left leg and arm draped over my body. His presence felt heavy. I wanted to vomit.

Colin acted oblivious. He didn't see my tears, and it wasn't because the room was dark. Within minutes Colin was snoring. I got up. I needed to shower. I wanted to wash Colin off me. OUT of me.

The next day Colin acted as if nothing vile happened between us. In Colin's mind, he had a roll in the hay with his wife and successfully prevented blue balls. It was his sense of entitlement that gave him the green light. Not me. Once again, his desires and wishes were prioritized, while mine were ignored or minimized. That sense of superiority that all narcissists have allowed Colin to ramrod, literally, his desires through mine.

To keep his Mr. Nice Guy facade intact, Colin convinced himself that he seduced me that night. His words, "See I told you," after he assaulted me, spoke volumes.

Colin's acting as if no boundaries had been crossed, and no crime committed the night before, forced me to operate in his reality. It's a behavior that I tolerated in my marriage because I grew accustomed to it in my childhood. There was no acknowledgment of poor behavior, no apologies, a simple act as if nothing happened. It was how many of my family members behaved, and how many still do.

Whenever I brought up the elephant in the room between us, Colin would say, "Let it go. That was yesterday. Why are you bringing up the past?" Sometimes he'd just use his favorite response of "Nuh-uh!" or flat-out stonewall me by staring blankly.

I didn't understand this reasoning or behavior as a kid. Growing up, there was a constant energy of distrust and fear. I didn't feel safe. Experiencing the same with Colin felt like a betrayal because I thought he would be different. I believed that Colin was my safe space. But, when the familiar feeling of distrust and fear arose, the pattern of silence or fawning that I developed in childhood often won.

In too many ways, I was comfortable with the people in my life not being safe. I had become accustomed to standing guard.

As a child, when my "no" had been ignored by sexual predators, I hadn't fought back. I had simply laid there and thought about other things, doing nothing to prolong the event. After the same began happening in my marriage, while Colin snored in satisfaction, I'd cry in the shower, sometimes scrubbing myself so hard that the scrunchie made tiny cuts which would burn when the soap got into them.

I never told Colin exactly how the pain of his actions played out in the shower. Part of me didn't want to risk his apathy. A bigger part of me couldn't understand why such conversations were necessary. Colin had known about the sexual trauma of my past, beginning at age five, clear up to my experience of date rape in college. Yet, that knowledge did not lead to him extending compassion, grace, and human decency. Therefore, providing love and safety as my husband was not a priority in his entitled mind.

I am positive that if someone brought up the matter to him now, Colin would feign ignorance, or indignation that I would write such a thing. In other words, after repeatedly assaulting me, he would play the victim.

* * *

The next day Colin's nonchalant attitude about raping me the night before triggered a memory of something that happened during the summer we first met.

Colin and I were at a festival held on campus. I noticed that some girl appeared to be following us. She had a unique look—white, 5'4" or so, close to 200 pounds with short light-brown hair. She wore a yellow plaid, men's Izod button-down, short-sleeved shirt, and denim Bermuda shorts. There was no confusing her with anyone else.

I finally said to Colin, "Don't look now, but I believe that girl, over your left shoulder, about 8:00 o'clock, is following us."

Colin looks anyway. He laughed and admitted he knew her. "She's some girl I met at a party. After fucking her on the bathroom floor, I left her there. She's been pissed ever since."

I thought he was joking. A very disturbing joke, to be sure. I punched him in the arm and told him how *not funny* that was!

"I'm not joking! We were drunk!" Colin looked disgusted by the fact that this girl was following us.

I asked her name.

Colin said he didn't remember.

The story was so bizarre. I couldn't figure out why someone would say such a thing, *and* so matter-of-factly, especially if it was true. I decided that Colin was lying, and I told him I was not impressed.

I saw this same girl in one of my health classes the following quarter. You know that creepy feeling you get when it feels like someone is watching you? Sure enough, I looked up and caught her looking at me. Two, three, four times. When class was over, although she was in the first row of seats closest to the door, she didn't leave. We walked out at the same time. This same girl looked like she wanted to say something. I wanted to ask her about Colin.

In the end, we both chickened out! We avoided each other for the rest of the semester, with the one exception of being assigned the same medical dummy during a CPR exam. Even then, we didn't mention Colin.

Suddenly, after several college graduations, giving birth to two babies, and being married for so long, the memory of that girl came back as if it all happened yesterday. I wondered if Colin really was telling the truth about that mysterious girl. I wonder if that girl had been forced to have sex without consent. I remembered that Colin had excused his behavior back then with the excuse of being drunk.

I wondered if the girl had pleaded for Colin to stop, and if so, had her pleas been ignored. I wanted to know her side of the story.

I felt like I already did.

* * *

It's a strange feeling to have to protect yourself from someone you love. The fact that I *failed* to protect myself was absolutely debilitating. Sometimes, the realization that I was sleeping with the enemy swept over my body quickly, reminding me to stay alert. Other times, it was a heavy, noticeable emotional weight that was ever present. Before I healed, I often went through life feeling as if I'd taken too much Benadryl—there, but not there.

After the incident shared above, my mind ruminated about the first time that Colin insisted on having sex with me without my consent. The time above was not the first time, nor the second. The first time was shortly before our youngest son was born. The next morning, I called Colin out for his behavior. I explained, "By insisting that I have sex on demand last night, you treated me as if I am a call girl." Colin had zero reaction. I went on to add, "Since I'm no cheap escort, you owe me a thousand dollars for last night's services."

Looking hurt and confused, but still with no apology, no request for clarification, Colin got his wallet. It held only three hundred dollars. With his hands shaking, he sat the money on my bedside table. He quickly exited our bedroom.

I wanted to scream. I refused to cry. I didn't understand why Colin had treated me that way. I didn't understand why *he* didn't understand the reasons I was so hurt, so angry. I didn't want to be with a man who needed me to explain such things.

The only thing that kept me from leaving Colin that day was knowing that, as a Jehovah's Witness, I did not have scriptural grounds for a divorce. Leaving Colin would mean being disfellowshipped and shunned by the entire organization, including my congregation and all baptized family members. Shunning meant being alone. And at the time, being alone felt terrifying.

Instead of leaving, I prayed for "long-suffering" as I had been indoctrinated to do.

More than long-suffering, I prayed for the return of the Colin that I had married. I replayed past events in my mind, looking for clues on how I could bring *that* Colin back. The constant brain-chatter made it hard to think through everyday tasks.

So, I didn't.

I numbly went through the motions, as if on autopilot. All of my energy was reserved for and spent on making Colin feel seen, loved and heard.

I did this in hopes of setting an example of how I wanted to be loved in return.

Colin's ego and sense of entitlement never left our bedroom. In one way or another *it* was there. In hindsight, I recognize all of its disguises.

It was what happened shortly after the birth of our second son that the connection between Colin and I in the bedroom changed forever.

The permanent damage came with a visit from the elders in our congregation.

The Elders' Visit

I rearranged the cheese and fruit plate for the fourth time and still it looked nothing like my mother's. I wished I had bought more grapes and strawberries. I removed the kiwis and then decided that their light green color brought more life to the ensemble. Finally, I put it all on a smaller serving plate. Voila! That was the key. The final touch was a sprinkle of powdered sugar on top of the coffee cake.

This was to be our first shepherding call from the elders in years. Elders in Jehovah's Witnesses are the equivalent to pastors in other religions.

Colin had given me four days advance notice about the scheduled visit, and I'd been fine about it until that day. Elders' visits were not new to me. When I was a kid, I accompanied my father on calls. He had been a favorite elder in our congregation back then. He took me along to babysit any kids that might be a disruption. Or so I was told. I wasn't aware until I was an adult that elder visits were done in pairs.

I could not pinpoint the cause of my anxiety. I wasn't necessarily worried about the purpose of the visit. I figured it was due to our lack of regular attendance and participation in field service since becoming parents.

Colin appeared more nervous than I was. He was socially awkward in these kinds of situations. He was extra nervous when it came to Brother JR. I didn't blame him. It was pretty clear that Brother JR was not a big fan of Colin's. He found my husband lacking in spiritual leadership and initiative. Although he wouldn't voice this directly, Brother JR's disappointment in Colin eked out in his sighs, and the tone in which he said, "Well, perhaps ..."

I, on the other hand, really liked Brother JR. I liked his calming energy and authenticity. I bought his favorite tea for the visit. I had spent enough time with him and his wife to know just how he liked it. In fact, we liked our tea made the same way. Steeped for about two minutes, because the recommended five tended to taste bitter, and with a small spoonful of sugar. I had been excited to see Brother JR and to hear how his wife was doing. When I started to feel nervous, I told myself that there's no need to feel that way, and that Brother JR was just coming to encourage us to get back to the Kingdom Hall and the book study. I knew that he would likely volunteer his wife to help with whatever I needed.

I put the boys to bed a little earlier than usual in hopes of calming our nerves before they got there.

As the time got closer to 7:30 p.m., the worse Colin appeared to be. I assured him there was nothing to worry about. Such visits were routine. I told Colin they would likely encourage us to get to all the meetings and to study our Watchtowers even when we couldn't make it. I told him that Brother JR would probably tell me to reach out to the older sisters in the congregation for help with the boys, and to help me to juggle household chores and field service time. I did my best to reassure Colin by saying, "Everything will be fine. Don't worry. Your words will come. If not, I'll be there with you."

At 7:20, I put on the tea kettle because Brother JR was never late.

Ten minutes later, the elders and I were sitting in our living room as I served coffee and tea. I had my Bible. They had theirs. Brother JR asked about the boys and my job. He was also a teacher.

We were waiting for Colin, who claimed to be checking on our boys. Since they should've already been sleeping, I knew that Colin was just buying time. I felt bad for him. I was proud of him when he finally came downstairs to join us.

Brother JR started with a prayer. During the prayer, I felt myself take a deep breath and exhale. I realized I had been essentially holding my breath for the last four months or so. I took another deep breath and exhaled. And another. I was feeling so much better. This was what I needed. When I heard myself say, "Amen," I was smiling, and filled with renewed energy.

Then I heard Brother JR say, "Monica, Colin asked us to stop by to speak with you regarding your wifely due."

Wait. What?

I was stunned, but I heard Brother JR continue: "I want to share a scripture with you. It's 1 Corinthians 7:3. It reads: "Let the husband render to his wife her due, but let the wife do likewise to her husband." I didn't need to actually hear Brother JR read the scripture. I could already recite it in my head. I'd heard it read often enough in the Kingdom Hall, read from New World Translations of the Holy Scriptures, Jehovah's Witnesses' version of the Bible. I knew what it said.

I couldn't believe what was happening.

Breathe! Breathe! I coached myself. *In. Out!*

But I was holding my breath. Literally. No matter how hard I tried, I couldn't seem to exhale.

Inside, I was screaming: *He knew!* Colin knew the whole time what this meeting was about.

How dare he?

I looked over at Colin for some evidence that this was all a mistake, a misunderstanding on the part of the elders. Colin said nothing. He just stared at the floor. I wanted to ask him for an explanation, but I feared the words, "You fucking coward!" would be the only thing to escape my lips.

I didn't want to look like the wrathful wife in front of the elders.

Brother JR continued, "Monica, as a Christian wife you must know how serious this is. By not rendering Colin your wifely due, you are leaving him vulnerable to committing adultery. You will be held accountable in Jehovah's eyes."

I wanted to respond, but I couldn't. Proverbs 21:9 began running through my head: "Better to live on a rooftop than in a house with a contentious wife."

Brother JR noticed my distress. He looked over at Colin who was still looking at the floor.

My vision was warped by what looked like Fourth of July sparklers—an aura that indicated an oncoming migraine.

I could taste the cinnamon of my coffee cake coming back up.

"Colin, do you have something to say here?" Brother JR asked.

I heard myself say, "Yes! Tell him about what happened again about six months ago. Tell Brother JR why I'm not giving my wifely due." Though tears filled my eyes, and my voice cracked, Colin could hear the venom in my words.

Our eyes met briefly but Colin said nothing to either of us. He simply swallowed hard and returned his gaze to the floor.

I wanted to sink my nails into his throat and pull out his voice box. Clearly, it was of no use to him.

Instead, all I could do was close my hands into tight fists, as tears exploded from my eyes. I began crying, a full-on ugly cry with running mascara and snot. My cheeks were burning hot under my fingers. I wiped at my tears, but they kept coming.

It all came pouring out of me with the realization that I was married to a backstabbing coward. I was afraid, humiliated, angry, and under attack. Yet, the one person I thought of as my safe place, as *my person*, was the cause of all of it.

Colin didn't respond to my tears. I wasn't surprised, but it still hurt all the same.

I had something to say, but the words didn't come. Instead, I crossed my arms over the front of my body, placing my hands deep into my arm pits. I squeezed and folded in on myself. Somehow this calmed me just enough to speak.

I told Brother JR, "I'm done here. Colin hasn't told you the full story. The next time you visit, it will be because I have committed suicide or homicide."

Brother JR held my gaze. He asked if he could say another prayer.

I got up and walked out of my living room, leaving Colin alone with the praying elders.

I thought to myself, *Fuck him!* I didn't say it out loud, but I knew that the elders knew how I felt.

I didn't bother to wash my face, brush my teeth, or even change into my PJs. I simply hurled myself onto my side of the bed, the bed I shared with the enemy, and curled into a ball. Then I wailed—a wail that came from somewhere deep, deep inside me.

I kept thinking of how Colin let me spend the day reassuring him about the visit, making sure he felt comfortable and taken care of. And yet, he knew. *He knew the whole time!*

Colin knew that the elders' visit was no routine shepherding call. He had reported me to the elders. He had painted himself as the victim of a wife who did not live in subjection, a wife who did not satisfy her husband's needs, and who therefore needed to be reproved by the elders.

I felt lost, stupid, and afraid.

How can I ever be safe when the one person—my person—who claimed to love me more than anyone else in the world, had forever betrayed me. How could I be safe when he believed he had every right to hurt me?

At that moment, I wanted to die. The only thing that stopped me was my boys. I loved them too much to leave them alone with such a monster!

That night, I fell asleep praying that Colin had the good sense to sleep on the couch.

* * *

Colin's behavior with the elders' visit was a clear case of using manipulation and control tactics to serve his sense of entitlement. Because I had started making myself unavailable to Colin sexually, he grew rageful. But, because covert narcissists are timid and fearful in comparison to the gregarious and bold overt narcissists, Colin's rage came out in passive-aggressive ways. Colin calling in the elders to admonish me regarding my wifely duties was triangulation, a form of psychological and emotional manipulation to get what he felt he was entitled to, namely my body.

It's ironic that Colin never displayed his rage toward me physically. Had he done so, we would have gone toe to toe. Other forms of abuse, such as marital rape, didn't register as abuse. Had Colin hit me, the form of abuse that I recognized, I would have left immediately (likely after hitting him with a bat).

I grew up seeing my father physically beat my mother. Maybe it's not ironic, but more so the nature of the beast. Narcissists seem to know just what buttons to push to control their targets. Colin knew about every incident of my childhood sexual trauma. He used that to his advantage. All that mattered was what he wanted, no matter the costs.

***

My body knew better than I did about Colin's toxicity. Over the years during our time together, I developed adverse reactions to Colin's sperm. Some days I'd have itching and swelling. Other times, an infection seemed to spring up overnight. Repeatedly, I was treated for vaginosis and yeast infections. I stopped taking bubble baths and started wearing all cotton underwear (no lace, not pretty). I started eating yogurt daily. Nothing seemed to help. Sex with Colin meant a vaginal infection, period.

Initially, I had attributed my recurring yeast infections to complications with my first pregnancy. Apparently, there was a tear in my amniotic membrane which allowed bacteria to enter my uterus. After the delivery, I had an infection and a temperature that required broad-spectrum antibiotics. Clearing up the bacterial infection led to a systemic yeast infection requiring a 30-day round of Diflucan to clear it up. That helped temporarily. Over the years, I also had regular STD tests at the insistence of my primary care physician, as part of my annual physical. Truth be told, although I never had an STD, I did have some anxiety anticipating the test results.

It was at the twenty-year mark, or so, when my doctor suggested that my yeast infections may be psychosomatic. She asked me how I felt about my sex life. I said nothing. I didn't have words to explain what my body was telling me. I came close to saying, "My sex life is great!" but I would have been lying to myself and my doctor. She recommended that I explore the question with a mental health therapist and wrote up a referral. I was too embarrassed to respond. I knew that if I spoke, bottled emotions and tears from deep down would spill out. All I could do was take the written referral, fold it, and put it in my coat pocket.

Now that Colin is no longer part of my life, neither are vaginal infections. This has also been the case following the few rounds of antibiotics I've had since my divorce. Antibiotics are notorious for causing yeast infections. This all leads me to believe that perhaps there was a psychosomatic connection. I am now more attuned to my body cues.

EXERCISES

The narcissists in our lives feel entitled to far more than is granted or appropriate. It's up to us to set and enforce boundaries. We cannot afford to project our values on toxic people and assume that they will treat us with the respect that we show them.

Setting boundaries with a narcissist is quite difficult because they often flat-out ignore them, and they tend to retaliate when you try to hold them accountable by enforcing a consequence. So perhaps, setting boundaries with mentally healthy people is a good place to start practicing.

Exercise 1: The Good, Bad, and Ugly

Use the following questions to take a personal inventory of your relationships:

- How do you treat people?
- Are you a doormat?
- How would friends, family, or workmates describe you?
- What about their possible descriptions fit?
- Are you the person who would "do anything, for anyone"?
- What about your way of being are responses to other people's behaviors?

Exercise 2: We Need To Talk

Think about one of your less-than-fabulous relationships. The person who makes you groan when you see their name pop up on your phone would be perfect. What about that person's way of being frustrates you? Get more specific about what troubles you about that particular relationship. In what ways would you like that relationship to change? Be specific.

Now construct a boundary around the issues you've identified. Here is a template to use:

- (Insert name) I feel (insert emotion) when you (insert specific action). What will it take for you to stop doing that and instead do (insert preference)?
- Example: Tricia, I feel unappreciated and taken advantage of when you borrow my car and don't replace the gas. Your cost of gas doesn't fit in my budget, not to mention that I don't have the time on the way to work to stop for gas. What will it take for you to stop borrowing my car, or to replace the gas when you do?

I find this template useful because you can use a little humor with a lilt in your voice when you ask, "What will it take for you to XYZ?" Also, if the offending person responds with an insult or invalidating comment, you have more information regarding the value put on the relationship.

Or try something like:

- (Insert name) our relationship is important to me. I get bummed out when I think that I may have to stop speaking to you. So that I don't have to fantasize about poisoning your coffee, will you please stop doing XYZ. It would mean a lot to me and preserve our relationship."

Exercise 3: Be Clear and Specific. Set Consequences

Dealing with a narcissist's sense of entitlement is challenging. It's important to set boundaries. Clearly express your feelings and needs in a specific and straightforward manner. Avoid being vague or overly accommodating. State the behavior that is causing an issue and explain how it affects you. Let the narcissist know the behavior that you prefer. Afterward, state the consequences that you intend to enforce should the narcissist cross the boundary. It's crucial that you are committed to following through with what you state as a consequence. Frame your concerns using "I" statements to avoid sounding accusatory. This helps to focus on your feelings and experiences rather than placing blame.

For example: "I feel taken for granted when you commit my time to be with your mother. I would like to be involved in the decision-making process. If I'm not included in the discussion, do not expect me to change my plans to accommodate you and your mother."

CHAPTER 10

LACK OF EMPATHY

Looking back, it's incredible how blind I was to all the signs pointing to Colin's lack of empathy. From the very beginning of our relationship, the signs were there. By projecting my values and ways of being onto Colin, I saw him through a filter that allowed me to tell myself, "He loves me, so he would never hurt me intentionally." As it turns out, humans have this amazing ability to see things not as they really are, but how we think they should be. Given that I was raised by a covert narcissist and had experienced significant childhood trauma, the lens through which I saw the world had some major blind spots.

I tried to rationalize and excuse all the red flags that popped up along the way. For years, I dismissed Colin's behavior with, "Oh, that's just how men are," or "Colin doesn't mean it, he's just stressed."

It was hard to fathom that what I meant when I said "I love you" was far different than what a covert narcissist means when speaking the exact same words. When I told Colin that I loved him, it was a reminder that I was the person he could count on, the person who would support him in building his dreams and getting over or around any obstacles. I meant that as long as I had food and shelter, so did he. I meant that he was the person that I chose to experience life with and to love unconditionally. When I say, "I love you," I mean for who you are—not for how you elevate my self-esteem.

From personal experience, I can tell you that a narcissist's love is self-serving, shallow, and conditional. When narcissists proclaim their love for you, what they actually mean is, "I love how I feel about myself when you are around," or "I love how others see me when I'm with you and what you can do for me."

The narcissist's love has little or nothing to do with you personally. Fortunately, neither does their disdain. The narcissist's reason for doing anything, including pretending to love you, is to get narcissistic supply—in other words, to validate their very existence. Narcissists may profess their love as a way to manipulate you, and to get you to pour more love into them. Ironically, these are also the reasons narcissists may withdraw their love from you. The manipulations could be to control your behavior and shift your thinking. Attention, adoration, and affection play their part throughout the relationship. However, the end goal is the same—to validate the narcissist's existence.

Over the years, I kept recommitting to my marriage. It happened each time Colin seemed to articulate back to me my feelings and frustrations about his behavior, along with promises to change. In those moments, I felt heard. I felt seen. Not only that, but Colin also had strategies to change, and at times I thought he had changed for the betterment of our marriage. Over the years, I noticed that the strategies Colin had were ones I suggested, the ones non-disordered responsible grown-ups use on a daily basis. I also noticed that with the everyday shenanigans of life with a narcissist, we fell back into familiar patterns because I was too busy taking care of our boys, or "putting out fires," to protest. Ultimately, Colin's behavior never truly changed.

When I am honest with myself, I can admit that Colin remained the same arrogant, condescending, entitled, cowardly, and untrustworthy person he had always been. It was me who had been changing. I stopped requiring Colin to step up and be the man he claimed to be. I stopped counting on Colin to keep his word, or to demonstrate integrity or accountability. I stopped counting on Colin for much of anything. Worse, I settled for the mediocre love he showed me, thus forfeiting the powerful, authentic love that I gave and deserved in return!

I did learn the lesson. Love should never be about manipulation, control, or requiring someone else to validate your existence. Love is meant to be about genuine affection, respect, mutual well-being, and support for one another.

* * *

The first time that my antenna went *way* up about Colin was when his father died. My initial concern was regarding his profound lack of emotion, rather than a lack of empathy. However, I was keenly aware of what I saw as a lack of emotional response, curiosity, concern, or compassion. I attributed this to the theory I'd been taught growing up, *that real men don't cry.*

My father was the same. I assumed that such men displayed their grief in other ways.

When Colin's father died, I was the one who answered the deputy sheriff's call. Colin's father was living in Port St. Lucie at the time. It was a Saturday, and I was studying for my statistics class at the dining room table. Colin was at work. The deputy had asked for Colin by name. When I explained he was not available, she introduced herself and asked if I knew Colin's father. I have to admit that when I heard his name, his previous transgressions came to mind. I feared he had been arrested and needed someone to post bail.

But it wasn't a call for bail. Colin's father had not shown up for work for three days, so the sheriff's office had been called to do a welfare check. That's when they found him on his living room floor. They surmised that he had a heart attack, which had led to a fall and a head injury. He died the previous Wednesday.

I didn't question it. I was filled with pain for Colin. The deputy must have been cued into my anxiety because she asked me to repeat the information back to her, including the assignment given to me, which was to notify the rest of the family members. I understood my assignment and started making calls.

Informing Colin's sister and her husband didn't go as smoothly as I had hoped. I worried that Colin would have the same reaction regarding his father. I decided to not tell him until he got home. My rationale was that a few hours won't change the outcome. Then, I changed my mind. I picked up the phone and then hung up. After the third time, I decided to wait again.

I kept putting myself in Colin's shoes. How would I react learning that my father was dead at the age of fifty-five—my father, who had met his new grandson just a few months ago, and would never see him again? I wondered how I'd feel to know that Colin knew hours before me and hadn't told me. I worried that his sister would call him before I did. Then, how would I explain not calling? Round and round, I went.

I finally decided that if I were Colin, I'd want to know. I made the call and reiterated what the deputy told me.

"Wow … okay!" was the response I remember. Then he said, "I have a few more patients. I'll be home later."

I was taken aback by the lack of emotion in Colin's response but chalked it up to Colin being in a bit of shock. Everyone responds to grief differently. I prepared to be there for Colin whenever he was ready to process the news. For months immediately following his father's death, the most emotion Colin displayed about his father's death was the anger he felt toward Bonnie, his step-mother, for being the beneficiary of his dad's life insurance, despite being divorced for several years by that point. In fact, his father had changed the beneficiary to his current wife and his grandkids. He had addressed, stamped, and sealed the envelope to the insurance company, but he had never actually mailed it. Colin's second expression of emotion was annoyance at his sister's singing when he and his siblings got together to spread their father's ashes.

Six months after his father's death, I asked Colin how he was handling it all. I let him know that I was a bit worried that he never cried or showed any sadness about his father's unexpected death. I knew he had a great deal of unspoken resentment toward his father. Part of it was because his father wore a toupee. Colin rolled his eyes and laughed about how ridiculous his father looked and promised me that he'd never wear one. I simply giggled along with him and thanked Colin for his promise.

On a more serious note, Colin's father had been involved in a teacher and student sex scandal. The crime was in the local papers and on the news. Colin was furious and embarrassed. His mother sent him copies of the articles which fueled Colin's reactions. His father had also married a mail-order bride that was younger than we were. Most of all, Colin resented having to make nice and pretend that none of these matters tore at his insides.

The relationship between Colin and his father caused almost as much tension in our marriage as the relationship with his mother did. Colin felt obligated to visit his father in Florida several times a year. As part of his conviction, Colin's father lost his teaching license and had to leave the state. I'm not sure why he chose Florida to start over.

I was baffled by Colin's stoic reaction to it all. In the end, the answer to my question was a shoulder shrug. I firmly believe that the only genuine emotions Colin is capable of expressing are irritation and rage. At least, that's what he has shown me. I'm curious if it's the truth for all covert narcissists.

I've read numerous times that narcissists experience schadenfreude. My Google research on the term led me to understand schadenfreude as: *the finding of pleasure, joy, or self-satisfaction that comes from learning of or witnessing the troubles, failures, or humiliation of another.* I can see that in Colin too.

***

It was the night that our marriage imploded, and over the two years following, that I experienced the full scale of Colin's apathy. Three weeks before that night, Colin started presenting himself as empathetic, full of compassion, and remorseful for what he had put me through since the day we met in college.

"I don't deserve you," he would say. "I don't blame you for wanting to leave."

I hadn't said that I wanted to leave. And by then, I knew this was a manipulation, a cue for me to *ooh* and *aah* over him, and to reassure him of my love.

True, I had asked Colin to leave the year before. However, the closest I had come to saying that I was done with our marriage after being hoovered back was telling Colin that I would not wait for him while he dated other women. Colin had proposed the idea of dating others during a therapy session. He wanted to be allowed to explore single life for six months, to get it out of his system, and then afterward, he would be able to make the required changes for the sake of our marriage.

Before I could speak up, the therapist said, "You can't have your cake and eat it too! It's clear to me that you want Monica as your home base, while you go out and play. Do you understand that you are asking for permission to have an affair and that Monica is saying *no?*"

This conversation resumed in my bedroom a few days later. Colin claimed he was torn between his life with me and the boys, and the adrenaline rush of being pursued by other women.

Colin had gritted his teeth and clenched his fists. "It's just so hard to choose!" He looked and sounded like a toddler not getting what he wanted.

At first, I laughed, assuming he was joking, being self-deprecating. I was wrong. Colin was serious.

I said, "Let me make this easy for you. If you walk out that door, do not ever come back. Your lack of clarity on the matter is quite informative, in my opinion."

Colin backpedaled. "I'm not saying that I don't love you. I am saying that I just can't shake the adrenaline rush that the idea of being pursued by other women brings. I mean, it keeps coming up."

In this situation, Colin's inability to see cause and effect, or natural consequences of certain actions, was quite familiar. One of the therapists along the way had said that it was due to Colin's immaturity.

Explaining the impact of his words or actions had become an automatic response on my part.

This was true for Colin's work life as well, not just in our marriage. It became my duty to explain human nature to Colin when he couldn't understand why his staff responded to his comments the way they did. Over the years, my role became emotionally and mentally exhausting.

Needing to explain why I wasn't interested in sticking around while Colin sowed his wild oats was beyond me. I had no more to give. Inside I screamed, "This isn't a multiple-choice quiz motherfucker!" By now, I was tapping into my anger—freely. I kept the words inside as I let the energy course through, then out of my body. I didn't want to give Colin any fodder for making me out to be the unstable one in the marriage.

Colin's constant and exhausting need for reassurance was what I was thinking about when he began to speak the night of the implosion. "You are such a good person, Monica. I am sure that you will find someone in six months or less."

Again, I hadn't indicated I was looking for anyone new. At the time, I was simply insulted by Colin putting words in my mouth as my father used to do to my mother. I also felt disdain for the victim tone in Colin's voice. At the time, I didn't realize that playing the victim was a form of gaslighting for the covert narcissists.

But I was keenly aware that this was all landing in my body in a different way than it had before. I believed that my awareness was due to the new grounding practices that I had learned from Iyanla Vanzant at her Wonder Woman Weekend a few weeks before.

Colin continued his nonsense. "You have done so much personal growth work. I'll never catch up with you."

I remained quiet.

"I want to be an equal partner for you, but I'm afraid that I will never be."

I remained quiet.

"You deserve to have someone who can love you better than me."

I felt pity for Colin. For him to believe that I would want to start something new within six months of our thirty-year relationship ending meant that he simply didn't get it. Or me. I felt sad for the woman he would be with next.

"You deserve someone better than me," Colin said again.

"Don't I have a right to make that decision?" I asked him. I was about to go on when a realization occurred to me. *Wait! This boy already has someone.*

My entire body sighed, confirming that this information was *known*. Yet here he was pretending to be granting me my freedom, pretending to be looking out for my well-being.

Anger sparked in my chest, hot and searing. There was also something new and powerful flowing through me. The more I focused on the growing warmth in my chest, the lighter I felt. I didn't know it at that moment, but that was a new way for my body to process my anger.

Then I reminded myself: no more swallowing it. No more twisting myself to feed his ego. Colin would need to say the words. *This cowardly, cheating motherfucker gets to say the words out loud!*

Part of me wondered if someone had given Colin an ultimatum—her or me.

I felt the heat of my anger ebb and flow in proportion to Colin's blabbering and my breathing in the possibility of freedom.

The two of us sat quietly across from one another, me on the sofa, him, on the ottoman, our left knees touching. We sat silently for an hour and a half. Colin took my hand into his and played with my fingers as he often did, but still refused to utter the words.

I waited.

And waited.

I knew this shtick. Colin wanted me to be the bad guy. Colin wanted me to end the marriage so that he could say I was the one who wanted out. He could then convince others, including himself, that he was the dutiful husband and father who had tried his best and who understood why his wife left, and that he honored her decision to leave.

I refused to let Colin off the hook. He needed to sit in his mess.

Eventually, he said the words, "I want our marriage to end."

They cut through me, but not in the way I expected. It was what I imagine a trapped animal feels once freed from a cage. A heavy weight was lifted from my body. No, not just my body, but my spirit. I felt expansive as if I filled the whole room ... floating above it all.

I was free of giving unappreciated and unreciprocated attention, love, and loyalty. I was free of the religious obligation of a dutiful wife. I was free of the promise to love Colin, despite his fuckups. I was free from recommitting to our marriage every time Colin asked me to give him another chance and begged me not to leave.

I was free!

After Colin said the words, he seemed just as surprised by my reaction as I was. There was a calm emanating from me, a newly found peace. He tried to get me to co-sign for his decision when he said, "I'll try not to be jealous when I see you with some handsome hunk in six months or so."

My response was, "That won't happen. I won't be looking for anyone. I won't be available!"

There were several minutes of silence. Then Colin said, "I'm going to miss what we have!"

"That hardly feels true," I said flatly. As I said, I wanted Colin to sit in his mess. I was done feeding his ego.

My responses put Colin's decision squarely in his lap. He would have felt better had I pretended to be grateful for his decision to set me free, and that I would indeed be with someone better (which no narcissist would truly believe).

I knew Colin well enough to know two things: 1) Colin needed me to be overjoyed with his decision, and 2) he had someone else waiting.

"You deserve someone better than me...so, I'm going to get out of the way," Colin kept saying.

Agreeing with this would free Colin of any guilt. I refused to sacrifice reality for Colin's benefit that night. There needed to be no doubt about who had ended our marriage.

In truth, Colin had been slowly killing our marriage from the beginning, starting with the wedge he drove between his mother and me. The night of the implosion, I wanted him to be accountable—finally.

I didn't want to give Colin an opening to blame me for the ending of our marriage. Within twenty minutes of my not feeding his ego to make him feel better about himself, the way I had for the past thirty years, Colin's inner rage surfaced. I felt it. Then, I looked up and our eyes met.

"Gawd Monica! You're unbelievable." The fingers of Colin's right hand were clenched. "I thought you were a smart woman. How much are you going to put up with?" Colin's voice was filled with contempt and resentment. He went on, spewing venom. "I've been lying to you for years, and you kept staying. I shit on your head, and you keep forgiving me. What do I have to do?"

I am not sure exactly what else he said, but the energy was dark and vile.

Colin's words landed like high-voltage electrical zaps into my body. I didn't know if I was dying or waking up.

From somewhere inside me, a voice whispered, *Don't say anything, just listen*. My heartbeat slowed down a bit. *Just listen*. I heard it again. I said nothing out loud. I simply held Colin's gaze and listened. I heard and felt everything.

He went on! This part I am certain of. Colin said, "Besides, we won't work out. Just look at you! I can't even get it up with you anymore." He looked me up and down, passing cruel judgment on my body. "You asked me before if the weight you gained with the kids bothered me. I said no, but I *lied!*" Then he added, "You know it's true. I haven't been able to get a decent boner for years."

The knowing inside me whispered again, *Just listen*. I took a deep breath in and held it. I bit the inside of my bottom lip to keep the thoughts running through my mind from spilling out of my mouth.

I wanted to yell: "What the fuck are you talking about, you cheating motherfucker! That's not what the doctor said six months ago. Don't you remember asking me if I'd be willing to give you shots in your penis to help increase the blood flow because you are afraid of needles and too chicken to do it yourself?" I wanted to defend myself and my body. But I didn't say a word.

As Colin went on, I thought about the first time Colin experienced erectile dysfunction. We were just a few years into our marriage, and he seemed to be suffering from seasonal affective disorder. He had been prescribed Paxil, and I remember him feeling embarrassed about the side effects the drug had on him. That is until he got angry, and the problem somehow became my fault. Back then, the story was that we were not having sex because I seemed to never be in the mood, or I was too busy. Whatever the excuse, I was to blame.

The thing I remember most about that time is that when I would initiate sex, Colin would say, "Down Girl! Not now." It took less than a handful of times for that to happen before I stopped initiating. Part of me believed that I was, in fact, the problem. On the other hand, I remembered the potential side effects of Paxil because Colin had read them to me. Low libido and erectile dysfunction were on the list. His flushed face and teary eyes had said it all. It was my fault then too, or at least I was the one being punished.

Remembering all these events from our past did nothing to lessen the sting of Colin's words as our marriage imploded. I folded my arms over my belly and tried to make myself smaller. The more I shrunk myself, the larger the stretched, scarred, and hanging flesh just below my belly button felt. It was the same tire of loose skin that I'd spent years trying to be okay with, the same part of my body that I thanked and praised in the mirror for carrying my babies to term. (The boys had tried to get out early, but my uterus and cervix hung onto my babies and stayed closed long enough for my boys to be born healthy.)

Colin knew that I'd wanted to have a tummy tuck. However,

whenever I brought up the idea, Colin would say, "You don't need that. I love your body just the way it is."

I believed him. I had credited him for being virtuous. I now believe that Colin protested my tummy tuck either to make me less desirable to other men or to punish me, or simply because he didn't want me to spend the money. In the end, Colin used my extra weight, my loose, stretch-marked skin, as a justification for his cheating and blowing up the marriage.

* * *

Colin called a few days later to "apologize" for blaming me for his erectile dysfunction. Although he never said the words "I'm sorry" or "I apologize," he did muster enough accountability to admit that he should have never blamed me. I have no reason to believe that Colin came to the realization that his words were hurtful. Nor do I have reason to believe that he hadn't meant to hurt me. It's far more likely that Colin mentioned his bluntness toward me to one of his karaoke friends and they did not praise his bravado. It's just as likely that Colin feared what others (friends and strangers alike) would say about him if I shared the details of our conversation.

Avoiding a wound to his Nice Guy facade is what motivated Colin to voice anything close to an acknowledgment of his behavior. He needed me to continue believing in the false persona he had created. My mental and emotional well-being were not a factor.

Colin asked if he could take me out for Mother's Day later in the week. I declined. His acknowledgment and the invitation were self-serving. Colin spoke of us remaining friends. He believed we could do it because of how we felt about each other. I noticed he didn't dare say the words *I love you*. I didn't give into Colin's silent pleas for approval. I just couldn't. I knew in my heart that Colin would punish me for not allowing him to readjust his mask. I would be punished for not playing my part in Colin's delusion. The punishment did come.

LACK OF EMPATHY

* * *

It was the end of May, just three weeks after our marriage imploded and just before summer break, when I got more information about what my body was telling me. Colin called me at work. When I saw his number, I assumed that he was calling to confirm a time to help me pack up my classroom. This had become our custom at the end of each school year. Things needed to be put away, or in boxes, so that the custodial team could deep clean the room, strip it, and re-wax the floors. Though our marriage was ending, Colin said he still really wanted to help me. At the time, I knew that he was simply trying to make up for the shitty things he'd said during the implosion. For that reason, I declined his help. I said I'd manage without him. When I saw his number, I planned to say no again. However, in my heart, I had given him credit for calling to confirm. That is until I realized why he had actually called. Colin wasn't calling to sync our schedules to work in my classroom. He was calling to do a different favor for me.

"I'm calling to tell you something that I think is best coming from me, instead of someone else."

"Oh, okay!' I said, cautiously.

"I want you to know that I am in a serious relationship with someone, and we may be—"

"What?" I interrupted. "It's only been three weeks since ... How is this possible?" I asked this already knowing the answer. "What happened to, *'I'm radioactive and I need to be by myself for a while and do some personal growth work?'* That's what you said." My tone was surprisingly flat. I sounded as if I was gathering time and location details from one of our boys about plans with friends.

Colin is the one who interrupted this time. He sighed a familiar sigh to indicate I was being overly sensitive, or too much, or too little, in some way. I didn't respond to the sigh. That's what he wanted. I noticed that my arms and torso started to feel hot. Colin sighed again. This time louder.

I didn't respond. I knew that he wanted me to lose my shit.

"I never said that I was going to be celibate. I have done some work. And I'll keep doing it … with her," he said. His tone was dismissive.

"Why would you call me at work to tell me this?"

"Like I said, I wanted you to hear it from me, and I didn't want to send a text."

A warm feeling of peace washed over me—a knowing, a lightness—just like the night of the implosion, only deeper. This is who he is. Colin is a liar, a cheat, and a coward. He already knew this woman. He had likely made promises to her as he was picking out new wedding bands for us. It was more likely that I was giving my opinion on the rings Colin had picked out for her. This realization flowed like a ripple through my chest. My entire back itched. My arms and torso felt as if they were on fire—along with the tops of my thighs.

My body was processing trapped emotions and the lies I had told myself. I didn't resist. Intuitively, I knew that what I was experiencing was for my good. I remember thinking Colin could have spared me this news, or at the very least called me *after* work. This was my punishment, and it was just getting started.

I heard Colin speaking but couldn't make out his words. I was caught by a subtle lilt in his voice. I pictured the glint that I was certain was in his eyes. The eyes matched the voice. I'd seen the pair many times before, sometimes with a pierced mouth trying to hold back a laugh. I used to scold myself for even thinking that Colin would be so cruel as to laugh at my pain. It had been impossible for me to accept that someone I loved, and who had claimed to love me, would deliberately hurt me. However, from that day forward, standing in the hall outside my classroom, after thirty years with Colin, I knew that I could no longer pretend not to know.

Nowadays, when that happens, I say to my body, *Burn baby, burn! Momma needs to see TRUTH.*

LACK OF EMPATHY

* * *

A few weeks later, as we were making arrangements to divide our belongings, Colin called saying, "I know how much you love your Sleep Number bed, so I wanted to see if you wanted it back."

"That's very thoughtful of you," I said. "I had been thinking about buying another one. But, if you aren't going to keep it, then maybe—"

Colin interrupted me. "Full disclosure," he said. "I want to be completely transparent with you as I promised. I did sleep with another woman on it ... well, several women. I just thought you should know before I brought it back to you ... in case that made a difference."

This time, I felt gut-punched. I wanted to trust that we could split amicably. However, it had been just a little over a month since our marriage imploded and Colin seemed to be going out of his way to hurt me, all while pretending to be the nice guy. I wondered if he'd been this way for the entire marriage and I was just too numb to notice. I tell Colin to trash the Sleep Number bed, and that I am not at all interested in having it back.

"Are you sure?" he asked, innocently, pretending he had no idea how cruel he was being.

"I'm a hundred percent sure," I said and hung up. I spent the rest of the day crying. It felt therapeutic and cleansing. I cried as I continued to put Colin's items in the garage. I cried with excitement that he would never step foot in the house again. I cried as I smudged the house to clear the negative energy and reclaim it as my own.

I was determined to be free of Colin.

I cried as I sorted laundry. I cried as I watched and sang along to the movie *Grease*—an old favorite that Colin used to cue up for me when I was saddled with painful menstrual cramps. I cried about that memory. I cried about the joy of being able to cry in peace. I cried because I could cry freely without having to reschedule my pain so that someone else would feel better.

***

As if the man I first fell in love with returned, Colin's first proposal for an amicable severing of our marriage was fair and leaned in my favor. I am not sure what prompted the shift. He had either gotten his needed dose of narcissistic supply, or he was acting out of shame and guilt. Colin proposed that he would pay off the house so that I could stay in it. He knew that I couldn't afford it on my teacher's salary. Colin also proposed that we'd transfer all of our investments into my name since I was the one that had started them—and because I hadn't been able to pay into my retirement throughout the years that I served as the family manager. This was all true and felt like a fair trade. I thanked Colin.

"You helped me to build the practice," he'd said. "I want you to have your share. It's only fair." Colin sounded sincere. I believed him.

I felt safe and that everything would work out. I thought that as long as I didn't have to worry about money, I'd be okay on my own. At different moments I allowed myself to believe that Colin and I could be friends. The possibility was palpable considering that we shared a lawyer at that point, and Colin texted me almost daily to check in. He appeared to be empathetic to the anguish I was feeling.

He didn't mention this new woman and I didn't ask. I understood this version of Colin. I wondered if that other woman Colin chose to love would understand his quirks. At times, I felt protective of Colin and anger toward this unknown woman! At this time, I still believed that Colin was dealing with a deep trauma, or that he had some sort of Asperger's. I was not connecting Colin's covert narcissism to the decades-old diagnosis, NPD.

Looking back, after doing my work to heal, I am astounded by how quickly I had slipped back into toxic hope. Even after Colin had shown me just what he was capable of only weeks before, I allowed myself to believe in the best of him, despite all of the evidence to the contrary.

I went through the process of dissolving my marriage to Colin, completely steeped in the familiar toxicity of Colin saying one thing and not completely following through, or while doing something entirely different. More specifically, Colin punished me while also claiming that we were going to have an amicable and fair dissolution of our marriage, repeatedly citing his sister's dissolution as an example. I didn't realize it then, but my coping mechanism for such cognitive dissonance was to numb out and distract myself with the boys or work. Not being emotionally or mentally present at times prevented me from seeing the extent of Colin's self-centeredness, emotional detachment, and complete inability to form genuine connection.

Matters got a lot worse with Colin before I let go of toxic hope and forced myself to accept the truth. Colin never loved me. Colin is incapable of love and connection the way non-character disordered people define it.

When you're in a relationship with a covert narcissist, it's absolutely imperative that you see them for who they truly are. Do not make the mistakes I made by falling into romanticizing and projecting your loving qualities onto the narcissist. Do not project your values and standards onto the narcissist by assuming that he will do the right thing. Your definition of the right thing is far different than the narcissist's definition. Be warned! In the narcissistic abuse cycle of idealizing (love bombing), devaluing, and discarding, you are becoming an addict, and understandably so. When your love is real, and you are looking for affection from and connection with a person who claims to love you, having those needs taken away through gaslighting, invalidation, and stonewalling hurts mentally, emotionally, and physically. Not having any power over the narcissist's behavior, you are left waiting, wondering, and longing, so when it comes you are ecstatic. Relieved. No questions are asked because you are grateful for the elixir. Without warning the love is withdrawn. We subconsciously adjust our behavior in hopes of earning a hit. In other words, we are subjects of good old-fashioned intermittent reinforcement, just like a lab rat. The programming is systematic and intentional to make us addicted to the cycle.

As we began dismantling our thirty-year relationship, I had come to accept that Colin no longer loved me. By the end, I was one step closer to accepting that he *never* loved me and closer to understanding that narcissists are incapable of love. What I had a problem with was the idea that Colin meant harm to me. I had proven my loyalty. I stayed faithful to the marriage. I forgave every time I was asked and ten times more often when no transgression was acknowledged. Yet, none of that mattered. Based on his behavior, Colin greatly resented me and regarded me with contempt. It was this inner turmoil that made the process so traumatizing.

* * *

A thousand years from now I would still maintain that Colin does not have his own core identity and that every aspect of his existence is a product of another person's image, impression, or opinion of him. It was before that summer got into full swing that Colin did a 180-degree turn regarding the splitting of our assets. I knew that somewhere along the way, Colin had spoken to someone that made him feel *less* than he believed himself to be. While we were together, whenever Colin felt *less-than*, I was to blame. Although someone else inflicted the wound to his ego, I was the one to be punished.

You will likely experience the same with the covert narcissist in your life. Remembering that the covert narcissist must be the victim and the good guy in any scenario, there can be no empathy for you, or anyone else. Someone else is 100% at fault. Narcissists in general need zero proof of their reasoning. Assumptions are made and arguments ensue.

Colin's lack of empathy showed the greatest during our divorce proceedings. An example is one of the circular conversations that we had as Colin justified an inequitable split of the assets.

Money For The Boys

"Could you just put all your cards on the table?" he asked. Despite my longstanding transparency about my finances, I agreed. However, Colin insisted on including the $50,000 in my savings as an asset.

"What $50,000?" I was genuinely puzzled. Colin accused me of playing dumb and claimed he saw it in my credit union statements. I clarified it was earmarked for the boys' tuition, not available for personal use.

"But it's in your savings account, so it goes in your column as an asset," Colin insisted, attempting to end the conversation.

Concerned about the impact on our promise to support the boys' education, I asked if he would handle their expenses. Colin avoided the question, leaving me anxious for my boys' well-being.

"They will need money this fall. I can't rely on this for both my expenses and the boys," I pleaded.

"It's going in your column. It's in your bank account," was Colin's only response.

Frustrated with Colin's semantic arguments, I realized it was a tactic to avoid responsibility and deflect blame. Despite my efforts to explain, he insisted on including the earmarked money in my assets.

"You can still use it for the boys, but it's going in your column as an asset. Besides, I can't trust you to give it to them," he sneered, baselessly accusing me.

The conversation circled with Colin unable to see reason, leaving me unsure how to make him understand my perspective—or to see logic. I now know that he had no desire to understand the issue.

Power

Playing his role as Mr. Nice Guy, Colin suggested filing taxes separately while his accountant handled mine in exchange for maintaining my job-provided health insurance. Months later, two days before tax day, Colin claimed that his accountant found doing my taxes a conflict of interest. Hearing my distress, Colin assured me that there was no need to worry because he had dropped off my taxes at H&R Block, and all I had to do was sign. During the appointment, Mr. B, the agent, hinted at his disdain for Colin. Something about the interaction with Colin led to Mr. B reviewing the tax forms that were dropped off. He discovered potential refunds that were available to me as head of household, which Colin was not entitled to claim. Colin had misrepresented the situation, leading to a $10K refund for me. When I questioned him and reminded Colin of his declaration to put all of our cards on the table and to have an amicable divorce, he reacted angrily. Colin wanted my refund to offset his increased tax payment. He insisted that it was absolutely unfair that I received a refund while he had to pay. Later Colin retaliated by withholding his share of insurance premiums and threatening legal action.

Looking back, I saw that Colin's actions stemmed from the same self-centered perspective and manipulation that was a recurring pattern in our relationship. The only difference was that the stakes were higher, and Colin became more vicious, determined to get his own way.

What Colin seemed to want more than anything was power and control. For so long, he had appeared aloof and indifferent to me and the boys. During the divorce, he was vindictive. When I reminded Colin of our original agreement of transferring all of our mutual fund investments into my name to replace my lost retirement funds, his response was, "I paid all the bills during that time. You didn't have to work. It's not fair."

Greed

When it came to getting alimony for thirty years of marriage, Colin threatened, "If you pursue this, I'll ask for alimony. You have a steady income; mine isn't. I can make it look like I earn less than you."

My heart raced; bile burned my throat. "Why, Colin?" I asked, my voice cracking. I clenched my teeth to stave off tears.

"Because you haven't paid any bills since you quit teaching twelve years ago and you haven't paid any bills for the last seven years since you started working again," Colin said, barely containing his rage.

"You know exactly where my salary has gone. Look around the house," I argued, noting his stonewalling. I listed major home improvements: "We got a new kitchen, a room addition, and a bathroom for the boys. Those alone consumed nearly three years of my salary. Then there was a $10,000 deck and a $6,000 whole house generator. Remember? More importantly, you agreed to the spending."

"I don't believe you. What proof do you have that you haven't stashed money?" Colin retorted.

I felt trapped, knowing this was an unwinnable conversation. "Colin, I ran down where my salary went. Add the $50,000 for the boys' tuition. I haven't stashed any money. Why would I?"

I suspected he was projecting his behavior onto me. Feeling powerless, I considered triggering his shame but hesitated, fearing further retaliation. Tearfully, I threw a Hail Mary, "I won't make it, Colin. STRS changed, and I'll have to work until 65, not 55 as we planned."

Silence from Colin. "Hello?" I said, feeling abandoned and as if I were suffocating. I didn't want him to know my fear. There was no compassion from this man who a short time before claimed to love me. A man that I still loved. It left me questioning everything.

Colin's cruelty escalated, revealing that our shared history and my loyalty meant nothing to him. Despite my enduring affection as the father of our boys, he showed no empathy during the divorce.

I believed in Colin from our early days when he was an undergrad. I supported him through grad school, shared my salary, and encouraged him to start another practice after his first one failed. Despite my contributions to his current private medical practice, from building his patient list to designing waiting rooms, he seemed to disregard my role. It didn't matter that I sacrificed my teaching career at his urging by repeatedly reminding me that he made enough money for both of us. Our history together simply didn't matter.

* * *

I slipped into a depression with the latest irrefutable truth that I was married to a monster. I had to laugh at myself remembering that this is exactly what I wanted when I stopped praying for long suffering and started praying for clarity. On the bright side, my prayers had been answered. On the other hand, I felt unstable. I didn't understand Colin's behavior. Before, I could delude myself with the excuses that he was exhausted … that he misspoke and didn't mean it … that he would come around. At this stage of the divorce, Colin was simply cruel.

When we were together, I was able to dismiss Colin's behavior with the idea that I was simply convenient and that it wasn't personal. During the divorce process, Colin sought me out. It was hard not to feel it as an attack. I grew to fear Colin's rage and punishment. Colin made another threat to petition for part of my retirement. When I asked him about it, he claimed not to know anything about it nor the clause that read, "Wife shall maintain married name." Colin blamed both on his lawyer. When I asked my lawyer about it, he suggested that Colin was lying and that such demands were not standard. Instead of feeling reassured and empowered, my lawyer's words sparked more fear of Colin. I wanted out. I wanted to retreat and lick my wounds. I wanted to protect whatever was left of my life and my sanity.

In the end, despite Colin's promises, I received no compensation for the twelve years I dedicated to managing the family, while not paying into my retirement. Colin, claiming financial constraints, said that he couldn't pay me alimony and pay off the boys' loans. I threw my lot in with the boys. Of course, trusting Colin was a mistake. I thought he'd do right by his sons. I thought it was just me that he hated. Instead, he prioritized his own lifestyle, leaving me struggling without alimony, and the boys saddled with debt. During my recovery, I revisited Colin's NPD diagnosis. This time, I saw it through the lens of covert narcissism.

LACK OF EMPATHY

* * *

Accepting the ugly truths of my marriage to Colin has been crucial to my recovery. I had to look at matters objectively. I had to call a thing a thing. Like *being coerced into having sex*—RAPE, because that's what it is, whether you're married to the perpetrator or not. I had to get brutally honest.

The relationship with a covert narcissist isn't all bad, all the time. That's why so many of us end up stuck for so long. The problem is that the good times are not enough to sustain you. The toxicity eventually poisons the entire relationship. By the time you realize the source of the problem, you are a mere shell of yourself. You may have little mental and emotional energy or hope to recover. It seems that turning back the hands of time, before your prince charming turned into a frog, is the only chance for happiness again.

Don't despair. There is a way out. Like me, it's time to get real about your relationship. Determine what you're actually dealing with—lying, gaslighting, and especially a lack of empathy. Then proceed accordingly with the realization that matters only get worse with a narcissist, not better. No matter how loving and sincere the covert narcissist appears to be, it is all a lie.

Complete the *I Remember* exercise below. Because it's a doozy, there is only one exercise. You are opening Pandora's Box. Remember, this requires brutal honesty. There may be tears. Thank goodness crying is cleansing. Let the tears flow. Repeat this exercise at least three times, being more honest each time.

EXERCISES

Exercise: I Remember

Make a list of all the times the narcissist in your life really hurt you. If you experienced the event as cruel and invalidating, list it, no matter how the narcissist dismissed it. Do not limit the hurt to physical violence. Abuse could be emotional, mental, spiritual, and financial. Abuse comes in many forms. Include them all.

Listing the memories of the narcissist's cruel behavior allows for radical honesty. It allows you to see the narcissist in your life for who he really is. Making a list of memories can also be validating.

Allow yourself some quiet, alone time to do this exercise. Be gentle with yourself the first time through. I chose a small coffee shop because the public space would keep me from getting caught in the story and the emotions. The truth is, I used my vanity of not wanting to break down with the ugly cry in public to my advantage. Do whatever it takes to muster your courage.

I ask you to do this *I Remember* exercise for several reasons:

1. Memories of Colin's abusive behavior came flooding back the longer I spent in no contact. Apparently, I had repressed some events. This makes sense due to the cognitive dissonance that being enmeshed with a covert narcissist causes. I repressed and suppressed my feelings and thoughts to protect my mental health. You likely have done the same. It's what you had to do to survive. I invite you to intentionally excavate the memories. Get them up and out, and into your consciousness.

2. I have found brutal honesty allowed me to call a thing a thing. Being forced to have sex against my will is rape, not whatever I was excusing it as before.

3. Remembering the truth about Colin also supported me in maintaining no contact and setting and enforcing boundaries. Best

of all, I harnessed the anger that radical honesty brought up and used it as fuel to create my new life.

4. Bonus! The anger no longer lived in my body. Hopefully, you will have the same result. Now, it's time to take a deep cleansing breath and get started.

At the top of your paper, write the words *I Remember When* ... Then begin listing the memories as they come to mind. Do this for 10–15 minutes. Do not censor yourself. Write down whatever comes up. Trust that whatever comes up needs to come out of your body.

Once you are finished with your list, take a few minutes to just breathe, slow and steady. I recommend the 4-7-8 Breathing Technique. Celebrate yourself for a job well-done. Remind yourself that you are *still standing* and moving on to bigger and better things.

Find your mantra, your rally cry. My most useful mantra was: *Keep going, Mon. Have faith in what will be!* I often chanted it while I rocked myself to sleep at night. If it resonates, then feel free to use it too. Switch out my name for yours, of course. Know that I'm with you.

If it makes you feel better, share your reality with a person you trust to get their take on the dynamics of your relationship. Make sure that the person can be objective and non-judgmental. I was surprised by the number of people who thought Colin was an asshole, but never felt comfortable about mentioning it to me. Turns out that these people saw his behavior more objectively than I had. Sharing your story will also validate your experience. There is something very powerful in feeling heard—something that is missing in a relationship with a narcissist.

Repeat this exercise at least nine times. Do not let too much time pass in between. Reread your list each time you find yourself romanticizing the relationship with the narcissist, or when you are feeling guilty about enforcing boundaries. Get clear. Stay clear about who the narcissist is.

Well done.

CHAPTER 11

NOW THAT YOU KNOW

So, what do you think? Are you enmeshed with a covert narcissist? As I noted in the introduction, I am sharing my story in hopes that you will learn from my experience. I want you to know how the traits of narcissistic personality disorder show up in the covert narcissist. This is information that I wish I had known from the beginning, after first hearing the NPD diagnosis. I don't want another woman to do thirty years with a covert narcissist because she was unaware of the hidden or subtle red flags.

If you are indeed enmeshed with a covert narcissist, then your next decision is to determine what you will do with that information. Will you stay in the relationship? Will you go? Will you simply sit on the information? Or will you apply what you've learned and establish boundaries? Will you start practicing radical self-care?

Your decision is not an easy one. I get it! There are risks and benefits that result from either decision. Whatever you decide, at least you will do so while informed and not out of ignorance or toxic hope.

When it comes to dealing with a narcissist of any kind, much less a covert narcissist, ignorance is *not* bliss and it is *not* folly to be wise. There is power in knowing. You are now wise enough to spot the manipulations. You won't waste time wondering if you are the problem.

Remaining in a Narcissistic Relationship

Being enmeshed with a narcissist is challenging. The relationship is emotionally and mentally draining. However, not all of us can leave, or for one reason or another we choose to stay. The reasons for staying in a narcissistically abusive relationship are deeply personal. The pros and cons are specific to your situation. When making your decisions, I implore you to realize that the drawbacks have a long-lasting impact. Staying in a narcissistic relationship will result in emotional and psychological harm, with the number one result being a loss of personal agency. Targets are conditioned to believe that they cannot live without the narcissist, that they are greatly lacking in some way and could never be loved by another person. The longer you stay, the greater the damage. A lost sense of self, as your needs and wants are overshadowed by those of the narcissist, is just the beginning.

Now that you have been reminded of the risks, here are some practical strategies to help you endure, or survive in case your relationship comes to an abrupt end. Think resilience and self-preservation. This is just an overview to get you started.

Resilience

- **Develop Radical Acceptance:**

    It's crucial that you fully accept that covert narcissists are who they are, and they do not change their nature. Remember, covert narcissists pretend to be Mr. Nice Guy/The Girl Next Door. They pretend to be modest and humble, but are full of entitlement, grandiosity, resentment, and hidden rage. They lack empathy and are manipulative and vindictive. You must accept that they will not change.

    To help with this the mantra I use is: *A dog barks, a cat meows, and a narcissist lies and manipulates.* Waiting for or expecting a dog to meow or a cat to bark is ludicrous. Likewise, the thought of a narcissist being anything other than self-serving is just as ludicrous. A dog barks and a cat meows because that's simply what they do. Narcissists do what they do because that's who they are. It's not personal. It's just a fact. Making important decisions based on this fact will serve you well. The narcissist will never love you the way you want to be loved. It's simply not in their nature. You have to accept that the narcissist doesn't value those moments of connection that you hold so dear.

- **Embrace Self-Care As A Priority:**

Much of your time and energy will be monopolized by the narcissist. As a result, your needs are absent from your to-do list. It's crucial that you make self-care a priority. This means believing that your emotional, mental, and physical well-being are essential for the resiliency needed to navigate the challenges of the relationship.

Essential self-care goes far beyond treating ourselves to a massage and pedicure. After hydration and quality sleep, the next item on your list gets to be whatever meets *your* personal needs. Here are some things to consider: stress reduction, practicing mindfulness, setting boundaries to protect your time and mental health, and doing things that bring you joy and a sense of fulfillment. Make the time. Take the time.

- **Maintain Independence to Preserve Your Identity:**

Narcissists often seek to create dependency in their relationships, making their partners rely solely on them for validation, support, and decision-making. Maintaining some form of independence will counter the narcissist's control efforts and provide protection.

Form a network outside the narcissistic relationship. Build connections with friends, family, or support groups that provide understanding and empathy. Maintaining your own friend base or work environment will allow you to see yourself in other contexts and relationships. Not only would you maintain a sense of self, but you'd be less likely to fall for the narcissist's gaslighting efforts to make you responsible for their poor behavior.

Do your best to keep separate credit and savings accounts (a secret account would be best). Keeping a separate credit and savings account will provide a safety net in the event of an unexpected discard, or a starting point should you decide to leave. Do your best to keep any professional degrees or licenses current, even if they aren't being used.

- **Practice Emotional Detachment:**

Enmeshment with a covert narcissist often involves emotional manipulation, control, and a blurred sense of boundaries. Therefore, practicing emotional detachment is crucial to preserving your mental and emotional well-being.

The first step toward emotional detachment is to recognize the manipulative behaviors of the covert narcissist. Being keenly aware of the tactics, such as gaslighting and playing the victim, will prevent you from becoming emotionally caught up in the drama. Name the manipulation and stay objective. Do not accept the narcissist's version of reality over your own.

Be mindful of the emotional energy you invest in the relationship. Limit sharing deep personal thoughts and feelings. Covert narcissists tend to exploit vulnerabilities and goals for manipulation. Such information can also be used to inflict emotional pain, or to engage in a smear campaign.

Envision a future for yourself beyond the relationship with the narcissist. Establish personal goals and aspirations for the future. This forward-looking perspective can help prevent loneliness and depression.

Creating a daily journal practice would prove to be tremendously valuable. In the morning, set an intention for how you want the day to go. Go into detail, as if watching a movie screen, scripting your response to the narcissist's behavior. At night, do a brain dump of your worries, anger and fears. Acknowledge your strengths. Brainstorm solutions to problems.

Self-Preservation:

- **Document Abusive Behavior:**

    Documenting the narcissist's behavior will validate your experience. It will help you to recognize patterns and to have a clearer understanding of the manipulative tactics being tried. Recognizing behavior and mood patterns will allow you to develop strategies to protect yourself and navigate the relationship more effectively.

    Confirm your sanity! The written, factual, objective records of events will ground you in reality and confirm your sanity when the narcissist is suggesting otherwise. Being grounded and confident in your reality greatly supports your sense of identity.

    If your situation reaches a point where legal intervention is necessary, documented evidence will serve you well. It can support your legal efforts to obtain a restraining order, file for divorce, or pursue custody arrangements. Be sure to date and note the witnesses involved. When there are visible signs of abuse, such as property damage or injuries, consider taking photographs as evidence.

- **Plan An Exit Strategy: Assess Your Options**

    Narcissistic relationships are characterized by manipulation, control, emotional and financial abuse, and often unexpected discards. Given such, an exit strategy is crucial. Plan ahead. Start immediately.

    Whether you are discarded, or choose to leave on your

own, leaving a narcissistic marriage is emotionally challenging. An exit strategy will help you to emotionally prepare for the process. Having an escape plan means you will not have to stay a minute longer than you choose to. It means you'll land on your feet in the event of a discard.

Financial abuse is a common tactic in narcissistic relationships. A discard often means that joint bank accounts are emptied before you are aware. Similarly, your leaving may lead to financial retaliation, which could mean that you have no access to funds or credit cards. So, it's crucial to secure financial independence beforehand and gather relevant financial information. This could be a secret credit card or savings account. Think of it as an insurance policy. Remember, the first suggestion should you choose to stay with a narcissist, or can't leave just yet, is radical acceptance of who and what you are enmeshed with.

As mentioned previously, you will want to have some funds set aside that will allow you to secure shelter, food, and other essentials for a few months. Think about car payments, utilities, medications, etc. Investigating the costs of apartments and hotels in your area will give you some idea. Knowing where the local women's shelters are would also be helpful information.

Of course, the needed funds will change if you are able to stay with someone in your support system. Be sure to include your support person in your plans.

Perhaps this person can keep copies of all important papers, a credit card, and cash. If they are off site, you won't have to worry about scrambling for them when matters are emotional or dangerous.

- **Embrace Self-Love:**

Being in a relationship with a narcissist means all of your

needs and wants are secondary to the narcissist's. Oftentimes, we aren't even on our own to-do list. As you navigate the relationship, embracing self-love will go a long way. Don't worry, self-love is not the same as being narcissistic.

Self-love means showing yourself grace and compassion. You are in a tough situation. Expect to falter at times. Forgive yourself for any moments of reacting in kind to the abuse you are living. Narcissists often trigger their targets with reactive abuse.

Allow time to reflect on your strength and the things you are doing well. State them as affirmations as often as possible. *I am loyal. I am brave. I am loving. I am a good partner.* Do not minimize your accomplishments. (That's the narcissist's job.)

Take time out to recharge. Take a nap. Get away for some alone time. Sit on the sofa and do nothing, if needed. Treat yourself to a new lipstick. Do whatever is needed to keep yourself going—guilt free!

Voice and enforce your boundaries. The narcissistic personality can't help but to challenge all boundaries. If you slip, acknowledge it and reset. Setting boundaries is about protecting your peace–mentally, physically, and spiritually.

Self-love requires intentional efforts and a commitment to recognizing one's intrinsic value. You deserve your love.

* * *

Whether you decide to stay or to go, being enmeshed with a narcissist will require work. There's work to do to maintain your well-being in the relationship and work to undo the damage once you've left or have been set free. In my experience, no matter how long you stay, there is great joy and freedom in being narcissist free.

Should you decide to end the relationship with the narcissist, you can begin to heal from the mental, emotional, and spiritual trauma. Best of all, you get to rediscover yourself, who you were before the narcissist, and who you are after. The person you were before the narcissist will give you clues as to how to become narcissist-proof in the future. You get to love yourself as you never have before and as no one else can. I promise you; the other side is worth it!

PART 2

*Don't stay stuck—not when reclaiming yourself
and creating a fabulous life is an option.*
— *Monica Linson*

CHAPTER 12

FINDING MY WAY OUT

Finding my way out of the darkness has been the hardest, scariest and most rewarding thing I've done so far. My path to recovery was not a straight line, but one made with switchbacks up a steep mountain. We're talking caves, sheer drop-offs, and a few 180-degree turns.

Your path will likely be the same. I told you that the path was scary, and I also said that it was rewarding. Better still, I've already proven that it is doable.

And if I can do it, so can you.

In the chapters that follow I share a summation of my recovery. Just like in part 1 of this book, I share part 2 in hopes that my experience will provide some perspective and insight to support you on your journey. Being enmeshed with a covert narcissist is a total mindf*ck. It's no place for a person to live long term. Once surviving, it's a greater injustice to stay stuck in the fallout. Don't stay stuck—not when reclaiming yourself and creating a fabulous life is an option.

When reflecting on and organizing my story, I noticed themes emerge: **self-awareness, self-empowerment, and self-love**. That's what I want to share with you. If you've experienced a discard then you know that at the start of my journey, I had to get my bearings and figure out *what the hell just happened!*

The hours and days following the implosion of my marriage felt like I'd been swept up in a tornado. I remember saying to myself, *Toto! I have a feeling we're not in Kansas anymore.* I would then picture Diana Ross and Michael Jackson, as Dorothy and Scarecrow, singing "Ease

On Down The Road." I'd sing to myself, "Just keep on keepin' on the road that you choose." In an effort to hold onto my drive and sanity, I became my own personal cheerleader.

I needed to get a clear picture, not only of the previous few days and weeks, but of my entire marriage.

I needed to know what had become of the young man that I had fallen in love with and married. Mostly, I wanted to understand why the latest version of this man who claimed to love me, and who professed to have my best interests at heart, was being mean, spiteful, and arrogant while acting in immature and resentful ways.

A big part of me knew that Colin's behavior had more to do with self-loathing and frustration, and absolutely nothing to do with me. But another part of me was nauseous 24/7 from the betrayal and lies. Just like everyone else who seemed to waste their love and youth on someone who didn't love them back, I felt stupid, unwanted, and unlovable. The pain was excruciating on some days. On other days, it felt benign and achingly familiar—the very pain that I was trying to escape when I met Colin.

Validating my experience was a clue to my healing, and I believe it will be a clue to yours as well.

Don't worry. Needing to have your experience validated is not the same as the narcissist needing validation. The intent is different. We are seeking to recover from psychological abuse, not trying to prove we are superior to others, thereby deserving of attention and praise.

When a person's experiences and points of view are dismissed as stupid or unimportant, that person is left feeling unheard, misunderstood, and unsupported. They feel unsafe. It's the *unsafe* feeling that had me in shambles for so long. Life with a narcissist is an environment of constant invalidation. We end up burying our feelings and trauma deep inside, having never given voice to our pain. That gets to change. In fact, writing my story has been a powerful tool in my recovery. Through the process I was able to face the reality of my experience and glean the lessons. I invite you to consider telling your story.

If you decide to do so, I know just the writing, editing, and publishing team to help you. I'd be honored to read your story.

Questions Are the Cure

There was something unexpected that showed up on my journey that is likely to show up for you too. It's that I kept asking questions and the more questions I asked the more answers I got.

Intuitively, I figured there must be a lesson that I was missing. Thanks to the work of Iyanla Vanznt, the number one question I kept asking is: *If this is for my good, then what is the lesson here?* Truth is, while it's easy to lie to ourselves, we can't lie to ourselves forever.

It's also true that our mind wants to take out the trash, so to speak, and as soon as we are ready, it unloads as slowly or as quickly as we allow.

This led me to another helpful question: *What am I pretending not to know?*

I uncovered dozens of subconscious blocks. I examined them and then wholeheartedly tossed them out or shifted them to a more empowering belief. My cleanse-by-questioning strategy required radical honesty. It's a hard patch of the journey. It's also the most significant because our subconscious beliefs determine the life that we create for ourselves. Turns out this is done with or without our conscious consent. It's why we keep finding ourselves making the same destructive choices shortly after declaring our intent to take a new path. Think of New Year's resolutions you've made.

Personally, I was determined not to rebuild my life with the same shitty bricks that made me vulnerable to a narcissist. As you've surmised, more years of my life than not have been spent in narcissistic toxicity. I wanted something different—something *I* created. It's essential that we tend to the parts of ourselves that made us vulnerable to the narcissist.

I did the hard work of looking at my part in the abusive relationship. I had to get honest with myself about why I accepted such poor treatment, why I worked so hard to fix a marriage that Colin was actively working so hard to destroy. I had been telling myself that Colin didn't know any better, that he didn't realize the damage he was causing.

Well, that bullshit justification was no longer going to work because in the end Colin had made it clear that he knew exactly what he was doing and had known all along. The truth is, he meant me harm!

More importantly, I had to ask myself: *Why did I think it was my responsibility to help Colin, and what made me believe that I could fix a toxic relationship when the other half had no interest?*

My heart-breaking questions started almost immediately following the night my marriage imploded. After all, I had to grieve the loss of the man that I thought I had married. I had to recognize that he was long gone, and in his place stood a monster. Later, I had to accept the fact that the man I fell in love with never existed. The personality disorder required that he project a false image. I filled in the deficits by projecting my values and faith in the world onto the situation. In other words, I gave the benefit of the doubt and refused to believe that a fellow human, let alone someone who claimed to love me, could behave the way the covert does.

To reclaim myself, I had to ask myself, *Why do you miss someone who treated you so badly?* It's that question that led to my creating a list of truths when it came to Colin. With such facts posted on my bathroom door, staring me in the face each morning, I had to ask, *What made me stay?* I kept pulling that thread and discovered the childhood wounds that created my subconscious beliefs of unworthiness, shame, and not being safe in the world. I did my work to heal that wound and shut down that old operating system. It was false and outdated.

Through asking hard questions, and demanding answers of myself, I became more self-aware. I shifted my beliefs and healed my subconscious wounds. Most of all, I accepted *my truth* in order to reclaim myself and rebuild my life.

With the decision that I would *never* allow Colin back into my life, so many new possibilities lay before me! I asked myself, *Now what?*

I took an assessment of my life with the purpose of determining what I wanted. Imagine that! There were no parameters that included someone else's dreams and well-being. To be honest, at first, I wasn't sure of what I actually wanted.

My entire life up to that point had been about putting others' needs ahead of my own and trying to prove myself useful—and therefore indispensable. Of course, it was cloaked under societal and religious convictions of being a good daughter, a caring big sister, and a loyal and supportive wife.

However, subconsciously, it was all about trying to *buy love to secure my safety.*

Fortunately, I was able to uncover the origin of such thinking and reframe it. I had to rediscover who I was before and on the other side of narcissistic abuse. I wanted to see who I could become once I was finally free of subconscious blocks. I wanted to reinvent myself and rebuild my world through new lenses.

And what an adventure it has been!

I wanted so badly to get to the other side of pain.

I was not able to tell this story in a linear fashion because life doesn't happen that way. Zig and zag went, and still goes, my journey. Yours probably will too. I hope I made the needed connection for you. If not, reach out to me. I'd be happy to clarify any points.

CHAPTER 13

QUESTIONING AND SHIFTING MY BELIEFS

"It is during our darkest moment that we must focus to see the light."
—Aristotle

For days following the discard, life just sucked. It was painful and made no sense to me. There was little reason to get out of bed, shower, eat, or leave the house. I forced myself to do it anyway, determined to do whatever it took to keep myself in motion.

During this time, my thoughts and emotions bounced back and forth between elation and fear. Looking back, I was elated that I was finally free of my life with Colin and also terrified of what life on my own would mean. The fear intensified when I remembered that I was married before I graduated college. Before college I was at home under my father's roof. I'd never been single, free, or on my own before. These moments were so hard. They often left me in tears and not trusting myself to make it on my own. The bouncing emotions seemed to have no rhyme or reason. Fear just seemed to pounce without warning— no regard for time, place, whether I was at work, taking a shower, or driving in my car. Thoughts of *what if* always ended in a worst-case scenario. What I was experiencing was different from what I'd heard about panic attacks before. The thoughts were more like memories or checklists of things to do. No racing heart at those moments. Yet, my body seemed to be on fire. My chest, arms, and legs seemed to be burning from the inside out.

There were days when I would wake between the hours of 3 and 4 a.m. feeling energized and full of joy. On those mornings I felt invincible and excited about whatever the day might bring. I'd savor that energy by meditating, feeling its power throughout my body. I would make a to-do list or dream list from that mental space. I'd purge the house of things that didn't match that energy. I started a 100 Things I Want To Do In Life list during one of these early morning escapades. I brainstormed new things to explore. I even added "learn to make sushi" to that list—something I still want to do.

However, on other days, I found myself feeling nauseated for no apparent reason. When such days coincided with a workday, I stood near the school exit door closest to my car, keys in hand, waiting for 4:00 p.m. to arrive, the official end of my contractual day. Then I'd walk as fast as I could to my car, lock the door, turn up the radio as loud as possible, and scream. The screaming released the energy pockets that seemed to be exploding inside me. The screaming would lead to tears, the tears to laughter! I had no rational explanation for any of it at the time. I simply knew that it had to happen.

So, I let it.

The most alarming events were those when I missed Colin terribly. The pain in my chest was so intense it felt like my heart was broken. Literally. As if that weren't bad enough, this was self-inflicted pain. What really had me stumped—and pissed at myself—was missing someone who had made it crystal clear that *he didn't give two shits about me.* I was so disappointed in myself that when the missing would start, at some point I started looking at myself in the mirror and asking, *Why are you missing someone who treated you like shit? Why would you want to be with someone who doesn't love you? Why don't you want better for yourself?*

I was determined to figure out what my body was trying to tell me. The desire was mostly out of curiosity. After all, the new and strange sensations—of burning limbs, energy swirling in my chest, and a presence—had to mean something. I also didn't want to break down in public because, these days, everyone has a video camera in their pocket!

The first thing I did was to start journaling. Well, journaling *again* would be more accurate. When my youngest son was born, I started working through the book *The Artist's Way* by Julia Cameron. I decided that it was time to do morning pages again—three pages of longhand stream of consciousness writing, done first thing in the morning. They had helped me in the past. There was no reason they wouldn't now. My variation was to add a question to prompt my fifteen-minute stream of consciousness. I asked myself the tough questions that flooded my mind, starting with: *What's the lesson to learn here? Why would you want someone who treats you so badly?* Then I added, *What lies are you telling yourself? What are you pretending not to know?*

Just like before, I bought myself a beautiful journal with acid-free, archival quality paper, and a box of Flair markers that flow well across paper. I put the markers in a beautiful, small makeup bag. The process of choosing a special journal and the bit about the pens are part of my healing ritual. When I got out my special journal and the bag of multi-colored Flair pens, my mind knew that it was time to work. It triggered my subconscious to ask, *What's going on here?* Remember, our minds are answer-seeking machines. Give it something helpful to focus on. These days, it's as if my mind sees the journal and markers and says, "Here we go! Get ready. This is gonna be good!"

This time my adventure with morning pages started out rough. I spent the first week or so hiding from myself. Nothing seemed to be there. I wrote the question over and over, never lifting my pen. No answers revealed themselves. However, the tightness in my throat told me otherwise, that something wanted to get out. My body and the tears running down my face also queued me to keep going. In order to find out what the hell was so painful that I'd want to hide it from myself, I kept asking the questions.

Within two weeks the answers started to flow. The more questions

I asked, the more answers I got. Nowadays, the answers are almost immediate. All I have to do is check in with myself.

It's important to know that my personal process started with writing the question with my non-dominant hand to tap into my subconscious, followed by writing the response with my dominant hand, writing non-stop for a minimum of fifteen minutes. The key was to write freely. No censorship and no judgment about whatever came up. I did not lift my pen from my paper.

The answer to the question *Why would you want someone who treats you so badly?* first appeared as *Who else is going to love you? No one.* Later the response: You're *dirty. You brought reproach on Jehovah's name.* It was this practice that led me back to the sexual abuse I experienced at five years old. It was hard to accept. I felt so defeated. I had done so much work around this already. Two different therapists during my college days urged me not to see myself as a victim even if I were just five … then eight … then eleven, and fourteen. We worked through each perpetrator. It was believed that seeing myself as a victim took my power away.

Neither therapist made it clear as to how I would get my power back.

Another therapist told me to acknowledge my victimhood and express my anger toward the perpetrators and my father. I allowed myself to feel this anger. I went further and gave words to my anger toward Jehovah God. I figured if Jehovah could smite me any minute, as he had David and Bathsheba's baby to show how aberrant he saw sexual immorality to be, then I was going to let him know my side.

Back then, I worked on forgiving myself. Those weekly sessions seemed to help. They allowed me to slowly embrace my sexuality. They allowed me to stop hiding behind bibbed overalls and baggy clothes. Yet, thirty years later, the childhood sexual abuse that I had spent years acknowledging and accepting was resurfacing.

The problem was that none of the past therapists supported me in addressing the subconscious beliefs that I had about myself surrounding all of it. It was those subconscious beliefs that had me missing someone who treated me like shit on his shoe. It was these subconscious blocks that had me believing that Colin was the best I could do—that he was what I deserved. All of that cognitive behavior therapy never addressed the self-hatred and self-blame. It never addressed the *dirty* label that my father put on me, nor the unclean fornicator label that I was told Jehovah himself tagged me with. It never addressed the feelings of unworthiness that I swaddled myself in every day.

* * *

The more questioning and listening I did, the more my journaling and body cues revealed. When my body longed for Colin while at the same time being repulsed by the idea of seeing his face, I had to acknowledge that I was trauma bonded. In short, a trauma bond is when the wounded (me) is seeking relief, help, and healing from the person who caused the wounding. To break the bond, I had to get real with myself. I had to accept that Colin *never loved* and *could never love* me.

After voicing out loud and accepting that Colin never loved me, the truths of my marriage to Colin became crystal clear. Memories came flooding back. I forced myself to write down each one. I forced myself to see and hear the evidence that I had been ignoring or had been too emotionally exhausted to comprehend. Stepping out of the fog into the reality of life with a covert narcissist became a project—my mission. In other words, my recovery was nothing casual, but deliberate and intentional. I had done enough personal growth work to know that it started with getting radically honest with myself.

More Questions

I paid someone on Fiverr to draw a picture of the ogre that I knew the true Colin to be. The image was a horned beast, standing on two legs, with arms that reached his knees, and a smile filled with shark-like teeth. I had the artist include a young boy who peeked out from the ogre's leg. The little boy was a crucial part of the image because seeing Colin as a wounded five-year-old boy played a huge part in overlooking his behavior. Once the image was created, each tidbit of proof of the true Colin was written on a copy of the image.

LIAR, CHEAT, COWARD were the first three words I wrote.

I added the name of the male friend that my gut told me Colin had an affair with over the years. Although I had no concrete proof, I honored my intuition. Despite Colin's gaslighting, I knew that I didn't make things up out of the blue. The picture and the list were posted on my bathroom door. It was the first thing I saw each morning. I no longer allowed myself to escape into toxic hope. Each time I got even a hint of missing Colin, or romanticizing our marriage, I stood in front of my bathroom door and read my list. I reminded myself that even if I didn't fully feel like I deserved better, I wanted better. When I heard my father's voice say, *Who do you think you are?* I answered: *I'm Monica, who has given too much to too many people, including you.*

I knew that when it came to this delusion, the only way out of this pain was through. I had to rip off those labels that my earthly and heavenly fathers had put on me. I had to uproot the damage that wearing those labels had caused.

Secondly, I had to take a good hard look at my part in the dynamic between my husband and me, starting with when I began to put up with the disconnect between Colin's words and actions. When looking at my part of the equation, I didn't allow myself to rationalize Colin's behavior. Being abused as a child, being tired, being confused, or having a personality disorder—none were an acceptable excuse. Worse! Colin being "sorry" for his behavior was not proof that he meant well, that he would try harder, that he would eventually get it. Nor did it mean that he loved me and was committed to our partnership. Those thoughts were merely positive projections I placed on Colin. I reminded myself that Colin was a liar, a coward, and a cheater. *That* was the truth, despite his words or my wishes.

At some point, I heard Pema Chödrön, a Tibetan Buddhist teacher, explain that true emotions only last for ninety seconds, and that any emotions beyond that time meant we were caught up in the story. Remembering that tidbit, I folded another important question into my shifting process. It's one that I still ask myself whenever I am reacting, instead of responding, to an event. It's the question that I now ask my coaching clients whenever they are triggered by the narcissist's behavior.

The question is: *What are you making this (event, comment, thought, feeling) mean about yourself?* I've found for myself, during my recovery and since, that the answer to that question is the story behind the story. It's what keeps the emotion going long after the ninety-second initial reaction. For example, Colin claiming to be in a committed relationship just three weeks after our marriage imploded surprised me. Surprise was the true emotion I felt. Although I had suspected it, to hear him admit it was unexpected. To have Colin confirm my suspicion, and to claim that he was telling me out of love and respect, turned surprise into hurt and despair, which meant that I was caught in the story.

The story that I told myself was that if Colin could move on so easily, then he was having an affair and I was too stupid to notice, that I was a fool for believing that he wanted to renew our vows as he had claimed, supposedly his sign of rebuilding and recommitting. I told myself that *she* must be prettier, skinnier, smarter, more cooperative … better than me. It all felt so true.

But was it? Is it? What proof do I have? None. I didn't even know the woman.

From there, I started to examine the story that I was telling myself. I asked, *Is that really true? If not, then what's another interpretation?* After coming up with another interpretation, I'd ask, *What's a higher interpretation?* Then, *What's the highest interpretation you can come up with—one that would serve you better?* These are questions that I had learned to ask during my training to become a life coach. At the time, I used the skills in my classroom to support my students in becoming more self-aware. I also used my training during parent-teacher conferences because more often than not, parents simply want you to know that they are doing their best. Who knew that I'd one day be my most troubled client?

When it came to Colin's bullshit story of having just met someone with whom he was now in a committed relationship within just three weeks after our marriage ended, before the official separation agreement was drawn up and signed, I called it just that—bullshit!

Allowing myself to simply acknowledge that fact, without guilt, was huge. Next, I looked for evidence of the opposite of the story I told myself. This answered the *Is it true?* part in the examination. I listed the evidence proving that I wasn't stupid:

- I had survived my childhood.
- I graduated high school.
- I earned several college degrees.
- I am becoming more self-aware.
- I can cook without burning down my house.
- I can drive a six-speed manual transmission.

I wrote down or spoke my list out loud.

When the wounded part of me yelled, *You were stupid enough to marry him!* I simply yelled back, *But he wasn't **that** person when I married him.*

Yes, I yelled it out loud, and it was tearful and dramatic! Giving voice to my pain and breathing through it all helped me to process the trauma.

The final item on the list of evidence proving that I was an intelligent, powerful woman was that I not only supported Colin through grad school, but I also helped him build a very lucrative practice.

Done and done.

Next!

When I caught myself blaming my own intelligence, body, or character for Colin jumping into a "committed" relationship so soon after our relationship ended, I put a stop to it with a simple reminder that if Colin had been having an affair, then that makes him a cheater and a liar. It doesn't mean I was stupid or unworthy. This was a higher interpretation of reality than the spiral of self-doubt I had become used to.

I also realized that Colin was making a mistake. He was jumping into a new relationship in hopes of feeling better about himself. But no matter where he went or who he was with, he wouldn't be able to escape himself. His true self is the one he has always truly despised, hidden just beneath Mr. Nice Guy. *Colin knows that I know the true story of who he is. He no longer sees himself as the knight in shining armor that we both previously imagined him to be. Colin is in pain.*

The point of reframing the lens through which you see your reality is to shift your perspective and open your mind and heart to another possibility. Doing this gave me another way to see myself—and Colin. It gave me something to do besides shit on my own head with the same blame and toxicity I'd received from both my partner in life and my own father.

Another mantra I created was a bit more crass. I'd simply say, "Fuck you, Colin!" when I found myself reliving traumatic stories. Sometimes, I would say the words out loud; sometimes I'd just whisper them under my breath. I had thirty years' worth of stories ruminating in my head. Saying a hearty, "Fuck you, Colin!" was invigorating, and it allowed me to carry on with the more important task at hand—like not falling into a trauma spiral in front of my students. My goal was to not be incapacitated by my memories.

I invite you to try the process for yourself. At the very least, ask yourself the important question: *What am I making this mean about me?* Ask this question every time you find yourself triggered and reacting to a comment or an event. *What emotions do you feel? What are you making either situation mean about yourself?* Questioning yourself this way, as your new best friend, will lead you to key subconscious blocks, sometimes known as limiting beliefs. It's a powerful start. Unraveling those subconscious blocks is essential to your freedom.

The Power of Exploration & Affirmations

Affirmations also played a role in my healing. Affirmations can be quite powerful when used properly. Most people seem to use affirmations as a way to confirm an already strong belief. The affirmation serves as a reminder and makes them feel empowered. Others use affirmations as a north star to hope and wish upon.

I used, and still use, affirmations as a catalyst for the change I wanted. I started by creating an *I Wish List*. Again, I used another beautiful journal reserved specifically for this exercise, along with my array of colored pens. I turned the lights down low and played soft music—the kind you would typically associate with massage or meditation. I usually had a glass of iced tea or kombucha. I would sometimes light a candle. I always burned Palo Santo. All of this was to signal to my mind and body that we were getting ready to get down to business, to do something special. I also set a timer for an hour. This gave me an escape hatch in the event that I found a big scary mess of memories or toxic beliefs. That escape hatch gave me courage to dive in despite my fear. It gave me permission to take a break if needed.

Let me paint the picture: Sitting comfortably on my sofa, I allowed myself to think about my relationship with Colin. Most often, I chose one of the memories I had most recently been ruminating about. After allowing myself to feel all the emotions that came with the memory and the stories that I made up to go with it, I'd put my pain into words. *I wish I had been enough. I wish I had listened to my gut. I wish I was courageous. I wish I trusted myself.* You know the drill. You've made similar wishes. We all have. No shame.

Next, I'd choose one wish and state it, not as a wish but in the affirmative. It became my affirmation. I'd doodle the words in my journal. While drawing the words and adding other embellishments to the page, I'd repeat the affirmation.

For example, *I wish I had been enough* became *I Am Enough!* As I stated and repeated the affirmation, I noted the emotions that arose and the body cues I felt. These alerted me to the resistance that lived in my mind and body. I wrote down the inner thoughts that ridiculed and laughed at the absurdity of my being enough.

All three of these events informed me of my subconscious blocks. They pinpointed a place to explore, a limiting belief to dismantle and shift.

Exploring meant asking more questions: *Why does this feel like a lie? Why am I about to cry? What's this tightening in my chest all about? Why is my throat burning? Why is this voice in my head laughing?* Exploring meant pulling the threads to see what would unravel. I would keep unraveling until I had an answer or until I was too exhausted to continue.

If you're anything like me, you will find yourself falling asleep shortly after the hour alarm. Sometimes, you'll be able to keep going. Trust yourself. You'll know if you've reached your edge. You'll also know deep down if you are letting yourself off the hook. My process was to repeat the same affirmation until I'd cleared the limiting beliefs, discarding outdated beliefs and reframing my memories and knee-jerk reactions through the lens of my wiser, more empowered self. I worked with the affirmation until it *felt* true.

Then I reinforced the affirmation by posting it on my mirror or somewhere in plain sight. I even made my affirmation into wallpaper on my phone.

Through affirmations, I'm able to set goals for myself and map out an action plan. However, some goals take more work than others. For example, in the process of writing this book, I was faced with impostor syndrome. Many authors suffer from this. It was on those days that I had to remind myself that I'm good enough to tell *my* story.

I realized that feeling a little unsure of myself when I'm setting big, scary goals will never go away. If I didn't feel that fear (and do it anyway), it likely meant I'm too comfortable and it's time to dream bigger.

When I was making my *I Wish List* I also borrowed some

affirmations I came across in magazines or online. I went through the same process of trying them on and seeing what needs shifting. Whether you come up with your own affirmations or swipe them from somewhere else, simply repeating them over and over will not result in a shift in your way of being. This is especially true if you already resonate with the message. If you already resonate with an affirmation, then it's unlikely to be attached to a subconscious block.

Uncovering, then shifting my subconscious emotional blocks through affirmations and exploration was my goal. I invite you to do the same.

Just so you know! Once I became more grounded in who I am, I continued using affirmations with my energy work. Following my chakras, I moved from the root chakra, I AM to affirmations of I FEEL, which align with the sacral chakra. I tried on sacral affirmations like: *I feel calm and grounded in who I am; I trust that my life will unfold toward my highest good; I feel safe and protected by The Universe/God.*

Again, whenever I ran into resistance to these affirmations, I would work to clear—unblock—them.

I worked (and still do) with my body cues and practiced Reiki to get my chi flowing.

The affirmation connected to the other chakras are:

- I DO for the solar plexus;
- I LOVE for the heart chakra;
- I SPEAK for the throat chakra;
- I SEE for the third eye chakra; and
- I UNDERSTAND for the crown chakra.

I invite you to move into these realms of affirmation work. Such intentional energy work will help you to embody the power and lessons learned from your experience of narcissistic abuse.

The Need for Safety

My greatest subconscious block was not feeling safe and yet it's what I wanted most. My desire to feel safe and to clear my feelings of shame and worthlessness kept leading me back to memories from five-year-old Little Me.

Considering that I have yet to master time travel, I came up with the next best thing. I posted pictures of myself at five, eight, and eleven years old. Starting with my kindergarten picture, I talked to Little Me every day. I greeted her each morning. I said, "Good night," before I went to bed. I told her that I loved her. On one random Saturday, I asked Little Me what she wanted to do, as if she were standing in the room with me. From somewhere inside, I heard the words, *play jacks*. So, I bought us some jacks. I wanted her to feel important and to feel heard. I wanted her to know she was safe.

One day through tears, I told Little Me how sad I was about what happened to her at the babysitter's house. I told her about how pissed I was that our daddy didn't believe her. I told her that I would keep her safe and that I was learning how to keep both of us safe. I showed her the steel security door with its keypad that I had installed in our bedroom, so that no one like the babysitter would ever wake us from our sleep again. I told her about my Glock 9mm.

I had similar conversations with each version of Little Me. I told the eight-year-old me that what happened on the stairs at 99 Riddle Road was not her fault. I tell her that I know how frightened she was when Eric grabbed her from behind, locked her in his long arms, and then rubbed himself against her. I explained the strange noises that Eric made. I listened to eight-year-old Little Me explain how she had no idea what was happening and how much it hurt when Eric crushed her enough to leave bruises.

I cried for her! For both of us.

I let the eleven-year-old me know what I had discovered about that heavy, floating feeling she felt, like watching herself on a screen, as Venetia touched her *Dee-Dee*. I reminded her that it was the same feeling we had when our mother gave us half a Valium at fourteen years old for really, really bad cramps. I also told her about a similar feeling with Percocet when we had our wisdom teeth out. I let her know that despite what the congregation elders had claimed, an inability to move did not indicate participation and guilt, but more likely the effects of a drug, or at the very least, shock and fear. I let Little Me know that, as an adult, I was on the lookout for such dangers. I assured her that I was on top of things and that I was very particular about who got to be part of our inner circle.

Reconnecting with Little Me this way allowed me to reclaim the parts of myself that had been stolen when I was a child. It was the first time I had really spoken directly to myself about what had happened. Speaking to empathetic therapists over the years had not been the same. As memories and thoughts, along with thousands of what-ifs came up, I was able to process the long-trapped emotions tied up in them.

Sometimes, processing meant journaling. Sometimes it meant crying to release the trauma. Sometimes processing meant taking a nap, or watching a favorite movie to show the compassion and support that wasn't available back when I was a child—back when I needed it most. It allowed me to shower Little Me with the love I so desperately wanted and worked so hard to get from my father. The love is here now, rock solid. There is no need for the once-wounded me to look for love in the wrong places or in the wrong people.

I invite you to connect with your inner child! Find pictures of your Little Me. Talk to her—**every single day!** Take her out for ice cream. Buy her a new coloring book. Eat cereal straight out of the box. Spend time with her. Help her to make sense of the past where needed. Love her! Be the parent to her that you needed back then.

If this sounds corny to you, I get it! But here's what I know. I trusted my intuition and I healed. The more I did these things, the more memories and information surrounding subconscious blocks were revealed and cleared.

Self-Awareness Is a Superpower

The more aware we are of the lenses in which we see our world and the patterns in which we operate, the more power we have to create the world we want to live in. In other words, we learn how to get out of our own way! Self-awareness is a superpower. By learning more about myself and recognizing my triggers, I am able to moderate my response to life and reality as it is now. When frustration or obstacles appear, I respond only to the current situation in front of me, *not* to fifty years of unrecognized childhood trauma. Knowing what my triggers are keeps me from spiraling into a fight, flight, freeze, or fawn trauma loop. (I learned from an early age to play nice—fawn—when situations were dangerous.)

Once I learned these techniques, I stopped viewing my world through fear, shame, and self-doubt. I was no longer in a constant state of feeling not good enough. I started interpreting the world and my experiences in a different way. Suddenly, new opportunities presented themselves. Warning signs began appearing in techno-color. These were red flags I hadn't been able to see through my outdated lenses.

Nowadays, I make sure I never leave my house without my correct lenses. If I do, or if I am triggered, I reset. I'm not gonna lie—there are people that have me shifting gears and switching lanes all day long in their company. Some days I choose to disengage from such people. I give myself permission to do so—whether family, friend, elder, congregation sister or brother, boss, or otherwise. If someone crosses a clearly articulated boundary, personal standard, or value, I give myself permission to sever ties. My subconscious beliefs and trauma response patterns used to run my entire life, especially when it came to putting everyone else before myself. No longer!

I also know now what my strengths are, and I use them as my jumping-off points to start anything new. My greatest strength is my strong intuition. My intuition is what I originally ignored when I first met Colin. I had learned to fear my intuition when I was growing up. When I ignored it with Colin, it's not that my inner self was unaware, it was that I was still choosing to not trust myself. Nowadays, my intuition and I chat every day, all day. She's the big sister that I wished I had. Other times, she's the cussin', blunt-as-hell, weed-smokin' hippy version of me. She's always my friend, my own personal inner goddess.

I invite you to make your intuition your greatest strength too. It is time to break the bad habit of not trusting your body cues. Reestablish that connection with yourself. When you have that personal body sensation, you know to pay close attention instead of rationalizing or minimizing the situation in hopes of keeping the peace.

When that special co-worker says, *Are you feeling okay today?* in that certain demeaning tone that is meant to put you in your place because you called her out on some questionable behavior, you will see it for what it is. You'll listen to your personal warning system and answer *I'm just fine, thank you.*

No more living on high alert trying to guess what the narcissist wants or needs from you because now, the only cues you're paying attention to are the ones inside you. Your gut intuitions.

The result of trusting your own instincts again is immediate. It gives you the mental, emotional, and physical energy to live stress-free, without fear of being caught off-guard, of the ball dropping.

You will even be able to date again, freely, trusting your early warning system to protect you. You may borrow mine until you refine your own. What works for me is being my authentic self in a relationship. Should any red flags appear, I honor my body cues and ask clarifying questions to get more information and to determine if I am projecting my past trauma onto the new relationship. However, if those answers lead to more red flags, then it's time to move on because I am no longer the person who ignores my body cues and red flags. My own personal warning system is three red flags, and a few clarifying questions. If those answers result in more red flags, then three strikes and you're out! Easy peasy, because that part of you that used to ignore red flags and body cues is now wide awake.

Ask yourself: What comfort are you looking for outside of yourself? Is it to feel safe? To be loved? To know that you're enough? How can you meet those needs for yourself? Consider the question and then try making a list of things you can do to meet your own needs. Whatever comes to mind, write it down. There is no wrong answer. Then review your list, choose one action to implement, and get to work.

CHAPTER 14

GETTING UNSTUCK

The belief that attention equals love will be responsible for a lifetime of unfortunate events.

— *Monica Linson*

When I look back objectively, examining my thoughts and behavior patterns, whether I sought answers from art therapy, meditation, hypnosis, or some mode of energy work, all roads led back to the same event.

When I am radically honest with myself, I am and have always been the five-year-old little girl who has been betrayed by someone who was supposed to love her. This is the vantage point from which I have seen and navigated the world. It's the lens through which I still see the world when I am overtired, dehydrated, or feeling anxious and overwhelmed. It's my default setting. There are some philosophies, like Imago Therapy, that suggest that this wound is the one my subconscious sought to resolve when I allowed Colin into my life.

Coming to this realization was difficult. It was hard to believe that after hundreds of hours in therapy talking about my childhood trauma, my frame of reference was still rooted in my childhood.

On the other hand, examining my adult behavior patterns while holding this possibility as true explained so many aspects of my life. Becoming aware of this personal lens and recognizing it as *my truth* has been incredibly empowering.

My First Assault

I was five years old when I had my first nap time visitor. He was my babysitter's son. I heard his steps as he came down the basement stairs. I held in my giggles. I was supposed to be asleep.

He woke me from my pretend nap by tugging on one of the plaits in my hair. "Hey!" he said and put his finger to his mouth as a reminder that I needed to be quiet. He didn't want me to wake my little sisters.

My mouth wouldn't stop grinning. I held my lips closed as tightly as I could, but it was no use. A giggle escaped.

"What was so funny?" he asked.

I shrugged my shoulders. I was excited to see him, and he knew it. I wondered what special treat he had for me today. Maybe I would get to watch *The Uncle Al Show* with him again, or *Hattie the Witch*. I secretly hoped he had a Bit-O-Honey candy for me. I knew he had some because I had seen him eating one earlier.

I sat up slowly so as not to squeak the bed. I had become quite good at this. This was our special time together while the little kids slept.

If I woke my sisters, I would have to share. I held my breath and pulled my legs out from under the blanket. Sitting up nice and straight, I was ready for my surprise.

He sat at the bottom of the sofa bed. I waited for the support leg to fold in on itself as it often did. It never seemed to lock in place. I didn't like that we never knew when it was going to cave in or hold. I also didn't really like the brown tweed fabric. It made me itch. I didn't like that it smelled like mothballs. Mostly, I didn't like having to take a nap on it.

But the sofa bed didn't collapse. My visitor motioned for me to join him. I inched a little closer to the middle, distrusting the sofa bed. Saying nothing, he put his hands around both of my ankles and pulled me to the bottom edge, right next to him.

He had yet to reveal my surprise. I was curious, still hoping for a Bit-O-Honey. And though Bit-O-Honey was my favorite, I would settle for a caramel Squirrel. The thought filled me with more anticipation.

I wanted to say, "Well?" and hold out my hand. But I had been told more than once that such behavior was uncouth. So, I waited.

He moved from the bed and knelt on the floor in front of me. I giggled. I waited for him to hold out his two closed fists. My Uncle Billy played this game with me, and he always had a candy in each hand. I was ready. How could I lose?

But my babysitter's son didn't hold out his hands. Instead, he pushed my forehead and I fell back. There was a familiar squeak on the sofa bed.

"Shh!" he said, and I strained my neck to the left and back to check on my sisters.

As I did, I felt him pulling down my shorts and then my panties. In my recurring nightmares, my panties are pink. The kind with tiny ruffles on the back. I felt something warm and wet. My babysitter's son groans. The sound reminded me of the noise my daddy makes after sneaking into the candy yams simmering on the stove until dinner. I pictured my daddy doing that little dance he does when something tastes *just that good!* I'm confused by the images in my head because the thought of candied yams, my daddy dancing, and the feelings in my body are a mismatch.

Again, I felt something warm and wet. This time it was followed quickly by a scratchy feeling. My body tensed. My legs straightened. Stiff, as if someone else has control of them.

My whole body was hot. There was a bah-bum sound coming from somewhere.

Bah-bum!

Warm and wet.

Bah-bum!

Then, a burning.

Bah-bum! Bah-bum!

The sound became louder and faster. But I still couldn't tell where it was coming from. I rubbed my right ear, then the left. No use.

Bah-bum!

Then I realized what was happening! My babysitter's son was licking my *DeeDee*. *DeeDee* was my mother's name for my private parts.

Bah-bum! Bum! Bum!

I squeezed my eyes shut when I remembered that my mother had told me repeatedly that no one should be touching my *DeeDee* other than… I ran the list of people through my head—my mother, my grandma, my aunt … *no*. My babysitter's son was *not* on the list!

Bum! Bum! Bum!

My ears burn.

Tears ran down my face. *Big girls don't cry*, I reminded myself. I covered my face with the blanket to hide my tears.

I felt a sharp pain from somewhere inside. My babysitter's son was sticking his fingers in places that I didn't understand—places on my body that I didn't even realize I had … places I knew nothing about.

BAH-BUM!

It hurt. His nails were scratching me. I held my breath. The tears flowed faster. They were hot on my cheeks. Or are my cheeks hot? I couldn't tell.

I bent my knees in hopes of using my feet to push on the bed, arch my back, put my hands by my ears, then push to flip myself backward. I'd made the move many times before on my own bed. But I wasn't on my own bed.

My babysitter's son quickly pushed my knees down. Once. Twice. I wanted to get away. I was trying to get away. I wanted to get back to the top of the sofa bed, back under the blanket.

I tried to tell him that he is not on the list of people who can touch my *DeeDee*.

"Shh! Be still," he scolded. "You don't want to wake your sisters."

That part rang true. I wanted to be a good girl.

I remained still, gripping my blanket. The scratches burned. "Stop! That hurts," I said.

He did stop.

I removed the blanket just enough to get a peak, to see if he was still there. Our eyes met and he smiled. My babysitter's son had the same smile he had when he gave me an Apple Now-and-Later the day before.

Bah-Bum!

He goes back to licking my *DeeDee*. My plea didn't matter.

Bah-Bum! Bah-Bum!

None of this made any sense to me. His mother, Sister Johnson, said he was there to help take care of us, not to hurt us! I think about how he sometimes made lunch for us, and how he turned the rope with me in double-dutch. He had said that I was a great rope turner!

I closed my eyes. My body shook with fear. I didn't know what to do. None of this made any sense.

Bah-Bum!

I didn't want to be here. I wanted to play jacks instead.

* * *

The next morning my mother and father were arguing. I could hear them through the register. I snuck to the top of the stairs; it was the best place for eavesdropping.

My mother had called off work in order to keep me and my sisters at home. "I'm not sending her back over there Tom. She …"

My father interrupted with, "Ray says that it didn't happen. No one saw anything… We need the money. There are bills to pay!"

"Why would she lie, Tom? Why would she make it up? How would she even know to make it up?"

I wanted to scream that I didn't make it up. That it was true. I wanted to explain that everyone else was asleep. That I didn't want to wake them up. I wanted to say all of this, but I didn't.

"I'm not sending them back over there, Tom," my mother said again.

"He says that he didn't do it. There were no witnesses, so how can we know for sure?"

"Why would she lie?"

I knew that liars tell lies, and that liars are bad. I wanted to yell out, "I'm not lying. I'm telling the truth!" I thought about how much trouble I must be in for letting someone touch my *DeeDee* and now I was going to be in more trouble because my Daddy thought I was lying too.

I couldn't move. I rubbed my belly to relieve the burning in my stomach. It didn't work. It never did. Every time my parents argued, my belly burned.

"We have bills to pay," my father repeated. "Get to work. We need the money."

I can tell that he was saying it through his teeth. I knew the sound well. My mother and I both knew what it meant. I prayed that my mother didn't say anything else. Defying my father at that point would have resulted in a slap across her face, or my daddy's hands around her neck, followed by him pulling her by her hair across the room to toss her wherever he saw fit. I folded my arms across my body and squeezed myself, and closed my eyes, as hard as I could. And prayed harder!

Later that day when I saw my father, our eyes never met. He didn't say, "Hey!" He didn't say anything. I waited for him to ask me to get him a glass of ice water, iced tea, or a cold beer. Whatever he wanted me to do, I was ready. But there was nothing. He wanted nothing to do with me.

A rift was created between my father and I that day. There wasn't a chance for me to plead my case. I didn't get to show him the proof that I was telling the truth. The blood on the inside of my panties would prove that I wasn't a liar. My daddy didn't say how sorry he was for my pain, and that we will figure this all out. He didn't say, *Your Mommy is going to fix you right up. Don't you worry!* I needed to hear those words.

I wanted my Daddy to say, "I went right over there and punched Ray in the nose. He won't be hurting you again!" I wanted my Daddy to kiss me on my forehead and tell me that I was going to be okay!

None of the things I needed to happen happened. Instead, my Daddy avoided me. That day, and for days after. There was no swinging me by my arms when he came home. No throwing me up in the air and catching me. No, "Hey, Gurl! Bring me a beer!" I would have welcomed any sign of recognition, of solidarity, love, or friendship.

I knew that I hadn't lied. Yet, my father said I had.

When he did decide to talk to me, my father told me that I had angered Jehovah God. He read scriptures, Colossians 3:5 and 1 Corinthians 6: 9–10, to prove his case. The best explanation that my five-year-old self could come up with was: *I am bad. I am a disappointment to him. My daddy is ashamed of me. God doesn't love me. I will be destroyed at Armageddon. I am not safe!*

I couldn't figure out what I did to cause my babysitter's son to think that I wanted him to do what he did. I did remember that I had been happy to see him. I remembered wanting to get up from my nap and watch TV and eat candy. It had been our secret for months.

Guilt, confusion, fear, and shame set in. These emotions are the first tint on my new lenses. My five-year-old self turned confusion, fear, guilt, and sadness into an intense need to win back her daddy's love. Quick, fast, and in a hurry! Somehow, I figured out that the best way was by proving myself to be useful. I do not recall the exact event that connected the two together. Perhaps it was when I crawled under the bed to get my daddy's dress boots and he gave me a big smile of appreciation. A smile on my daddy's face signaled his approval. It meant attention. Attention meant love—this woefully lacking idea of attention equals love will be responsible for a lifetime of unfortunate events.

My daddy's attention often came with words like: *What would I do without you gull?* (Gull was my daddy's special word for his daughters. His way of saying girl.) I loved it—even into adulthood! Back then, for me a smile on my daddy's face often led to a toss into the air and being caught in his arms. Something that I loved a hundred times more after the babysitter's son.

As I grew up, I found more sophisticated ways to be useful to my father. For instance, there was no dirty taste, or gritty texture, after I cleaned a mess of collard greens. When I cleaned chitterlings for my daddy, although they still smelled like boiled feces when cooking on the stove, they were pristine. In third grade, I learned to pour beer with no foam. By eleven, I had learned to make highballs for my daddy and his friends (in a specific set of glasses I was to pour two fingers of Jim Beam, two more of Verner's Ginger Ale, then add two ice cubes). I also cut slices of lemon for them when lemons were available, and not being saved for my mother's lemon meringue pie. I knew that my daddy would rather have the pie. I learned later that the lemons were to hide the smell of alcohol on their breath on days when they stopped by before going to the Kingdom Hall.

At nine years old, I learned that having lunch for him when he came in from mowing fields on his tractor gained me a great return on my investment. I perfected *his* cheeseburger! I'd learned that the ground beef could be just a little bigger than the size of a tennis ball. That way, there would still be enough left over for my mother, my sisters, and me.

I rolled it in my hands until it was perfectly round, followed by three squishes to flatten it. He liked his cheeseburgers pink in the middle. So, my mother taught me to let the meat cook on the starting side long enough until I could see the edges turn brown before flipping. When I was first learning, it seemed that my mother was constantly having to adjust the temperature on the stove.

More of a simmer than a fast fry! My sister always did it wrong. For the life of me, I could never figure out how she managed to cook a burger that was burnt to a crisp on the outside *and* somehow still cold and raw in the center. More baffling is that she seemed to be doing this on purpose, so that my daddy would stop asking her to whip him up a cheeseburger.

In the meantime, I'd slice an onion as thinly as possible. Then, I'd add that to the skillet, moving the onions around to coat them in just enough of the grease. Just smelling grilled onions put my father in a better mood. Time to flip the burger, also meant time to add the cheese. At that point, I'd cover the skillet with the lid, or a larger skillet, or even a cookie sheet. Whatever was clean or handy.

Over time I figured out that if I skipped the part of squeezing out all the excess grease with the spatula, the way my mother had taught me, and let the cooked burger rest on a paper towel for a minute or two, it made it the perfect kinda juicy that my daddy loved.

My father liked his bread toasted. He seemed to like white and wheat bread equally. I discovered that he liked Thousand Island on his cheeseburger just as much as on his Reuben sandwich. I can't recall if this was a desperate move because we were out of Miracle Whip and I tried it myself, or because my mother told me to use it for the same reason. Either way, it became a thing.

I'd present his cheeseburger with lettuce and fresh tomato slices from our garden. Sometimes with french fries. Sometimes with fried okra. I'd wait for his happy giggle (my sign of a job well done).

From the age of five, I internalized the lesson that earning my daddy's love, and God's approval was, subconsciously, my top priority.

A job well done meant I had proven myself to be useful. Being useful meant that I was valuable, worthy of existing.

Over the course of my life, my daddy and I have had a special relationship. Our unspoken transactions became more significant—for both of us. When I was very young, trying to connect with my daddy felt just like being at the drive-in with my cousins who were in a different car, two rows up. Not quite the same as snuggling under a blanket on the hood of the same car.

Later, I pictured our relationship as an impenetrable wall—a wall that wouldn't budge no matter how hard I banged my head on it, begged, or cried, all in hopes of my daddy seeing and hearing me. That didn't stop me from longing for the closeness and working hard to get it.

Something to Think about

For five decades after the sexual assault, I lived my life through the eyes of a scared little girl trying to feel safe and to be loved by her daddy—and God Almighty himself. Of course, to many on the outside looking in, I presented as a powerful, smart, professional woman who spoke her mind and had her shit together, or at least most of it.

I invite you to ask yourself if you might relate to this need to earn someone's love. Ask yourself: *Where am I going above and beyond to prove myself worthy? From whom am I trying to buy love or prove my worth? From whom am I accepting the love I think I deserve, instead of the kind of love I give and want in return?*

The File Marked "SAFETY"

Everything that science has proven about how our mind works is very intriguing to me. Our subconscious mind seems to be an individualized storage and filing system. It files all the events in life—everything we've seen, heard, touched, tasted, done, or thought. And the greatest, most important file is the one marked "SAFETY."

Our subconscious mind reminds us of the possible risks of injury or death. This was especially important in the early days of human existence. The best example I've heard over the years considers the days of the saber tooth tiger. Just imagine yourself leaving your home to visit your bestie down the path. You *must be aware* of all the dangers afoot! It's a matter of life and death. There is no time to smell the roses or listen to a bubbly brook. Those are nice, but not life preserving concerns. The human subconscious is so efficient that it does not fill important files with such *nonsense* as lovely, joyful, and pleasant things and events. That is until we tell it to do so.

This primal wiring is why we tend to recall the worst moments of our lives more readily than the joyful parts, so we can avoid potential dangers.

My five-year-old subconscious mind interpreted the events

surrounding my babysitter's son and my father's dismissal as abandonment, being unworthy, and being unsafe. As it's programmed to do, my subconscious mind thus made safety priority one. The lessons and tasks within the safety folder read something like:

People who love you don't hurt or abandon you—get people to love you.

People who find you helpful don't hurt or abandon you—be helpful.

People who you love and care for will love you back—they won't hurt or abandon you.

Love people for who they are—they will do the same.

Jehovah doesn't like a haughty person—be humble.

Turn the other cheek—overlook others' shortcomings.

Meet their needs—they will love you for it.

Give people the benefit of the doubt—good people are loved and safe.

Be a good person—being a good person will keep you safe.

These rules were helpful in many ways. One, they kept me alive back then. Two, they made me a good and loyal friend to people who appreciate me today. Three, they made me a good person. I like who I am.

However, on the whole, my operating system that I constructed as a five-year-old was problematic. The first problem is that I was coming from a subconscious place of *lack and need*. I needed to feel safe. In order to ensure my safety, I needed to appease people and make them a friend, rather than a foe. I wasn't coming from a place of personal power and choice the way I do now.

The second problem is that not all human beings operate under the same notions. Not all the people I love, and the world says should love me back, do. Instead, they love what I can do for them. They love me when I am agreeable and complacent. They love how I make them feel about themselves. This includes family members. Worst of all, this giving and giving in order to feel safe and loved made me vulnerable to narcissists! Vulnerable to the likes of Colin.

My childhood wounds and the lessons learned have been running my life ever since, just as they were when I met Colin. They are also the reasons I ignored my intuition. When Colin and I first met, my body sent me warning signs, and continued to do so. Instead of listening to my instincts, I listened to lessons learned from trauma.

I opened up to the possibility of having misread him or being judgmental when we met in passing the very first time. I made excuses for him. I turned the other cheek. Once I ignored my body cues and intuition, my subconscious mind ran plays straight out of its default playbook.

It's extremely noteworthy to me that my subconscious mind allowed me to shift easily to accepting Colin into my life because his toxic energy felt familiar to the energy I had known growing up with a covert narcissistic father. It was an energy I was used to, one I understood. Although it was the soul-sucking energy of the covert narcissist, it felt like home to me.

I knew how to respond to Colin's needs. It was like riding a bike. Once you know, you know. I mistook familiarity for love. My subconscious programming was keeping Little Me safe, as if to say: *We know how to play this game. We're good at it. Proceed!*

The third problem that I see wrong with the lessons, beliefs, and responses learned by my five-year-old self is that, although they kept me relatively safe regarding my physical needs, they did not keep me safe emotionally, mentally, spiritually, financially, or energetically.

Once I no longer felt safe with Colin, I did what I knew how to do to protect myself. I mistakenly believed my outdated, imperfect safety protocols were working. Then the love-bombing phases reinforced my toxic hope. It was toxic hope that kept me going for thirty years, blind to my subconscious beliefs.

My toxic hope had me dismissing the evidence showing I was in a no-win situation and an abusive relationship. The survival plan that I came up with as a deeply wounded five-year-old is what required me to not only overlook Colin's behavior, but to see it as good enough.

It wasn't until I took a good hard look at the truth, through exploration, affirmations, clearing my blocks, energy work, therapy, and taking care of the soul of five-year-old me that things truly began to change—for me and inside me.

When I look at my behavior patterns, I can draw a big red line connecting them to the subconscious beliefs that began when I was five. It took me most of my life to fully peel back those layers. That's a long time. I hope that, because you have this book in your hands, I can save you some time and heartache.

I invite you to take a look at your patterns and beliefs and start peeling back the layers that make you, you. Free yourself of the outdated subconscious blocks that prevent you from living a life you truly desire.

It's astonishing to me—or at least it used to be—how often and where the experiences and choices dictated by the five-year-old version of myself presented themselves.

The confusion and fear planted in my body by my babysitter's son when I was five years old kept me frozen when I was sexually assaulted by another babysitter at eight. The same happened at eleven years old, when I was sexually assaulted by a congregation sister, and then later when I was repeatedly assaulted by a family friend at fourteen. It kept me in a marriage that was rife with sexual assault.

Each time, I was told by my father and the elders of the Jehovah's Witness congregation that I lost Jehovah's favor for not fleeing as Joseph did from Potiphar's wife (Genesis 39: 6–12). I felt deep-seated unworthiness and shame, which led to shaky boundaries and a state of long-suffering regarding other people's bullshit. Remember, I prayed for long-suffering during my marriage—until five days before its implosion, at which time I asked for clarity. And thank God, I got it.

For years, I asked: *Who am I not to tolerate such a nice guy? Who am I not to forgive again and again for the same offenses?*

I asked *Who am I* with the same disdain that my father had in his voice and the congregation elders had in theirs. They asked with the overt intent of keeping me humble, and in my place—*good Christian qualities.*

Because of a lifetime of programming telling me that I was unworthy and shameful, I had a tendency to go above and beyond in order to prove my value. This tendency showed up not only in my pursuit of multiple degrees and certifications, but also in my relationships and career.

I was the friend who would do anything for you, asking nothing in return. I never asked for help because *who am I* to cause such a disturbance in another person's life. *Who am I* to expect support? In truth, I was afraid that if I let people know my needs, they would say no and that no one would come to my aid.

So, I stayed humble. I stayed safe, the whole time wishing that I had a friend like me.

The deep-seated feeling of unworthiness and shame has played a role in my beliefs about what I am allowed to have in this world. It has dictated the career path I've taken and the amount of money I am allowed to make (or spend on myself). If my dreams and desires brush up against my programming, I tend to self-sabotage. I'm still working on this one!

The unraveling that I have done so far, the exploration, the self-care, and energetic clearing of blocks and bad beliefs has opened my world to new possibilities, people, and experiences. Now, I look forward to more gifts as I continue to shift my energy and beliefs.

* * *

I am no longer operating from a place of fifty-year-old subconscious wounds and lessons. I no longer need nor have expectations of another person to make me feel safe, whole, or worthy. I am once again in touch with my intuition and body cues that alert me to covert narcissistic shenanigans.

When a person bumps against one of my boundaries or standards, I do not fawn by automatically minimizing the behavior or comment in hopes of keeping myself in someone's good graces. I've done my work. The more I release the trauma from my mind and body, the more space I have for peace of mind, joy, and creativity. I'm no longer living on guard. I have the confidence to dream and to ask for help when needed. I know that I am loved. I trust that I am safe and that there are people who will come to my aid should I ever sound the alarm. That is a far cry from how I've felt most of my life.

* * *

Something to Ponder: I want the same for you. I urge you to do the work that will free you of your subconscious, outdated beliefs. When I was little, fawning to please the adults around me, despite their dysfunction, was the absolute smartest thing to do to keep myself safe. However, that default response was outdated and needed to be updated. I am no longer little and in need of the adults in my life to provide for me. Now I get to be in charge. I am not required to put up with toxicity for my safety.

* * *

Ask yourself: What childhood experience is casting a large shadow over how I operate in the world today? Write down whatever comes to mind in your journal. This will likely lead to more questions. Journal about those too. The more you dig into your childhood, the more you will unearth the outdated beliefs and strategies you've created. This is your time to adjust or eliminate your beliefs.

CHAPTER 15

SELF-DISCOVERY: AN ADVENTURE GUIDE

And you? When will you make that long journey into yourself?
—Rumi

I learned that being enmeshed with a covert narcissist means to be systematically erased. A little each day, by transgressions large and small, my needs and wants, my feelings and thoughts, were invalidated. It's as if I had to scream to be heard, to be seen—to matter.

Being raised in a toxic religion by a covert narcissist for a father meant that my opinions, needs, and truths were repeatedly disregarded with scriptures. My daddy's favorites were Romans 12:3 and Luke 17:10. They read, "Do not think of yourself more highly than you ought," and "So you, also, when you have done all the things assigned to you, say, 'We are good for nothing slaves. What we have done is what we ought to have done.'" During my teenage years, I was often required to recite these scriptures whenever I stood up for myself or gave any rebuttal to my father's demands. The scriptures got harsher when I thought I deserved to go skating, or to the movies.

I wish my daddy had taught me how to advocate for myself rather than shaming me for having self-esteem, confidence, or pride. I wish he had been an example of how a good man treats his wife. My relationship with my father made me the perfect target for someone like him—a covert narcissistic abuser. The only difference between my father and Colin is that, in many ways, my father admired me, whereas Colin resented me.

By the time I came to grips with who, or more accurately, *what*, I was married to, I knew two things for sure: First, I had no real sense of who I was, or what I wanted out of life. Second, I didn't have a lot of time left. Although I was no longer living in terror of being destroyed at Armageddon with fire and brimstone, I was shaken by the knowledge that I was starting over at age fifty. There wasn't any time to waste. I wanted to figure things out as soon as humanly possible.

Three Rules for Self-Discovery

I read somewhere that targets of narcissistic abuse tend to isolate themselves. As a teacher, I knew about the negative backlash of social isolation. As humans, we are meant to connect with others. Reading that social isolation can then lead to agoraphobia sealed my resolve to bounce back faster. There was a part of me who refused to *go out like that*. I didn't want my story to end as a fearful, depressed, shut in. Sheer determination goes a long way. This time I was tapping into my resolve and stubbornness to reclaim my life.

To rediscover myself I committed to Three Rules:

1. Question everything I think I know
2. Say yes to any invitation for adventure
3. Check in with my intuition and follow it

Ten years before my liberation from the narcissist, I had already freed myself from the Jehovah's Witness organization. I knew that their Jehovah, the one seeking to destroy me for bringing reproach on his name by being sexually assaulted from the age of five to fourteen was *not* my God. Yet, I knew that there was something, if not someone, who had always been with me over the years. It was a voice that whispered *that's not true* when I heard something from the podium that rang false, or when I read scripture interpretations in Watchtower articles that set off alarm bells in my body.

There was always something, or someone, deep inside, in my moments of fear and despair assuring me that I would be okay. I didn't know what I believed. I didn't know for sure what I had been experiencing. I simply committed to finding out. I committed to finding My Truth—not the truth I was indoctrinated to believe and tried to make fit out of fear, obligation, and guilt, but rather what I knew to be true on a cellular level.

I have since found my truth. I have a spiritual practice that allows me to navigate the world powerfully and with confidence, knowing that life is unfolding for my good. I know that we are all here to love one another. I know that our greatest task is to learn from our experiences and grow into the best versions of ourselves. I believe we are here to remember who we are, our purpose, and to do less harm than good while we're navigating this human experience.

I now know that domestic abuse goes far beyond physical abuse. I also believe that emotional and psychological abuse can leave some of the deepest scars. I know that that's the kind of abuse a narcissist—especially the Mr. Nice Guy—inflicts.

Whether it is my relationship with a higher power or a life partner, I now get to decide what a healthy relationship is. I get to determine how I want to be treated. My definition of a toxic relationship is now one where I feel less like myself, where I am being asked to act in ways that are not me, where I feel less than powerful and confident in my decision making, where I am physically ill or mentally and emotionally drained after being in the other person's presence.

Now that I have these guidelines, I don't fear being enmeshed in an abusive relationship with a narcissist again, because I know in my heart that I will walk away long before it gets to that point.

Saying YES

In 2017, I committed to reclaiming my authentic self, the me without all the trauma, religious indoctrination, and societal expectations. Since I knew very little about who I was without the road map dictated by trauma, I set out on a mission of self-discovery. For the entire year, I committed to saying yes to *every* invitation for adventure. Saying no because of fear or preconceived notions was not an option. Since then, this call to adventure has had the greatest impact on my recovery; it's how I found myself hiking in the Swiss Alps, riding in a pink jeep up the mountains of Sedona and being stung by a warrior wasp in the Amazon jungle.

It all started with a beautiful woman named Lorri Hanna. She and I were partnered together at a women's retreat meant to ground women in their bodies again. I was there to learn how to stop living on high alert. Lorri was there because she wanted to connect with her body after experiencing breast cancer. She told me about her business Soltreks, an outdoor behavioral program for adolescents who seemed to be veering toward trouble. The young folks were trekked into the wilderness and given the opportunity to build a community, develop trust, to think, and practice problem-solving.

The teacher part of me was genuinely impressed. I remember commenting about experiential opportunities being the best way for kids to learn. I explained how self-awareness and problem-solving have always been my umbrella objectives as a teacher. I was impressed with how Lorri was empowering each student in ways that I could not. Lorri's program was a tremendous opportunity for kids to become more self-aware and to grow in self-confidence and esteem.

That's when Lorri hit me with the fact that she did it for adults too. "You should come on my next hike of the Swiss Alps. We hike from Switzerland to Italy," she said.

Wait! What? I heard a voice inside me say. I know that my face was red. I felt busted. Lorri didn't know about my commitment to saying yes to every invitation, but I did. My first thought was, *No! I don't hike. I don't have shoes, or a backpack. I have asthma.* It would have been easy to say, "No. Thanks anyway!" But it would have meant not honoring the commitment that I had made to myself. I wanted to be someone that I could count on. Betraying myself had become the norm in my marriage. I intended to shift that. I was determined to follow through for myself as I would for a best friend.

Lorri could tell I was thinking about it and reassured me, "You have time to train."

It was as if Lorri was reading my mind when she said, "There will be about ten women. It'll take ten days. I'll be with you every step of the way."

She went on describing a mountain pass, the views, and how we'd stay in lovely chateaus that she had already arranged. As she did, I silently reconnected to my personal commitment and my healing journey. This was a part to rediscovering myself ... to become more self-aware ... to show what I'm made of.

"Count me in!" I said—out loud. I surprised myself.

Since my travel buddy Lindsay was also interested in going, I had built-in accountability. I was both grateful and terrified about the accountability. I knew Lindsay would challenge any excuse I came up with for not following through with the commitment I made to hike the Swiss Alps.

By simply saying *I'm in*, I was keeping my promise to myself to accept every invitation for adventure. That was a big step for someone who had, first of all, never hiked a day in her life, and second, had been at the bottom of her own to-do list for half a century. I felt a bit of pride.

I had months to go before my official training started. Thank goodness! It gave me time to work up to it, to get frustrated, to quit, and to start again. I told a few key people about my plan. I was very selective about who I shared my recovery story with because I wanted to do my own thinking, not be discouraged by the people who didn't understand narcissistic abuse. I kept my head low and committed to my training. Weight training. Endurance. Stairs. Many, many stairs.

The training schedule required me to recommit to myself

daily—even on the days slated for rest and sleep. In the past, sleep was the first need I'd forgo, sometimes out of necessity to get things done, other times due to stress.

This adventure happened the year following my divorce. Parts of me were still battered and worn out, but I had completed the heavy excavating of my mental and emotional blocks. Essentially, I had done my work. My only desire for the trip was to allow myself to feel joy and peace, to trust that I was safe, to relinquish the need to control the outcome of things, and to discover if hiking was my sort of thing.

To my surprise, during the actual hike I had a great deal of quiet time with my thoughts—literally, miles and miles of thoughts.

While there were many opportunities to get to know the other women on the trip, many of the paths required that we trek single file. We gave each other time and space to navigate the tough terrain. A few of the paths were narrow with a sheer drop on one side. Those were the times when I focused on nothing but what I called my Beyoncé walk—skillfully putting one foot directly in front of the other. There wasn't room for my feet to be side-by-side.

Being without distractions was not new to me. However, it was the first opportunity since my divorce. I was curious about what would surface. As with most survivors of narcissistic abuse, I met the criteria of what a trauma therapist called Complex Post Traumatic Stress Disorder (C-PTSD).

Unlike many survivors, I found ways to address the resulting fallout and welcomed whatever came up, knowing it would be more priceless information about myself. I welcomed the possibility.

After my Swiss Alps adventure, I knew what I wanted more of—like the sound of running water and real Italian gelato, for instance. I also learned what energy and trauma remained trapped in my body, psyche, and aura. During this trip, I got to practice perseverance. I had become familiar with six-hour hikes. Just like during the training, my mind started longing for a break by hour four—more like hour three when a mountain pass was involved.

I had to trust that my training would serve me. I had to trust that if I fueled my body the way I was instructed, then I'd have enough energy to make it from Switzerland to Italy. It became a true mental exercise— mind over matter. When the inclines got steep, I reminded my feet and hamstrings of the stairs at Alum Creek Dam. I told myself: *We trained for this. Keep going! You've done hard things before. You can do this! This is the meaning of mind, over matter. You've Got This!*

With each mountain pass, we'd look back to take in the landscape we had just trekked. Each time I marveled at the beauty. Each time I felt my self-confidence grow.

I had another reason to be proud.

Since my Swiss Alps adventure, I have not seen water as green as the water in Griespass. The water in Switzerland that flowed from public fountains tasted like nothing I'd had before my trip, or since. Because it flowed from a mountain stream, this water was pure and clean, with no metallic taste, nor chlorine. At the same time, this water tasted delicious. It was not tasteless like the water that comes from my home water filter. The word delicious doesn't seem to capture the experience. For me, the taste is beyond words.

The feeling of freedom opened for me in that moment throughout my chest, then up and down my body, unfurling like a fern opening to the sun. You've seen them in National Geographic film clips. As corny as it sounds, this experience was mine. Me. Monica. Not Monica the daughter, the sister, the ex-Jehovah's Witness, the mother, the abused, the target ... Just me!

I knew that my lesson was to find the beauty in my everyday life, and to find *me*, while loving my brand-new life.

I had an asthma flare-up during my hiking adventure. I started getting wheezy and headachy the higher we climbed. I'm not sure if my body was responding to the steepness of the incline or the quality and temperature of the air at the higher altitudes. I had plenty of inhalers and a hefty stash of Prednisone, so I wasn't worried about having a fatal attack. What bothered me was an accusation that I recalled Colin making during the night of the big implosion. He had accused me of dampening his spirits and limiting his opportunities for an exciting life because I couldn't do much of anything due to my asthma and migraines. Besides feeling betrayed by this accusation, I suspected that he, as the greatest source of my stress, had been a catalyst for my worsening allergies, asthma, and migraines.

On top of that, I could count on one hand all the times that my conditions prevented him from doing something. The truth was, I would medicate myself ahead of time to stave off any possible reactions to any environment that would inconvenience Colin or ruin an outing. The greater truth is that he rarely invited me to—or planned—any epic adventures.

As I ran out of breath on the mountain path, I thought about the time I over-medicated myself, so as not to ruin his mother's commitment ceremony (her fake wedding, as we called it, considering that it was not a legal union, but a symbolic one). The reception was in an old musty church. Unfortunately, someone had tried to mask the smell with an abundance of potpourri and cheap, scented candles. Even Colin found the artificial scents of the candles overwhelming.

"We don't have to stay if you don't want to," he had said as soon as we walked through the door.

"I'm okay, for now," I assured him and took two puffs of my inhaler, just in case. I wanted to be there for Colin. I wanted my boys to participate in the family event. I added hot, black coffee to my regime. Hot, black coffee seemed to help my lungs to open their airways more. The key was to drink it fast. It worked. However, an hour later, I felt a tightness in my chest. My lungs were shutting down again.

When I mentioned this to Colin, he seemed not to hear me. He was busy talking with people *who knew him when*, as the saying goes. It wasn't until the four of us sat alone at a table with no one paying much attention to us that Colin decided that it was all very boring and beneath him. It was then that he was ready to leave. Of course, the excuse he gave his mother was my reaction to the musty air, potpourri, and candles.

Colin pretended to be exasperated by having to leave. I went along with the story because I was just happy about the possibility of breathing easier.

I realized that this memory had left me shaken. My body seemed to be reminding me of all those self-betrayals now. My arms and legs were hot. I was familiar with this burning sensation. I knew that my body was processing trapped emotions, unresolved energy.

I was angry. So angry. Thoughts raced through my head—and my body.

How could I have been so stupid to think that I was protecting my marriage by giving myself away and risking my own health? Colin didn't appreciate any sacrifices I made. In fact, it is clear that he had an entirely different interpretation of events—one centering on entitlement.

As the memories flooded my mind in the midst of my mountain trek, I noticed that I'd gone from gentle climbing to stomping. I caught myself stabbing the ground hard with my hiking stick. I hit a rock and the energy reverberated up my arm. I think of Newton's Three Laws of Motion. For every action, there is an equal and opposite reaction. I wanted to cry. *Fuck Colin! Fuck Colin!* I said to myself. *Fuck Colin.* Stab. *Fuck Colin.* Stab. Step. Stab. Stab. *Fuck Colin!* I knew that I was releasing emotions that were not safe to express when I was married, and definitely not when I was a kid trying to earn my daddy's love.

My breathing got raspy. I felt like I was going to hyperventilate. I stopped with my left leg anchored and my right poised for a climb, my toes in a crevice. My body knew what to do. My training was coming in handy. I took a sip of water. *God Bless the inventor of the CamelBak!* Drinking the water slowed my breathing. I thought to myself and giggled. *Note to self: It's hard to have a panic attack and swallow.* I did a few rounds of my 4–7–8 breathing.

I was ready to continue, and I had a new mantra for the remainder of the day's climb: Stab. Lift. *Fuck Colin!* Stab. Step. *Fuck Colin!* Stab.

Stab. Lift. I let the tears flow. They tasted like sunscreen and dirt. *This is important work*, I told myself. *You Go Girl!*

I vowed to never betray myself again, in the name of keeping the peace, or making someone else feel better about himself or herself, or in hopes of someone liking me more or loving me better.

I vowed that I would no longer take part in my own abuse. I vowed to go above and beyond for Monica, just as I always have for others, and see how that feels.

***

I invite you to find yourself. Reclaim all the little pieces of yourself that were stolen. Forgive yourself for all the pieces that you gave away! It doesn't have to be done during a two-week trek through the Swiss Alps (although I highly recommend it!).

One of the things I did when I decided to say yes to every invite for adventure was to make a bucket list. I listed all the experiences I think I might want to have in the time I have left. I added all the things I wished I had been able to do as a kid, but couldn't because money was too tight, or the experiences I did get to do but had a miserable time because I was with a narcissist.

Since making my list and accepting all invites, I've gone horseback riding in an Alaskan rainforest, I've seen an iceberg calving (both sad and spectacular), and I've done the Pink Jeep Tour in Sedona, Arizona. Turns out I love Sedona. Who knew? I didn't. I've seen Christ The Redeemer in Rio de Janeiro and sat on the Selarón Stairs—something I've been curious about since seeing them in a Snoop Dogg music video nearly two decades before.

I spent three days in the Amazon rainforest. While there, I was stung by a warrior wasp, or it's cousin, on my freakin' face! It hurt like a mo' fo! Our guide, Pepe, was worried and worked hard to keep me distracted as he kept an eye on the swelling. His grand idea was to take me tarantula hunting. I said *Yes!* despite a long-standing spider phobia. We found a few. "Babies," he said. I'm grateful that they weren't the bird eating size. The next morning, Pepe took me to the forest and put something on my cheek that smelled like camphor. He then cut lemongrass and made me some tea.

I've also had a one-night stand. Yes! That kind. I wanted my body to know someone new. I was also experimenting with the ideas of no expectations, no judgment, and enjoying the best part of a man, with none of the bullshit later. I'll never forget how that man's muscular body felt against mine, nor the sight of his many tattoos. I won't forget the freedom in knowing that I'd never have to feed his ego. Best of all, my body and mind woke up to new possibilities about sex.

I've learned so much about Monica since setting the intention to rediscover myself and taking deliberate action.

- Turns out that I love traveling. I just didn't like traveling with a covert narcissist.
- I was reminded that some people, maybe even most, can be trusted.
- I learned that I could navigate my way through Italy with the words *mi scusi* and *grazie*, a smile, and lots of pointing.
- I can do the same in Mexico with the phrase, *Hola Papi*.
- I am resourceful.
- I've learned that I'm a no-nonsense kinda woman when it comes to accountability and personal growth. I've earned the right to be.
- I've learned that some people find me intimidating, and that I am not for everyone. I love that such a thing doesn't bother me a single bit.
- I know that I am one of the most authentic people on the planet.
- I also discovered that I enjoy laughing and that it's helpful to find the humor in most things. Laughter can be so random, so absurd at times!
- I rediscovered that I am likable—even by complete strangers.

- As proof, complete strangers have trusted me with intimate details of their lives. More times than I can count I have been a witness to others' deep pain.
- To my surprise, I am really an old hippie in that I value peace, love, and the medicinal benefits of cannabis.
- I love essential oils and burning Palo Santo.
- I like to cleanse my crystals by the light of the moon, then use them to balance my chakras. (By the way, whether or not you believe in the healing energy of crystals, the act alone signals a message to your subconscious that you are doing things differently. That signal is powerful.)
- My fashion sense is bohemian. I love the freedom of sundresses and plan to wear them more often. I prefer sneakers over heels and being barefoot over anything. Forget fashion trends!
- I am an energetic healer and a powerful intuitive, both of which were demonized growing up as a Jehovah's Witness. I've reclaimed them both as a gift from Source, The Universe, God, or whatever you prefer to call it.
- There's very little to fear.

The Greatest Man I Never Knew

While I learned about myself, I also found a path to forgive my daddy and have compassion for Colin. It wasn't during a therapy session or as I wrote in my journal. It was when listening to Leann Rimes sing Reba McEntire's song "The Greatest Man I Never Knew." Hearing that song touched me in deep, deep places. My response was so unexpected.

All the other Reba songs in *The CMT Giants* special had been fun to belt out at the top of my lungs. I had heard the songs before. But this time something long buried wanted to come up and be seen, heard, and understood. This time the lyrics landed in my body differently.

I wondered why I was reacting this way. What was my body trying to tell me? What had been buried?

After all the digging, the feeling deeply, the questioning, and the listening, I found out that my father had also experienced sexual trauma as a child—at age six—from a White woman in Mississippi. None of his siblings who were still alive wanted to speak about the details. But, using those context clues that every good teacher preaches about, I could infer that my father was not likely to be believed when he reported the incident. That is, *if* he reported it. It was 1948, in Mississippi, USA, where I heard that my father had also witnessed a friend being deliberately run down in the road by a horse and buggy, and no one protested.

I doubt that my daddy told anyone anything. It's no wonder he was not able to reconcile my experience. I could feel the fear, the feelings of inadequacy, the powerlessness, and the stifled feelings of anger. Unable to admit any of that to himself, he made it about money and the need for my mother to get to work.

Who was he to question Sister Johnson, an older woman in the congregation? He wasn't able to deal with his own pain, so he passed it on to me.

Ironically, his self-esteem suffered greatly. It's possible that my father felt less about himself due to his inability to protect me or to get justice. Maybe that pain had been too much. As a result, the next best thing was to make me responsible for any pedophiles that might show interest in me. What I wore and how I sat became big issues that made me responsible for the bad behavior of grown men—so-called Christian men. My father was woefully unqualified to be present for me, to protect me emotionally, and to keep me safe.

Just to be clear! There is no room for the likes of my father or Colin in my life. I choose to love myself better than that, and to love them from afar.

The Freedom of Forgiveness

Most importantly, I learned to open space for self-forgiveness and compassion. I know that I am trustworthy enough to be my own best friend. Evidently, I had once believed that everyone was deserving of forgiveness, except one particular five-year-old girl who allowed herself to be molested, and the fifty-two-year-old lady who gave up thirty years of her life loving a real-life dementor.

I now know that those two humans are deserving of forgiveness, especially *my* forgiveness.

* * *

Something to Ponder: I invite you to take my cue and set an intention to discover yourself, maybe for the first time. Try new things, especially things that may have been incorrectly stamped as forbidden or taboo. Welcome whatever comes up, examine it, question it. Keep what's useful and truly yours. Burn the rest. No judgment. It's all part of the journey.

* * *

Ask yourself: Who am I really? Not who you've been told you are, not who society has labeled you to be. Who are you as defined by YOU? Write yourself a love letter acknowledging who you really are.

CHAPTER 16

CELEBRATING LIBERATION

"You can't go back and change the beginning, but you can start where you are and change the ending."
—*C. S. Lewis*

Since May 3, 2015, I've celebrated my liberation from narcissistic abuse on the third of every month.

The first celebration was a simple acknowledgment that I was still standing. Despite Colin's efforts to annihilate me emotionally and mentally, I was still intact—bent and twisted beyond recognition, broken in some places, but not beyond repair. I celebrated with a big slice of three-layer chocolate cake with buttercream frosting. I ate the entire thing by myself, solo, in a fancy restaurant.

When the waitress asked if anyone would be joining me. I smiled and said, "Thankfully, NO!" I thought of Colin and how I no longer had to share anything with *an ungrateful ass ever again*. I giggled. So did she.

The second time, I put on my PJs, ordered a large pizza with *my* favorite toppings, drank spiked kombucha, and then sang and danced to some of my favorite music videos—Adele's "Send My Love To Your New Lover" and "Fighter" by Christina Aguilera. I made a Badass Bitch soundtrack with lots of JLo, Leela Jones, Tina Turner, some Miranda Lambert, Reba McEntire, and Joss Stone. That playlist was my early recovery soundtrack, my fuel that helped me get into my warrior headspace. It strengthened my resolve to keep going, whatever that looked like. I've added to my playlist over the years, and I still have a morning dance party to set my morning intentions.

I discovered that how you start the day will define your day.

The third time, and many times after, I treated myself to red lipstick. Not only red, but the fifteen dollars or more variety, the kind I had previously denied myself. (Turns out that a cheaper version has more staying power. But I wouldn't have known that had I not allowed myself to buy the more expensive brands.) My goal in wearing red lipstick was to reclaim my beauty and sexuality. Growing up, I was taught that only harlots wore red lipstick. Call me a harlot if you want. My maternal grandma probably would. In fact, she'd call me a floozy. That is, until she knew my story. Once she understood, she'd cheer me on.

I am no longer hiding my femininity in hopes of avoiding sexual assault by a sexual deviant who lacks moral values and self-control. I no longer believe that Almighty Jehovah God holds me and my pink, ruffled undies responsible for my own sexual assault.

By month four, my cognitive dissonance was at an all-time high. Colin had upped the ante during divorce negotiations. He had forgotten the part I played in his financial success. He started believing that he had accomplished it all on his own and decided not to keep any of the promises he had made regarding our finances. So, I bought myself a half dozen cupcakes—vanilla cupcakes with three times more frosting than needed. I ate each one, starting with the icing, and wrote myself a love letter. It went something like this:

Dear Monica,

Believe me when I tell you that you are an incredible being. Life hasn't been easy. Yet, you've found joy. Those who should have protected you were the very ones who took advantage of your trust and innocence. Yet, you've shown kindness and compassion to others. You've lived with integrity, striving to live by the values you were taught, despite how fallible they were. You've learned from your mistakes. As you've come to know better, you've done better. Keep doing all of that!

The fact that you finally see Colin for who and what he truly is, is an astronomical feat. Well done! You had so many blinders—society, religion, and childhood sexual trauma. I know the guilt and fear that you had to overcome—guilt for thinking that Colin was indeed an abusive monster, and the fear that you could never make it on your own. I know the fear still appears at times, especially given the financial betrayal, but trust yourself. You'll figure it out. In the meantime, show yourself compassion and grace. Love yourself better! Give to yourself what you so freely give to others.

You gave Colin thirty years to get himself together. For thirty years, he failed you. He failed to be the person he presented himself to be. He failed to do the work he promised to do. He failed to do right by your boys. The only thing you know for sure is that Colin is a cowardly cheating liar. You get to move on knowing that you are not those things, and that he is out of your life.

Never feel shame for showing others unconditional love and unshakable loyalty. Their ungratefulness and cruelty are not your weaknesses. They are theirs.

Keep going! You've Got This!

I love you!

~Monica

I put the letter in an envelope. Then I decorated the envelope with doodles of a big-ass sun, hearts, spirals and the like. I then put the envelope in my underwear drawer so that I could see it every day. Just the sight of it reminds me of my inner resilience and beauty, and that I am loved. Starting my day with this mindset each morning has been cathartic and transformative.

One of my favorite celebrations included a complete redesign of my bedroom. I painted. I ordered a new king size bed with a purple tufted headboard, and gel topped mattress. I also got new curtains and plants. In the past, I couldn't have curtains or plants in my bedroom thinking that they were the cause of my nighttime coughing spells— you know, dust and plant spores. Well, turns out that after removing Colin from my bedroom permanently my coughing spells ended. I bought myself the most luxurious comforter set I could find. I hung fairy lights and large glass orbs. I added a faux fireplace and hearth. I framed affirmations that resonated with my energy and goals. I hung them so that I could see them as I lay in bed. (For a long time, they served as comfort when I woke in the middle of the night from a nightmare about my time with Colin.) I bought myself a Bluetooth speaker so that I could fall asleep to the sound of rain, far away trains, or crickets, the way I loved to do as a kid. Going to bed and waking up in such a nurturing space designed just for me was extremely supportive to becoming the best version of myself possible. Waking up to my new space shifted my default setting from walking on eggshells and high alert to excitement and possibility. It's a powerful shift.

Try it.

At this point there have been many celebrations, big and small, ranging from a nap, to decorating, to planning a pilgrimage to the Camino de Santiago, to writing this book.

The point is that I get to celebrate myself and my journey. I've spent too long focused on validating and supporting others. It's time that I got in on the action. Sure, you and I don't *need* validation the way a narcissist does, but it does feel good.

However I decide to celebrate the third of every month, my

Liberation Day will always be an acknowledgment of my strength, my tendency to love hard, my desire to laugh, and my determination to fill my life with as much love and adventure as I can handle.

And, obviously, it will likely include a confectionary treat of some sort.

* * *

I invite you to celebrate your Liberation Day! Celebrate it every month. Let it be a reminder of how far you've come, and a motivator for how far you can go.

Celebrate your choice to go no contact, then celebrate your follow-through. Celebrate that you are still standing. Acknowledge that the narcissist in your life does not have your best interest at heart. In fact, if you were married to one, it's likely that they actively plotted against you during the discard phase. Yet here you are.

Celebrate that you are paying attention to your body cues and that you are beginning to see the red flags that you missed before. Maybe you've learned to do all the "typically manly" things your partner used to do such as kill spiders, cut the grass, check the air in your tires, and fix things around the house. Or maybe, you've found someone who can do those things for you. Either way, celebrate that too!

If you do nothing else to celebrate your liberation, please do this: set a monthly reminder, an alarm even, on your phone to remind yourself of your journey. When it goes off, take a moment to cheer yourself on! Dance! Pump your fist. Feel the boost in your energy that comes from just being reminded of your tenacity. Recommit to yourself, if that's where you are in your journey. Open yourself to all the goodness that's headed your way. You deserve it!

One word of caution though: *Be careful what you ask for!* When I declared my intent to learn more about myself by accepting every invitation for adventure, the opportunities seemed never ending. The synchronicities seemed magical. For example, as circumstances unfolded, my two weeks in Brazil and the Amazon jungle ended up costing less than three thousand dollars including accommodations, most meals, and airfare. Be ready!

Also: Every once in a while, treat yo'self to an overpriced cupcake. You know the one!

* * *

Something to ponder: It takes ingenuity, resourcefulness, compassion, amongst many other attributes to navigate the world of narcissistic abuse. You are still standing, which means you have survived.

* * *

Ask yourself: What personal qualities supported me thus far? Make a list of them. Post the list somewhere you can see it every day. Remind yourself of your favorite three attributes by saying out loud, "I am (fill in the blank)!"

CHAPTER 17

DATING AFTER NARCISSISTIC ABUSE

Knowing what you want and with no expectations of another person to make you feel safe, loved, and enough is a powerful place to be.
— *Monica Linson*

Dating is a bit weird for everyone these days. Multiply that by a thousand if you've been a target of narcissistic abuse. I feel that I've outgrown the bar and club scene. Wisdom has taught me not to date where I work. Besides, the teaching profession is primarily a female sport at the K-5 levels. So, both options were out of the question for me. That left online dating. Ugh!

I waited a full year and a half and did some deep personal growth work before I even thought about maybe, possibly wanting to date. I know that you know what I'm talking about.

I had already fallen in love with the peace and quiet of my own freedom. I was beginning to love my own company. I was reminded that I had never been on my own before. I had gone from home (as the oldest child) to college to being married to being a mom. I liked not having so many responsibilities.

On the other hand, I wanted to be sure that I was choosing the single life powerfully, not out of fear.

Online Dating with Better Instincts

Bumble was the first app recommended to me. I was advised to commit to a paid plan. According to friends in the know, I didn't want to bother with anyone who was too cheap or too broke to pay for a plan. My immediate thought was, *Note to self: This sucks already.* Because I'm not chicken-shit and because I wanted to find out more about myself, I pressed on. My profile had pictures of me on my adventures to Italy, and Brazil. They were an accurate representation. I included a few of my favorite quotes that served as my north star at the time. I answered all of the "About Me" profile prompts in complete sentences—automatic for me as a writing teacher. It wasn't until a day or two later that I realized that I had a bias against profiles that were difficult to read due to improper spacing or no punctuation. I learned that photos of men lying in bed or standing in a bathroom felt cringy to me. I found that I didn't even bother to read the profiles of men my age who posted high school photos of themselves. I was already learning more about myself. Score!

Within an hour of my profile going live, the responses poured in. That was a huge ego boost. I hadn't been in the dating scene for thirty years. The boost was even greater when I read compliments about my smile, my positive vibes, and my travel adventures. Some of the comments were propositions that made me blush. Others made me delete the user from my feed. I was proud of myself for that last one. I mentioned nothing about my divorce.

I was part of the online dating world for less than a week when I was scolded by a handsome, supposedly rich man for not responding fast enough to his message. I was also propositioned by a foreign prince who needed someone like me by his side. *WTAF?!*

I wondered why no one had warned me about how blatant these situations could be. I deleted both men immediately.

Fortunately, my feed was on fire, so during that first week I also had some fun chats with a number of grounded, funny, thoughtful, and handsome men. They were also in other states. Within the three months, life happened, and those connections faded. No regrets. I wasn't willing to travel, nor did I want to feel indebted to a man for traveling several hours, one direction, to see me. Something told me that I would be setting myself up for disaster if a man felt that I owed him in any way.

I trusted my instinct.

As those fun out of state connections were fading, things were starting up with a man who was only an hour away. We chatted on the app daily and often. He appeared attentive and thoughtful. He repeatedly told me how excited he was to see my smile in person. He kept me curious. My only concern was that he never made me laugh, nor did he respond to my sense of humor. I love to laugh, but at that time laughing together wasn't high on my list of requirements. Fortunately, when the idea of meeting in real life came up, this man said that he needed my email to send me something. I had an email just for dating, so I gave him that address. The next day, I received an email with an attachment. It was two pages filled with a wall of text detailing his expectations of a capable, God-fearing woman. He made me laugh. Hard. Finally!

That seemed like a perfect time to delete my app and work on my list of standards and non-negotiables. I also wanted to get clear on whether or not I actually wanted a close relationship.

I was proud of myself for not fawning to placate the man who demanded that I respond to his texts immediately. I was not flattered, or duped, by the handsome prince that needed me by his side. Nor did I compare myself against the list of requirements that a would-be-suitor sent as a PDF.

At the top of my What I Want In a Partner list, I typed:

- Has sense of humor
- Wants to get to know me as an individual, not as a role to fill
- Uses proper English conventions

Dating in Real Life

There were a few dates where my under arms alerted when first laying eyes on the man. (Yep! Itchy underarms are my primary body cue to pay close attention.) I dismissed the cue as first date jitters. Ha! I was so wrong. Although I was not in danger, the dates were unbelievably horrific.

The first of such dates was with a man named Mike. He was local, which was exciting. His profile said that he was five years younger than I was. I don't recall his listed profession. I was happy that he was gainfully employed. Mike looked nothing like his photo, but he recognized me. I remember thinking, *Why don't you look familiar?* But almost immediately my attention was drawn to a large bouquet of flowers and a bottle of wine that he was presenting to me. That's when my armpits began to itch. *This is a distraction! I'm allergic to flowers and I seldom drink.*

My response was, "Oh! For me? Thank you." It seemed like a lot for a first date. My body cue was raised a notch higher. It got weirder from there.

It was summer and the restaurant I had chosen had a baby back ribs special. Risky for a date, but with his encouragement, I went for it. The problem arose when Mike insisted on holding my hand. How on Earth does a person eat ribs with one hand? I didn't know, nor was I interested in finding out.

"I'm gonna need this hand to eat," I said with a friendly giggle as I took my hand away. That solved the problem until I finished one bone and he grabbed my hand again. *What the—you need to get out of here.* I heard my intuition warn. The itch in my armpits grew more intense. That scenario repeated itself three times, even after I put my hand in my lap.

When the waiter came to check on us and gave me the same *What the hell?* look that I felt, along with a *Come on now, sis* head tilt, I knew then that it wasn't just me.

I asked for a box to take my dinner home. Clearly, I wasn't going to be able to finish it there. Plus, I figured this move would clue Mike into the idea of this date coming to an end. While we waited, Mike spoke about his gift of wine and flowers. My stomach alerted me that I needed to show appreciation. Of course, this felt familiar after being raised by one narcissist and then married to another. I decided that the gratitude I displayed initially was enough.

"Please go for a walk with me," Mike asked. "I'd love to take you for an ice cream."

I agreed because I was afraid to go to my car. I didn't want to risk this guy following me home. I was buying myself more time.

As we were leaving the restaurant, I stopped by to see the maître d'. His name was Ian, who voluntarily served as my secret bodyguard. I introduced hand-holding Mike to Ian and added, "Mike wants to take a walk to get ice cream."

Without missing a beat, Ian said, "I'll still be here. Why don't you leave your stuff with me and just pick it up on your way to your car." I was grateful for Ian's quick thinking and willingness to look out for me. I strongly recommend that you find yourself an Ian at an upscale restaurant and have all of your first dates there.

Mike insisted on buying me an ice cream cone. In fact, he ordered one for me. I had to stop the ice cream scooper as she headed for the tub of chocolate. "I am lactose intolerant. I don't want ice cream. He must not have heard me. I'll have a scoop of raspberry sorbet. Thanks." I know that I had spoken loud enough for Mike to have heard me. Maybe he simply ignored me. This felt very invalidating. Note to self.

On our walk back, Mike said, "I've never been on this side of town. It's very nice. My car is close. Will you show me around?"

I declined.

Moments later he said, "I bet there's a park nearby. Wanna go?"

"No, I'm ready to call it a night. Thank you for dinner." I could not, did not give an explanation. I turned to collect my belongings from Ian. Then, I lingered in the restaurant before going to my car. When I finally went to my car, something told me not to go home. So, I drove to a Target on the other side of town. I browsed until my body felt safe.

Setting Boundaries and Raising Standards

The next day, I made a list of all the boundaries around first dates. But I knew I needed to do more than just list them. I needed to be able to say them at the right time, in the right tone, no matter who I was saying them to.

I rehearsed them out loud in varying tones: *I'd rather we keep our body parts to ourselves on the first date. Thanks anyway! No kissing. I might fall in love.* (Giggle! This is to stroke the male ego.) *Let's keep our hands to ourselves* (rehearsed in my matter-of-fact teacher voice).

Here are a few more:

- No! I'd rather drive myself or take an Uber.
- Thanks, but no.
- I'm feeling uncomfortable. I need to go.
- It doesn't feel like you're hearing me.

Do not underestimate how strange and difficult it will feel to speak and enforce your boundaries. It's not what we're used to doing. I found it important to give my body options other than fight, flight, freeze or fawn. I wanted my body and mind to be familiar and at peace with setting and enforcing boundaries.

If you opt to do this, practicing them out loud should help. Remember; our minds can't tell the difference between a visualization and the real thing. Visualize setting boundaries. Speak them out loud—boldly.

Another reason to practice your boundaries out loud and often, until you get good, is because toxic people will push back. People who have been taking advantage of your openness, or who plan to, will become angry about your boundaries. As I mentioned in part one, narcissists often become angered by another's audacity to hold them accountable for their poor behavior.

Until I did the work to no longer attract narcissists, I encountered many of them in the dating world. You may too. Be ready!

Besides practicing my boundary-setting phrases, I continued my list of non-negotiables. I wanted to set standards that weren't born of trauma and not-enoughness. I wanted to be in a place of high standards and zero expectations. Knowing what I want and with no expectations of another person to make me feel safe, loved, and enough is a powerful place to be.

With clear non-negotiables, I measure any new relationship, ask any needed clarifying questions, and respond accordingly. I do this, even if the man is tall, funny, handsome, financially stable, and flattering.

Must haves for me are honesty, emotional intelligence, accountability, and mutual respect. I list these because strikes against these standards show up early in dating life.

With a concrete list, you have a firm, tangible measuring stick to determine if a relationship is headed down the best path for you. Your list of non-negotiables will serve as your grounding rod for when your love and happiness hormones are high, or when you're just longing to be held. Your list will support you in assessing the new relationship objectively.

I am not inviting you to do something that I haven't required of myself. I have my list. I have faith that my adherence to my list has saved me from more than one toxic connection.

My favorite was with someone I will call, Dan the Man. In short, Dan showed up when my vibration was high and I was simply looking for some fun. The first time we met my curiosity was piqued by his energy and sense of humor. He made me laugh—my kryptonite. I find a sense of humor to be very sexy. Score a point for Dan.

Within a week I received a few unexpected texts from Dan. They made me giggle. But there was no call to action, so to speak. The next time was an invite to his hot tub. *Okay! That's a clear direction.* I thanked him for the invite, but I declined because I was already booked for the night. However, I did take inventory of my swimsuits and got my situation … situated. You know the routine we have for a night when minimum clothing is involved.

Dan the Man sent a few more texts. One included a photo of himself and a few family members at the zoo. I wondered, *What the hell? Why would I give two shits about him being at the zoo?* These were my thoughts, but I didn't respond.

Later that day his text was, "How does it make you feel to know that I was thinking about you? I remembered you said that you were working from the zoo and while there, you were on my mind. I kept thinking about all the things I'd like to do with you."

This time I wondered to myself, *What the hell?* in a good way.

I texted back, "Are you flirting with me Dan?"

The answer was, "Yes! I guess I am. How am I doing?"

That made me laugh. I then entertained some things I'd like to do with, and to, Dan. My imagination scored all sorts of points for Dan.

The following weeks were filled with awkward moves. I was in my masculine energy and invited Dan out for a movie. I also opened my own car door and bought the tickets. It was at the concession stand that Dan called me on my behavior. He blocked my path, faced me and simply said, "I've got this!"

I suddenly felt vulnerable. Note to self: *Relax. Some men actually do this.*

The movie I chose was on my Oscar nominated must-see list. It was a good movie but also terribly sad. Ugh!

"That was really sad." I said. "I feel like I owe you another movie." Then I asked, "Have you seen the latest Mark Wahlburg movie?" And smooth as whipped butter, Dan asked, "Do you mean the one about …" From there he spews a plot summary that fits just about every Mark Wahlburg movie ever made, including the scenes where Mark usually ends up half naked. I can't repeat what Dan said or capture the tone.

I'd never be able to do it justice. All I remember is that it was spot on and funny as hell.

So funny that I had to do Kegels to keep from peeing as we rode down the escalator. Night saved. More points for Dan!

Later a financial transaction between us got muddy. However, he cleared it up promptly and with integrity—something I'd never experienced with a man before. He took it one step further and asked if we could meet face to face and talk about things. Dan was scoring points in categories that weren't even officially on my list. Funny how I wasn't expecting a man to be financially integrous, let alone requiring it. That was my trauma and subconscious limiting beliefs making an appearance.

Another few weeks passed by before Dan and I had a firm agreement that we would be *friends with benefits*. (Remember! This is a judgment free zone.) When I was honest with myself, I didn't want a boyfriend. I didn't want to give up the time it takes to nurture a committed relationship. I had a book to write, a business to create, courses to complete, and bath bubbles to take. Nor did I want to give up Saturday mornings in my PJs should the need occur. But a scheduled night of laughing and physical connection? That I could do.

Even now my time with Dan makes me giggle. I still dream about him at times. Dan was to be my fun-loving friend who provided laughter and physical connection. There were nights when we lay completely naked physically and emotionally. He told me about spending a great many days as a young boy, left to his own devices, riding his bike on the Oval of The Ohio State University. He shared how such days shaped who he is today. He shared how joining the military was a much better choice for him than going to college. When asked, he also gave his heartfelt opinion on how I could better enrich the experience for my students who saw school as an impossible mission. His suggestions worked. I was grateful.

I usually massaged Dan's face, chest and arms lightly with just my fingertips as he spoke. It's the same pressure I used to calm my boys when they were babies, and what I learned to do for lymphatic drainage in massage school. He involuntarily moaned, "That feels so nice."

Dan craved human touch. I loved listening to people's stories, especially his. Being together was a win for both of us.

It turned out that Dan and I have the same outlook on life. Our shared belief is that life is made up, and outcomes change depending on our interpretation of events. It's all a game and the objective is to keep learning and adjusting. The prize is *happiness*—and after that, whatever else you want.

Dan was handsome, smart, funny and had an interesting way of interpreting the world. He reminded me of my goals when my vision got fuzzy. Dan was fun, a stress reliever, a muse for how to navigate life as a teacher in a broken education system.

We provided each other with physical connection and great sex without the complication of bills, children to raise, household chores, bad moods, and all the other stressors that come with married life. The best part of our nights together was that my body responded to Dan in ways that left me feeling like an old dishrag (as my grandma used to say), drunk, and near comatose—then Dan got up and went the fuck home, locking my front door behind him, until the next time! My definition of a near perfect relationship.

The problem for me was that in my experience of Dan, he proved to be a less than honest person. I had two clear and simple requirements at the start of our arrangements. Dan lied about one of them. Strike one. When I asked for clarification, his answer was dismissive. Strike two. I told him so and that I'd like to have an actual answer the next time I asked. When that time came, Dan deflected. Strike three.

Shit! Dan had to go.

The specifics don't matter. The only part that matters is that honesty is the number one thing on my list of non-negotiables. In this situation, by lying, Dan denied me my freedom of choice. Isn't that what dishonesty really is? The person being lied to is denied the opportunity to make choices based on full, accurate, current facts about a situation.

Months later when I spotted Dan standing outside his house, my mind flashed back to the fun and connection we had. However, my body responded in a way that could only mean one thing: *Dan's a liar. We closed up shop. Get over it. The end.* By the way, I had a legitimate reason to be passing by Dan's house.

In the end, there were a few other matters that came to light, confirming that Dan was less than truthful. I made the right decision. Dan is free to be dismissive with another woman. I am free to create something with a better man. Someone who will be straight with me, and himself.

Options

I've been open and transparent with you so far. I'm not going to stop now. So, I gotta tell you that I am not sure that I ever want to get married again. I spent the first two years after the implosion of my marriage not dating for obvious reasons: I needed to heal. After that, I had fun seeking adventure. Sure, they may have been fun with a love interest. However, I doubt that they would have been as nurturing as they were with the groups of women I traveled with. At the time, I needed to be nurtured. I needed deep conversations and connections. Now that more time has passed, I find that I enjoy my alone time. That means a man would have to offer a great deal of laughter, fun, and adventure to have me give up my solo life.

I never expected this to be the case. Fear of being alone and not being able to make it on my own were some of the thoughts that kept me enmeshed with Colin for so long. Now that I'm on the other side, I find it hard to believe that I had been so fearful. I had to do a great deal of self-forgiveness work around this.

I've been able to meet so many of the needs that I thought could only be filled by marriage. It makes me wonder how many young women get married because it's the expected thing to do. I wonder how a shift in societal norms would change the dynamics of romantic relationships and marriage. What if the idea that "relationships are hard" was never something I heard growing up? Would I have put up with so much? Would other women?

Having said that, there is another side of me that believes that having the right person beside you, the person who is capable of reciprocating the empathy, love, and respect that you give, could make life more enjoyable—even the mundane tasks. The thought of traveling the world, cuddling on the sofa, and making each other's dreams come true excites me. There are days I'd love to have a soft place to fall when life gets tough. I am curious about what it would be like to face life's challenges with someone by your side. I wonder if the partner that Colin was pretending to be really exists. But I don't *need* any of it in order to be okay with myself, to love myself, to feel safe, or to be happy. I'm grateful to have options.

* * *

Something to ponder: My most heartfelt advice is to please take time to heal and rediscover yourself before risking the possibility of losing yourself in someone else again. When you don't fully process your trauma emotionally, mentally, and physically, then dating too soon can make you vulnerable on many fronts, making you a perfect target for another narcissist. But if you are healed, you could powerfully and intentionally walk away from the red flags or choose to remain solo. I invite you to give yourself options.

* * *

Ask yourself: What do I hope to get out of a romantic relationship? When I consider the fact that parts of me have been systematically erased, or invalidated, who am I really? Do I know? Who exactly will I be presenting on a date? How can I be sure what I want in a new partner if I don't know who I am anymore? Will I see the red flags this time? Remember, they were there all along. You missed them, just like I did. Don't do that to yourself again.

CHAPTER 18

THE GREATEST LESSON

"As I began to love myself, I found that anguish and emotional suffering were only warning signs that I was living against my own truth."
—Charlie Chaplin

The greatest lesson I've learned is that I get to love myself better. Notice that I said, "get to." I chose the word "get" because it shows that I am giving myself permission to love myself better.

Somewhere along the way, self-love had become vilified as selfish, bad, dirty in my mind. Somehow, the definition of a good person, or even a good Christian, became equated to giving myself away, putting others' needs above my own, giving until I bled, and then giving some more. It's what I understood a good daughter did, who a big sister is, and the job of a faithful wife. To be or do otherwise was prideful, sinful, worldly ... not loving.

I had seen countless inscriptions on wooden plaques or vinyl cutouts, social media posts, or t-shirt slogans, all suggesting to *fill your cup*, to *put on your own oxygen mask first*, and to *give from your overflow*. However, without concrete examples, they were nothing more than nice sentiments and lofty platitudes.

Worse than that, more than one medical professional advised me to practice self-care in the form of bubble baths, overpriced coffee, and lavish vacations. I guess the goal was to have fun and relax. What would have been better was to have concrete examples about how to reduce stress and to get better sleep. Thank goodness, I learned about polyvagal nerve theory in massage school.

During my recovery work, self-love came to mean accessing my personal needs and putting myself on my to-do list, right at the top. Not because I'm being selfish, prideful, or uncaring, but because I matter. I now know that self-love, in the form of self-care, is essential to my survival.

Meeting my needs has meant maintaining the morning routine that I started in recovery. I lived so many years living in survival, not grounded in my truth and purpose. It's important to me to connect with myself each morning, getting grounded in my intentions and purpose. Some days I journal. Some days I have a private dance party. I've since added chakra clearing and energy healing to my routine. Self-love in this regard has meant putting forth the effort to create a source of income that will allow me the privilege to spend as much time as needed for my morning routine. Being able to meet my personal needs is my definition of freedom.

The next act of self-love that I attended to was to use the word "no" more often. I stopped feeling obligated to honor every request for support or accommodation. This was especially true regarding events that were not aligned with my mission of healing and recovery. I freed myself of obligations to family and friends who never seemed to reciprocate. Saying no to people in this category became easier after I took an objective look at the fact that there were people in my life who not only never came through for me but who were also vindictive and entitled when it came to their needs. (Upon close inspection, I was surprised how often such dynamics are excused with the words like, "Well, that's just the way she/he is!" as if that's the reason poor treatment should be tolerated.)

Besides saying no to things that didn't serve me, I tightened my inner circle even more by allowing myself days of needed solitude. There have been full weekends where I am the only one who gets to enjoy my company. I've come to love those times. I've found that I need such times to recharge, to reflect, and to reconnect with myself. I delve into *my* core values, and remind myself of what truly matters to me, despite societal trends or religious indoctrination. Reaffirming my values and goals allows me to keep moving forward as I create my new life.

As I learned more about covert narcissism, I discovered that those traits appeared in my work environment. In my experience, once you see the patterns of narcissism, it's impossible to unsee them, and there appears to be far more people with such tendencies than I had ever imagined. When feeling the impact of such toxicity in my body becomes too much, I stand up for myself by calling out the behavior. As you can imagine, when this happened with a narcissistic boss, there were repercussions. However, I chose to ride the roller coaster of documenting and taking my concerns to my boss's boss. Making the choice to fight back wasn't easy. However, I refused to participate in my own abuse by not speaking up for myself.

At this point, I am loving myself enough to admit that our US public education system is currently broken. A quick Google and YouTube search would reveal the evidence. I know firsthand how difficult the job has become. I am so proud of the teachers who are loving themselves enough to walk away from the toxicity. Loving myself better means that I get to transition to a vocation that feeds my soul the way teaching once did. In the meantime, I have chosen to put a stronger boundary around my personal time and my contracted work hours. I get to do that guilt free.

Loving myself better has meant becoming my own best friend. I've learned to make my inner critic an ally. Instead of reinforcing the abusive words of my narcissistic father and Colin, I embrace the truth of who I am. I am a genuine, compassionate and loving human being who has been taken for granted by broken people in my life. Loving myself means forgiving myself for believing that I had to tolerate toxic people. Nowadays, my body alerts me to the red flags and my inner critic and intuition guide me from there. Loving myself means I get to listen to all three!

I invite you to embrace and celebrate the truth of who you are. Be your authentic, empathetic, and compassionate self—not who the narcissist says you are, not who your parents demand you to be, or religious doctrine expects you to be, but who you really are. You get to reclaim yourself!

EPILOGUE

"So, when your eulogy is being read, with your life's actions to rehash would you be proud of how you lived your dash?"
—*Linda Ellis*

I invite you to live your life to the fullest. Life is short! It's even shorter if you've wasted decades enmeshed with a narcissist.

Ask yourself, "What do I want?" That's a question we haven't been able to ask. Now is the time. Ask yourself over and over. Put it into words. Find a picture to symbolize your heart's desire. Make it your focus. Take a step toward your dreams—every single day. Big or small.

If you want to be wealthy, then determine how you define the concept. (I've found that it's far more than money.) When you find yourself blocked from the life you desire, remove those subconscious beliefs that are blocking your dreams.

If you want to travel the world, mention it every chance you get, even if you get teased. The universe is listening. The connections will happen.

If you want to find the love of your life, become the energetic match to that person. Strap on your intuition and go on some dates. Listen to your body cues.

My current mission is to support at least one-thousand women to grow in self-awareness, self-confidence, and self-love. Those three qualities will make her narc-proof! Being narc-proof is the best feeling in the world. We deserve it!

What will you do with your dash?

CREDITS

Narcissistic Personality Disorder Diagnostic Criteria is reprinted with permission from the Diagnostic and Statistical Manual of Mental Disorders, Fifth Edition, Text Revision (Copyright © 2022). American Psychiatric Association. All Rights Reserved.

Excerpt from The Dash poem by Linda Ellis, © Southwestern Family of Companies, used by permission.

ABOUT THE AUTHOR

MONICA LINSON has learned firsthand just how mentally and physically damaging a lifetime of traumatic covert narcissistic abuse can be. She lost herself in decades of gaslighting, rejection, criticism, self-doubt, and mental and physical abuse before she finally found her way out of the darkness.

In her first book, *Surviving Mister Nice Guy*, Monica calls out the covert narcissist's red flags that hide in plain sight so that others can see and avoid them at all costs. She is now a narcissistic abuse recovery coach, supporting victims as they navigate through and out of their harmful relationships. Monica lives in Columbus, Ohio and has two sons.

www.ingramcontent.com/pod-product-compliance
Lightning Source LLC
Chambersburg PA
CBHW071232070526
44583CB00017B/2147